Slow Media

Slow Media

WHY "SLOW" IS SATISFYING, SUSTAINABLE, AND SMART

JENNIFER RAUCH

OXFORD
UNIVERSITY PRESS

OXFORD
UNIVERSITY PRESS

Oxford University Press is a department of the University of Oxford. It furthers
the University's objective of excellence in research, scholarship, and education
by publishing worldwide. Oxford is a registered trade mark of Oxford University
Press in the UK and certain other countries.

Published in the United States of America by Oxford University Press
198 Madison Avenue, New York, NY 10016, United States of America.

Library of Congress Cataloging-in-Publication Data
Names: Rauch, Jennifer, author.
Title: Slow media : why "slow" is satisfying, sustainable, and smart / Rauch, Jennifer.
Description: New York, NY : Oxford University Press, [2018] |
Includes bibliographical references and index.
Identifiers: LCCN 2018008354 (print) | LCCN 2018009519 (ebook) |
ISBN 9780190641801 (updf) | ISBN 9780190641818 (epub) |
ISBN 9780190641795 (alk. paper); 9780197626023 (pbk.)
Subjects: LCSH: Mass media—Social aspects. | Mass media and technology. |
Mass media and culture. | Mass media and the environment. | Sustainability.
Classification: LCC HM1206 (ebook) | LCC HM1206 .R376 2018 (print) | DDC 302.23—dc23
LC record available at https://lccn.loc.gov/2018008354

9 8 7 6 5 4 3 2 1

Paperback printed by Marquis, Canada

*In memory of my mother, who taught me to love
books, vinyl records, the public library,
postcards, printed maps, stationery,
clock radios, typewriters,
and creativity.*

Contents

Preface: The Bearable Lightness of Slowing   xi
    CLOSER TO THE TIPPING POINT   xiii
    I HEART DIGITAL MEDIA   xv
    THE PROVERBIAL FISH OUT OF WATER   xvii
    IMAGINING THE ALTERNATIVES   xix
    USERS OF THE WORLD, UNITE   xxii

1. Introduction: Alternative Visions of Sustainability   1
    SUSTAINABLE MEDIA AND THE POPULAR IMAGINATION   4
    CULTURAL CREATIVITY BENEATH THE RADAR   5
    SUSTAINABILITY IN MEDIA AND COMMUNICATION   7
    SLOW MEDIA AS ALTERNATIVE MEDIA   8
    SATISFYING, SUSTAINABLE, AND SMART   10

2. Slow Media: Lessons from the Food Revolution   13
    LESSONS FROM THE FOOD REVOLUTION   14
    CINEMA: AN EARLY INCARNATION OF SLOW MEDIA   18
    DISENCHANTMENT WITH DIGITAL LIFE   20
    THE EMERGENCE OF SLOW MEDIA   21
    VALUES AND PRACTICES OF SLOW MEDIA   22
    THE SLOW MEDIA MANIFESTO   24
    PROGRESSIVE ALTERNATIVES, NONCOMMERCIAL FORMS   26
    DISPELLING MYTHS ABOUT SLOW MEDIA   29
    MOVING SLOW MEDIA FORWARD   31

3. "Good, Clean, Fair": A Sustainability Framework for Journalism   33

THE PROBLEM OF FAST JOURNALISM   35

A QUICK DEFINITION OF SLOW JOURNALISM   37

SUSTAINABILITY PRINCIPLES FOR JOURNALISM   38

BEING "GOOD" IS NOT ENOUGH   40

A "FAIR" ANALYSIS OF JOURNALISM   44

ALTERNATIVE ECONOMIC MODELS   45

EMPOWERING NEWS CONSUMERS   47

TOWARD SUSTAINABLE JOURNALISM   49

4. Greening Media: New Directions in Environmental Citizenship and Scholarship   53

THE MATERIAL EFFECTS OF "VIRTUAL" MEDIA   55

CONSIDERING CULTURE AND CONSUMPTION   57

MEDIA ECOLOGY, UPCYCLED   58

GREEN MARKETING AND GREEN REALITIES   61

RECLAIMING GREEN MEDIA   63

ECO-FRIENDLY ALTERNATIVES   65

WORMS IN YOUR APPLE   68

A GREEN LIGHT FOR SLOW MEDIA   71

NO LONGER OBSCURED BY CLOUDS?   73

LESS IS MORE   75

FROM GREEN CONSUMERS TO GREEN CITIZENS   76

5. Mind Your Media: From Distraction to Attention   79

IN SEARCH OF MINDFULNESS   82

MEDITATIONS ON MEDIATED LIFE   83

NEUROPLASTICITY, MULTITASKING, AND THE DEFAULT MODE   84

EXPERIMENTS IN MINDING YOUR MEDIA   86

BRINGING MINDFULNESS INTO MEDIA PRACTICE   90

YOUR BRAIN ON SPEED   93

LESSONS LEARNED FROM MINDFUL MEDIA   95

LET'S TREAT CAUSES, NOT SYMPTOMS   96

6. We Are All Post-Luddites Now   99

LUDDISM IN THE 19TH CENTURY   101

HEROES OR VILLAINS?   103

THE RISE AND FALL OF NEO-LUDDISM   104

OF METHODS AND MADMEN   109

TURNING TOWARD THE ENVIRONMENT AND GLOBALIZATION   110

BEYOND REDEMPTION?   112

GOING POST-LUDDITE   114

GETTING REAL ABOUT TECHNOLOGY CRITICISM   117

PARAGONS OF POST-LUDDISM   118

MOVING THE CONVERSATION FORWARD   120

7. Conclusion: Toward a Sustainable Future   123

AIN'T NOBODY GOT TIME FOR THAT   125

SATISFYING AND SATISFICING   128

POST-LUDDITES WANT BOTH   129

SLOWNESS AS SECULAR OASIS   130

SLOW MEDIA NATION   131

NOW IS THE TIME   134

Acknowledgments   137
Notes   139
References   161
Index   175

Preface

The Bearable Lightness of Slowing

> If you're just operating by habit, you're not really living.
> —*My Dinner with André*[1]

> Disconnection is the new counterculture.
> —Nicholas Carr[2]

Not long ago, I found myself on the sidewalk in front of a friend's apartment building in New York City, throwing rocks at her third-story window. My arm and aim were good enough to strike glass on the second floor, but her apartment was higher than that. I puzzled over how to get her attention. Wait for someone to come outside? Set off my car alarm? The problem was, she didn't have a doorbell. The disappearance of buzzers is one of the ripple effects in our new communication environment, where many people assume visitors will use cellphones to announce their arrival—and some property owners don't install doorbells, considering them optional. In the end, I hunted down a payphone to call my friend because while most pockets and purses hold digital devices, mine did not.

The reason? After reveling in the wonders of digital media for 20 years, I had abandoned the Internet for six months and cellphones for a year. An exhibit of exquisitely illustrated letters by the whimsical, macabre artist Edward Gorey had got me thinking about the loss of material artifacts that accompanied digital communication. I missed the creativity of making printed correspondence and the fun of receiving it. This mild wistfulness sparked me to try and reshape the contours of my mediated life. I hoped that going offline for a while would help me revive analog habits like sending letters and postcards, which used to bring such pleasure. My digital disenchantment was about much more than mail, though.

Once upon a time, I devoted hours to tactile and corporeal activities: poring through cookbooks for new recipes, hiking and camping on the Appalachian Trail, teaching myself calligraphy, hanging out with friends, printing photographs in the darkroom. I browsed through record stores, libraries, booksellers, and other purveyors of "printed, bound media artifacts," as Gary Shteyngart wrote memorably.[3] With a swell of nostalgia—partly for the free time I no longer had—I realized that offline leisure had gradually been pushed aside as I spent more and more of my life looking at screens. I had always imagined myself being a renaissance person, but digital media left me feeling one-dimensional. Like many of us, I began to find the blessings of digital media more ambiguous and the burdens heavier. The prospect of temporarily living offline aroused my curiosity. (Maybe you wonder what it would be like, too.)

It struck me that people could apply lessons of the Slow Food movement to the way they used media. I didn't want to do everything slow all the time, just create space for a gentler tempo that counterbalances and complements Fast Media. At the time, I felt alone in having connected Slow Food with digital media. Yet I speculated that a movement of like-minded people might be out there somewhere. I grappled with these ideas in the blog *Slow Media: A Compendium of Artifacts and Discourses about the Possibilities for a Less-Mediated Life*, where I shared my skepticism about technological "progress," my project of sending dozens of postcards to friends and family, and my encounter with a Slow Media group on Facebook (no, it's not ironic; stay tuned to find out why). As recounted elsewhere, I gladly learned that others had co-discovered the notion of Slow Media with me.[4]

I devised an ambitious adventure for myself: to go offline—not just for a day or a week, as many do, but for six months. This experiment attracted me for many reasons. I yearned to re-direct time and energy toward unmediated pastimes. I wanted to reassess the role of media in my life from a detached perspective, inspired by Marshall McLuhan's quip that "We don't know who discovered water, but it probably wasn't a fish." In other words, you can't clearly perceive a substance or situation that you're immersed in. People often analogize media to "the air we breathe," although unlike the fish out of water, we can live without digital devices and networks. Here was a chance to engage in participant observation, gather data, evaluate digital culture from the outside.

My plan was to revert to media technologies from two decades earlier: the year 1989, before the Internet and cellphones began their ascent. This meant that any print would be kosher: newspapers, magazines, books (no Kindles, iPads, e-books). I would listen to vinyl records, audio-cassettes, and compact discs (not MP3 players and their kin). I would watch cable television and videocassettes (not DVR or DVDs). I would use a typewriter or an offline computer for word-processing (nothing networked or downloaded or "in the cloud"). I would make calls on a landline phone (not a mobile one). I would listen to terrestrial radio (not satellite or online broadcasts).

When it came to other people's uses of technology to connect with me, I exerted no preference. I appreciated that many friends, family, and colleagues were willing or even eager to cooperate with this Slow Media experiment of mine. I would not direct them to do (or not do) anything for me that they would not normally do on their own. If someone used a cellphone, I would talk to them on it. If a travel agent went online to book my flight, so be it. If people providing me products or services required the Internet to do their jobs, *que sera sera*. Whatever they did behind the scenes did not essentially change my experience.

A conversation with reporter Sally Herships sparked a story about Slow Media on the popular radio program Marketplace that spread through the blogosphere and captured the public imagination.[5] After announcing my unplugging project to global audiences of National Public Radio, there was no turning back. According to press coverage (an unreliable indicator of reality, to be sure), by the end of 2009 Slow Media had gone from a budding counterculture to a fait accompli, a "movement" that news organizations namedropped without explanation, so familiar did they presume the phenomenon to be. It was covered by major news outlets throughout the United States as well as in Australia, Canada, Chile, England, France, Germany, and elsewhere.

Closer to the Tipping Point

As a society, we are smitten with happiness projects, the power of now, and the joy of less—to name a few best-selling titles. Many of us seek a sense of well-being, presence, and ease that seems lacking in daily life. We know that intensified media use contributes somehow to our feeling distracted, anxious, alienated, forgetful, overworked, stressed out. Few people think that digital technology is the sole source of modern discontent, or even the primary one. However, in the early years of the 21st century, many people discerned that the manifold benefits of devices and networks came at a price. A large and growing minority is seeking—and finding—new ways of interacting with media and with other people.

When wrestling with my qualms about Fast Media, I created my own vision of taking a virtual break. Little did I know that a considerable number of other people were arriving at the same solution: mindfully renegotiating their media use. Others were, like me, inspired by the Slow Food movement to savor simple pleasures by balancing digital media with slower activities. The Slow Media Manifesto captured this spirit. Written by three German scholars, it made waves in the global blogosphere by encouraging people to savor books, records, and other durable alternatives to cheap, fast media technologies.

At the time, prolific authors like Malcolm Gladwell and Stephen King were talking about their own efforts to resist media's intrusions on creative endeavors. King, for one, fessed up to a "screen addiction" that claimed 7.5 hours of his every day: 3.5 hours writing on a computer, an hour handling emails, an hour surfing websites, and two streaming video. (That's slightly less time online than today's average American.) King offered no solutions—"Uncle Stevie doesn't do advice"—but hoped to spend more time with his family, friends, dog, and motorcycle. "I don't think any man or woman on his or her deathbed ever wished he or she had spent more time sending [instant messages] or playing online poker," he wrote.[6]

For his part, Gladwell talked about re-balancing his time portfolio with less digital media. For instance, he gave up blogging in favor of writing books and articles—work that he considered more meaningful. "There are limits to what one can accomplish in a day," the author told *The Globe and Mail*. Gladwell explained that putting his smartphone out of sight helps him find peace of mind and focus— even when he's working in public places like coffee shops. "I find all kinds of small ways of finding moments of solitude," he noted.[7] Observing limits can enhance our productivity and our enjoyment of life.

As I was planning my digital retreat in 2009, Oprah Winfrey joined the fray. She dared her audience to try a weeklong experiment in voluntary simplicity in the "What Can You Live Without?" challenge. Winfrey proposed that people would find more meaning in life if they scaled back on stuff and cut out the noise— especially by disconnecting from digital devices. Rule No. 1 was to stop using media technology: computers, cellphones, television, and video games. Viewers were invited to download a 14-page guide with tips for coping with digital withdrawal, a journal for tracking successes and temptations during the trial, and a chart for setting future media limits to avoid old habits.[8]

That same year, a nonprofit group called Reboot launched the first National Day of Unplugging, aiming to secularize the ritual of shunning electronic gizmos for one day each week. The event encourages people to try unplugging at least once, and maybe make it a habit. Reboot's founders were media-savvy, nonobservant Jewish professionals who "felt a collective need to fight back against fast-paced living."[9] Their "Sabbath Manifesto" urged everyone, regardless of faith, to slow down and observe a day of rest. The central tenet: avoid technology by turning off cellphones, logging out of email, signing out of Facebook and Twitter, or however else you choose. Several other principles share a nondenominational orientation: lighting candles, drinking wine, eating bread, finding silence. The manifesto preserves the spirit if not the letter of the Old Testament, loosening Sabbath restrictions to make the practice more accessible and appealing.

At this time, an array of journalists, celebrities, and extroverts were trying "media diets" and "digital detox," too, including news anchor Katie Couric, food columnist Mark Bittman, and actor Josh Radnor; among countless others. People like Kim Kardashian, Lady Gaga, and Serena Williams briefly gave up their Twitter lives (presumably a great personal sacrifice) for the benefit of World AIDS Day. *The New York Times* and *Huffington Post* challenged people to cut back on device use—an unusual request, perhaps, for media to dare people *not* to read their content. Educators from Amherst, Stephens, and other colleges were holding campus events such as days of mindfulness and device-free vespers. Giving up digital or social media for a day, a weekend, or longer became a bona-fide lifestyle choice.

Bittman is a perfect example. A self-declared "techno-addict," he used to keep a laptop near his bed to check email first thing and last thing each day. He had started swiping his credit card when he couldn't resist the siren call of email during long flights. The author of books such as *How to Cook Everything*, he had learned how to work everywhere. Bittman was uncomfortable with his media cravings—and 70-hour workweeks—and decided that he would start disconnecting more. Though he grew up celebrating Passover, he had never regularly practiced a day of rest from technology based on religious principles. Bittman extolled the digital Sabbath as a means of combating excessive work and finding a sustainable pace for everyday life.[10]

The best-selling book *Hamlet's Blackberry* expressed a kindred attitude. In it, William Powers drew lessons from Plato, Seneca, Shakespeare, and other great minds in how to prevent devices from diluting family life. Techie tastemakers invited Powers to talk at the annual South by Southwest conference (SXSW), which featured unplugging parties hosted by Sabbath Manifesto founders. SXSW organizers were inspired by the National Day of Unplugging to hold a "tweet-free, in-the-moment" event where tech leaders and entrepreneurs shared secrets for doing a weekly digital detox to create "sacred 'no-connection' time" in their lives.[11]

My initial reaction was: Huh? SXSW people pride themselves on being tech-addicted, uber-connected, multi-deviced, and happily distracted. They were early adopters of Twitter and FourSquare and whatnot. Why are they turning off, tuning out, and dropping into the offline counterculture now? The involvement of people who produced, promoted, and enthusiastically participated in digital media and networks made this trend more intriguing.

Then there's me.

I Heart Digital Media

Somehow, people have gotten the idea that I hate digital media. Before we go any further, let's make one thing clear. This book is not about how life was so much better in [insert decade here] before there were [insert technology here]. You should not be surprised to hear that I love many things about digital media. Really, wouldn't my unplugging project have been boring if I hated the Internet? There would be no challenge, no sacrifice. It would be like me giving up pickles or sardines for Lent.

I realize how lucky we are to have digital technology, especially for communicating with each other. It was lonely living overseas in the 1980s, when I was out of touch with friends and family back in the United States. I also lived abroad in the 1990s, when the Internet was too slow to be very useful and land-line calls to the States were prohibitively expensive. Like most of us, I was dazzled by all the things that we can do with the Internet: sending free messages across the globe, finding information instantly that used to be practically inaccessible, sharing blogs and photos and videos with everyone, everywhere. Information technology was setting us free! And people who didn't use new technologies? So backwards. Luddites. They just didn't get it.

It wasn't an easy decision to put digital media on a back burner. I chose that path because it felt like—still does, sometimes—there were just too many days when I woke up and had coffee and breakfast, and went on the Internet to check email, and before I knew it, six or eight hours had slipped away while I was reading email, sending email, clicking on links, checking Facebook, just roving around the Web. At the end of the day, I often felt like—still do, sometimes— I had not achieved enough meaningful things with my limited time on earth.

While my experiences as a teacher, a scholar, and a human being drew me toward the Slow Media project, being a contrarian drove me as much as anything else. The more I talked with people about going offline, and the more they said it was impossible, the more it stoked me to prove I could. A lot of people laughed when I told them the plan. My friends and colleagues generally think that digital media are indispensable tools without which life would be daunting and dreary. Reactions fell into two camps: (1) it's an undesirable plan and cannot be done; or (2) it's an admirable plan and cannot be done. Their resistance only strengthened my resolve.

Other friends teased that I should dig out my long-lost Walkman and rabbit-ear antennas. One dear old friend showed faith in my ability to carry out the project, claiming that I was good at denying myself things. If I do have any such proclivity, it's toward asceticism that can help me become a better person and live a better life, to paraphrase Foucault.[12] Unplugging does not feel like self-denial when you focus on what you're getting, instead of what you're giving up. My ostensible self-deprivation was more like "philosophical self-denial," as Benjamin Franklin called it: refusing to do something desirable that would cost you more than it is worth.[13] This kind of positive denial offers a way of escaping the "hedonic treadmill" that turns novel pleasures into mere comforts and, eventually, into disappointments that no longer bring any joy.[14] In other words, periodically abstaining from digital media would help me get *more* satisfaction from them.

Yet the greatest allure of Slow principles is time politics, rather than pleasure. Despite the perception that indolent professors work a couple of days a week, it's more typical for an academic like me to spend 60 hours on teaching, research, and service. Professional duties have colonized our nights, weekends, and leisure time in part thanks to—you guessed it—*digital media*. Mundane activities such as health, personal care, and household maintenance are often pushed aside (suggesting that the stereotype of absent-minded, style-challenged professors might be justified). Studies show that physical and psychological strain in academia exceeds that found in the general population. Academics are not alone in their struggle to regain work-life balance, of course, but they feel the time crunch keenly. In an MIT survey, 78% of faculty reported that "no matter how hard they work, they can't get everything done," compared to 48% of CEOs.[15] Universities have slashed resources for professors while increasing workloads, productivity expectations, competition, assessments, and scrutiny. Meanwhile, there's less time for those things that beckoned people to the academy in the first place: reading, writing, reflection, deliberation, collegiality.

I could not change university culture or its acquiescence to corporate values like efficiency, quantification, accountability, and speed. But I could resist the incessant pressure to work more, better, faster—by curbing my own media use. Slow Media offered a method of personal intervention. Nonetheless, in light of social and professional obligations, I could only consider going offline during a break or sabbatical (such an opportune word). Like many careers, mine entails compulsory duties as well as negotiable ones. Research leave got the former off my plate and emboldened me to drop many of the latter. (Coincidentally, a colleague who took leave at the same time engaged in a similar effort to fortify work-life boundaries; she called it "The Silence Project.")

It took months of preparation to plan and implement the Slow Media project. I began in April 2009 by renting a post office box, digging out old videocassette and record players, installing a landline, removing my email address from hundreds of lists, and tracking down Polaroid film and typewriter ribbons. After much anticipation, I abandoned my computer on July 4, with a nod to Independence Day as well as the start date of Thoreau's legendary retreat to Walden Pond.

The Proverbial Fish Out of Water

Quick: Where's the nearest payphone to wherever you are now? Chances are good that you passed one recently and didn't notice. During my Slow Media project, I regularly had to locate coin-operated phones.[16] When I asked store clerks, bartenders, and strangers on the streets of New York City where to find one, they could rarely direct me toward a payphone—even if there was one within eyesight, on a path they trod daily. People would say there were no payphones nearby, and I would soon spot one a few yards away.

Like many people, you probably do not notice public phones in your physical environment. Unless you are alone somewhere with a broken-down car *and* desperate for a ride or tow *and* forgot your cellphone (or you have a dead battery or you cannot get a signal), they no longer seem relevant. When you do not have a digital device in your hand, your powers of observation kick into higher gear. Your perspective on the world shifts. Living offline feels like being an ethnographer, like doing fieldwork on your own culture. It gives the same kind of intercultural stimulation that you get from traveling, without leaving home or spending a dime. (Except, perhaps, a little spare change for payphones.)

Some questions to gauge your readiness for taking an Internet sabbatical: *Do you keep printed road maps in your car? When's the last time you used the yellow pages or sent a postcard? Do you have a landline? Turntable? Film camera? Fax machine? Clock radio? Stand-alone calculator? Manual or electronic typewriter? Wristwatch?*

Newspaper subscription? Address book? Do you care about the quality of your penmanship?

When spending significant time without a cellphone or computer, these are some things to stock up on and think about. Many digital immigrants (like me) have printed materials and analog gadgets like these in our homes, even if we do not use them anymore. I frequently ask my students if they have or use these items. They typically do not have—never had—any of them. They do not use—never have used—such things. Often their parents or grandparents do.

This might make unplugging sound so awfully inconvenient that you rule out the idea of trying it. Not so! Don't get me wrong: it *is* inconvenient. Yet the experiment brought me pleasure, opened my eyes, and defied my expectations. Some of the dialogue about our experience of reality in the 1980 movie *My Dinner with André*—which I watched on VHS during my offline experiment—struck a special chord, in this context.[17] André tells Wally that boredom is an illusion, a tool of oppression, used to suppress dissent. Analog media became the new lens through which I viewed the world.

People assumed I would suffer horribly by depriving myself of the Internet and cellphones, but to me it felt more like liberation. Conventional wisdom says that going online saves time and helps you get more done. On the contrary, I felt like unplugged days were longer and more productive. Things often got done faster in analog mode than digitally—like when I found phone numbers in the printed directory quicker than my husband did with a search engine. The Internet is our default resource, but it's not always the best one.

There's also the myth that older people dislike digital devices more than young people. You might expect Baby Boomers and Generation X-ers who grew up without smartphones to show more sympathy for my analog lifestyle than Millennials did (people born in the 1990s, roughly speaking). However, my 20-something friends entered into the spirit of the experiment more readily than older adults, who chided me for not conforming to their own habits and cultural expectations, as well as for "inconveniencing" them.[18]

I did allow a small release valve, letting myself go online for a total of one hour per month. I guarded that time carefully, meting out 15 minutes per week with a kitchen timer ticking nearby. On the first of each month, I was always excited to get my new hour. As I recounted in a Marketplace segment, I did fall off the wagon a couple of times, mostly when planning my wedding.[19] (Unless you, too, have recently spent six months without Internet access while shopping for a wedding dress, I refuse your judgment.) Having a limited amount of time online makes you focus on the things that really matter. It's a microcosm for setting priorities in life beyond the screen.

Living more mindfully in the material world prompted me to form a panoply of new habits that persist today. Borrowing movies from the library, instead of streaming entertainment. Keeping a printed dictionary and thesaurus on my desk, instead of using online resources. Shopping in brick-and-mortar stores, instead of ordering online. Making phone calls, instead of sending emails. People thought I was closing myself off from experience and connection by going off-line. Paradoxically, I was opening myself to new experiences and different kinds of connection.

Since replugging, I shift more consciously between online and offline modes, weighing the advantages and disadvantages of each. Like many of us, I get sick of staring at screens for too long. I like to support local businesses. I enjoy making vocal and ocular contact with human beings. I continue to downplay Internet use on nights and weekends, check email and Facebook less often, and keep my cellphone out of sight and mind much of the time.

Some digital habits that I gladly retrieved: Looking up directions in Google Maps (though I still like keeping a road atlas handy). Paying monthly bills online, instead of mailing checks. Accessing bank accounts on the Web, instead of going to the local branch. Buying plane tickets through websites, not travel agencies. Checking the weather forecast online, not on the radio or TV. Good riddance to those dull minutes of teasers and fillers one must endure before learning whether to carry an umbrella.

My unplugging experiment ended on New Year's Eve three years ago, at the very time when my husband happened to break his cellphone. The story goes: We were en route to a party right before midnight. The destination address was on his phone—which he had left at our house, too far away to retrieve. Having failed to find the party, we returned home, where he tossed the device across the room a little too hard. There we were, a professional couple—a journalism professor and a creative technologist, no less—with nary a cellphone between us. The scene was a trenchant reminder of digital devices' centrality in the modern world to which I was, somewhat ambivalently, returning.

Imagining the Alternatives

While my Slow Media project began with personal musings, it quickly took on professional meanings. Unplugging put a new twist on my work as a scholar and teacher. It was also the genesis of this book.

My objects of research expanded beyond "alternative media" to encompass "alternatives *to* media." Earlier, I had explored how certain news sources and communication models provide alternative content, forms, and practices. My scholarship had considered questions such as: Why do activists say they don't use mainstream media, when they actually do? What does the notoriously slippery term "alternative media" mean to people who use it? How is making printed zines different from producing blogs, according to people who have published both forms? The experience of being offline and discovering the creative energy that people showed in *not* using media piqued my academic curiosity. Most media research focuses on how people *use* media; relatively little work is concerned with how they *don't* use it. (This is partly for practical reasons: how do you study people when they're *not* doing something?)

After the experiment, I dove into research on the innovative practices through which people deliberately resist the influence of mainstream culture and create sanctuaries from digital media. As I dug deeper into Slow Media and unplugging, I became fascinated by the imagination and courage demanded by rituals like these. Scholars often distinguish between communication that serves a "transmission" (instrumental) purpose or a "ritual" (symbolic) one. In the first mode, we value speed and effectiveness. In the second mode, we participate in activities that aren't meant to be expedient but rather spiritual, emotional, aesthetic, communal. Communication rituals often mark a special place and time, a sort of *time out*, in which ordinary life is briefly suspended and an alternative reality is experienced. Unplugging aspires to these symbolic goals; it is not about going fast, being productive, and getting things done.

A familiar ritual involving media non-use is the Orthodox Jewish practice of a weekly Sabbath or *Shabbat*, a Hebrew word meaning "to cease" or to "rest." This tradition is rooted in the Fourth Commandment prohibiting work on the seventh day. In modern times, "work" is broadly interpreted to include writing, shopping, and activities requiring electricity, appliances, computers, and cellphones. People observe the Sabbath to obey God's will and community expectations as well as to maintain a space for contemplation and communion. Many people without strong religious motivations voluntarily adopt similar rituals from a humanist sensibility, limiting media use in favor of reclaiming personal time and re-engaging face to face with other people and nature.[20]

Other communities of faith uphold shared values by constraining media use, too. For instance, the Amish and Mennonites typically prohibit electricity and electronic media (including radio, television, and computers) in the home—not just one day per week but always. However, many of these communities have collectively decided to allow certain media in certain contexts, such as away from homes. Some Amish groups originally adopted household telephones, later rejected them when family life seemed to suffer, and finally accepted community phones located outside of homes.[21] People in these Old Order sects are not incapable or afraid of adopting new technologies. Rather, they want to use media deliberately, weighing the gains and losses, and deciding what works best for their society. Indeed, you could argue that Amish attitudes toward technology are more sophisticated than ours because their societies are capable of discriminating among innovations, as Bill McKibben notes.[22] We might choose different criteria than theirs, if we did discriminate. But we don't even try.

Many secular people choose to draw boundaries in time and space delineating what kind of media to use *here and now* versus what kind of media (if any) to use *there and then*.[23] Often they use spiritual language like *sabbath* and *fast* to convey the periodic separation from dominant cultural values achieved by eschewing media. Others have used corporeal metaphors of *diets* and *detox* to describe their pursuit of productivity and purity through media non-use. I like using the concept of *ritual* to highlight commonalities among unplugging activities, which might seem like anomalies if studied alone. The ritual perspective shows that abstaining from media can be constructive. Unpluggers aren't just criticizing mainstream culture—they're also enacting an alternative vision of life.

This positive approach to unplugging had a big impact on my teaching. I used to routinely assign students to do a "digital detox," instructing them to avoid the Internet, cellphones, television, and the like for a single day. Usually, a few people in each class report getting through a whole day without media. Many admit to failure and explain how and why they finally gave in to their digital urges. (The scant claims of success can't be verified, of course, since I have to take the students' word on how they spent their time.) Reasons range from possible or actual emergencies to poor preparation to irresistible curiosity to mere boredom. This brings to light a major weakness of focusing on what you *can't* do: forbidden mediated activities. It can create a void in which people get bored and time seems to drag unbearably slowly.

Inspired by Slow Media, I shifted the strategy. Instead of presenting the experiment as a negative—"you can't go online or use your cellphone"—I reframed it as a positive: *You have an opportunity to enjoy any unmediated activities of your choice.* Color me surprised when most of them loved the Slow Media experiment. Students wrote about how they wrote in paper journals, practiced calligraphy, watched movies on videocassette, listened to audio-cassettes or vinyl records, played musical instruments, and made pottery. They described the experience as *easy, relaxing, special, sacred, fun, interesting, old-fashioned, engrossing, therapeutic,* and *weird*. As it happens, many of these 19- to 23-year-olds felt nostalgic for things that they enjoyed and made time for during high school—activities that have been pushed aside, in part, by increased connection to cellphones and computers.[24]

I highlight the power of Slow Media as an alternative model in my research, too. Revivals of printed zines and vinyl records were more than just nostalgic—dare I say Luddite?—reactions against modern culture. (And nostalgia, like Luddism, is unfairly demonized; it can be a productive, progressive force.) In fact, Slow Media buffs enjoy digital technologies as much as anyone else. Resurgences of old media help reveal the structural and cultural factors that drive product development. Old technological forms are nudged offstage by commercial needs, design decisions, distribution policies, regulatory environments, advertising, and publicity campaigns—not simply because they are inferior or because consumers don't want them anymore. Slow Media proposes practical solutions that merit consideration, akin to community-supported agriculture and other networks fostered by the Slow Food movement.[25]

Alternative food systems blossomed partly because consumers wanted wider choice, higher-quality products, and greater pleasure in eating. But there's more to it than self-interest. Slow Foodies are driven also by concerns about fair trade and ecological health. These values apply to how we make, buy, and use media, too. I long hesitated to get a smartphone (I have since opted in) because I was uncomfortable with the device-industrial complex, whose business practices are often unfriendly to customers, employees, and the planet.[26] Society has gradually realized that the production, use, and disposal of digital devices have troubling consequences: depleting scarce natural resources, threatening public health, and polluting the environment. Slow Media gives us a useful framework for thinking, talking, and doing something about such obstacles to human and planetary well-being.

Users of the World, Unite

All these experiences in life and work put me on the path toward writing this book and envisioning a slower, more sustainable mediated future for all of us. In the years since my offline experiment, unplugging has grown into more than just "the new counterculture," as Nicholas Carr once called it.[27] Turning off devices and dropping out of networks have become a fairly mainstream way of tuning in to one's life. For example, one US survey found that most online users have taken or considered taking a social-media vacation, saying they didn't have time to keep up with multiple profiles and irrelevant updates.[28] A UK survey found that 34% of all adult Internet users sought time away from the Web—with 11% having done so in the previous week alone. Another 32% of respondents said that they would like to try a digital detox in the future.[29] Of the unpluggers, 25% spent up to a day offline; 20% took up to a week off; and 5% went Web-free for a month. In another US survey, 66% of adults and teens said they observed a "no devices" rule at the dinner table.[30] Sixty-five percent of Americans think that periodically "unplugging" or taking a "digital detox" is important for their mental health, but only 28% of those who say this actually report doing so.[31] Maybe we could all use some more encouragement.

Slow Media helped launch a public conversation that continues apace under many names. People have agitated for movements of Slow News, Slow Journalism, Slow Art, Slow Books, Slow Words, Slow Blogging, Slow Reading, Slow Professors, and Slow Communication. A concurrent stream of innovation swirls around cultural practices of unplugging, digital detoxing, media fasting, information dieting—call it what you will. This book weaves together these disparate strands to fashion a new banner, an identity that conveys the depth and breadth of a transformation in how many people think about digital devices and human lives. We need a visionary name to rally around.

Some people in affluent societies are reluctant to abstain from media, shopping, and work. Many North Americans, especially, have been apathetic or even hostile toward campaigns for "Buy Nothing Day" and "TV Turnoff Week" (later rechristened "Digital Detox Week" and devoted to "screen-time awareness").[32]

Our culture tends to value productivity, abundance, speed, and busyness over the absences thereof—namely, slowness, leisure, moderation, and idleness. Spiritual types might say that we're just racing toward our demise.

My motives in introducing Slow Media to a wider audience are not entirely selfless. Today, it would be harder for me to go offline for six months than it was in 2010. I would like to do it again someday, and I need help. What's more, I want *you* to be able to unplug when you want to. Now is the time for a silent majority to speak up and seek better ways to live by promoting human and environmental sustainability through slower media use and production.

None of us can do it alone. That's why popular appeals for downsizing (better yet, *rightsizing*) media use often take the form of manifestos. There's the Slow Media Manifesto, which focuses on sustainability and monotasking. There's the Sabbath Manifesto, whose prime directive is "avoid technology," followed by a list of to-do items: get outside, nurture your health, connect with loved ones. There's a Slow Communication Manifesto by John Freeman, author of *The Tyranny of E-mail*, whose solution to information overload is "Don't Send." There's a Slow Books Manifesto by Maura Kelly of *The Atlantic*, which takes a cue from food activist Michael Pollan in recommending "Read books. As often as you can. Mostly classics." There's tech pioneer Jaron Lanier's manifesto against gadgets, which argues that we need to shape technology instead of letting it shape us.

We find inspiration in manifestos like these that confirm we are not alone in seeking change. As individuals, we can only go so far in tackling the dilemmas posed by media, which are social and cultural in nature. The word *manifesto* is related to *manifest*, which means easily perceived. As the 21st century wears on, we realize that while the problems with digital media might be obvious, the solutions are less so. This book is about the quest for imaginative alternatives.

Slow Media

1

Introduction

Alternative Visions of Sustainability

The personal computer and Internet had a significant impact on the Sustainability Revolution by facilitating the dissemination of information and the organization of sustainability-oriented groups, which have better access to media outlets traditionally controlled by well-established institutions.
—Andres Edwards, *The Sustainability Revolution: Portrait of a Paradigm Shift*[1]

Due to the power consumption of all the processing that humans use, from Web searches to mobile phone calls, one's computational footprint is becoming a nontrivial part of one's carbon footprint.
—Bill Tomlinson, *Greening through IT: Information Technology for Environmental Sustainability*[2]

Since the 1970s, a growing awareness of the impact that human activities have upon the planet has spurred real-world changes that are widely likened to a "sustainability revolution,"[3] guided by a new sensibility of stewardship toward the Earth. This paradigm shift has prompted people to re-think their relationships to the natural world as well as each other and to regenerate the world through organic farming, renewable energy, green design, and related practices. The sustainability revolution offers alternative ways of life that support economic viability and healthy ecosystems by modifying consumption patterns and implementing a more equitable social framework, according to sustainability educator Andres Edwards.[4]

The movement toward sustainability dates back to the 1972 United Nations Conference on the Human Environment, which urged protection of natural resources and wildlife alongside human rights. It has deep roots in the Transcendentalism of Ralph Waldo Emerson and Henry David Thoreau, the conservationism of John Muir and Rachel Carson, and the pre-sustainability environmental activism of the 1960s. This revolution bloomed with the first celebration of Earth Day in 1970 and the green counterculture of that era, exemplified in the US by sustainable philosophies and lifestyles that Bay Area innovators advocated through Stewart Brand's *Whole Earth Catalog*. For a generation of hippies, do-it-yourselfers, and others seeking independence from mainstream American culture, it was more than a publication: it was a way of life.[5] Through the 1960s and 1970s, Brand's catalog promoted a pragmatic philosophy and a utopian agenda that celebrated technological achievement, human ingenuity, and sustainable living.

Sustainability ideas gained traction with politicians, economists, policy analysts, and environmental activists in the 1980s, when the Worldwatch Institute's first "State of the World" report announced that we were "living beyond our means, largely borrowing against the future," and the UN's Brundtland Report (a.k.a. "Our Common Future") popularized the notion of sustainable development. The 1992 "Earth Summit" in Rio added fuel to the fire, by negotiating a Climate Change Convention that later led to the Kyoto Protocol and Paris Agreement. Climate change is perhaps the biggest and most urgent challenge facing humanity today. Global temperatures are rising at an unprecedented rate, with 15 of the 16 hottest years on record occurring between 2001 and 2016.[6] If you were born after 1977, you have probably never seen a year of below average temperatures.

Another revolution coincided—in both time and space—with the one for sustainability. The Digital Revolution began to emerge in the 1970s, largely through widespread adoption of new communication technologies: first personal computers and later the Internet, mobile phones, and social networks. Sometimes called the Third Industrial Revolution, this radical transition is epitomized by a shift from analog, mechanical, and electronic technologies to digital ones. The Information Age ushered in sweeping changes that hardly need enumeration here, as they have profoundly transformed our culture, economy, politics, and daily lives. It is notable that many digital innovations arose side-by-side with sustainability ethics in San Francisco and Silicon Valley. Stewart Brand played a central role on this front, too. In the 1980s, he founded The WELL, one of the first virtual communities. In the dot-com era, he co-founded (with Kevin Kelly) *Wired* magazine, which famously named Marshall McLuhan its "patron saint."

Wired editors were perhaps unaware of the media theorist's pessimism about many forms of electronic media, which he called "pure poison." Our means of communication had begun to overwhelm our messages, he said—a state of affairs that he found deeply dehumanizing and depressing. Although people often interpret McLuhan's vision of the *global village* as positive and hopeful, he predicted that electronic media would produce pain, stress, and anxiety in the world—not peace, love, and understanding.[7] By contrast, *Wired* took an optimistic view of media's effects on mankind. Like the *Whole Earth Catalog* before it, *Wired* espoused a techno-utopian philosophy that saw little conflict between technological development and sustainable living.

As the quotes from Edwards and Bill Tomlinson at the start of this chapter suggest, the relationship between sustainability and media is complex—and double-edged. The digital revolution has been a boon to the sustainability movement in some ways and a bane in others. Information technologies have made it easier for sustainability activists to coordinate protests, spread information, raise public awareness, and garner support for a cornucopia of causes. People can more easily learn about companies' environmental and social performance by researching data and reports available online, which helps the public hold businesses accountable. Some critics worry that networked media too often distract people from meaningful social action and undermine movements against the status quo.[8] Our perception of new media technologies as empowering ordinary people, more so than corporations and governments, might be exaggerated.

Similarly distorted is our vision of "virtual" digital media as more eco-friendly than older print and analog forms. The effects of information technologies are not uniformly favorable to the environment, according to Tomlinson, a leader of the Green IT movement. For starters, digital media consume a considerable amount of power. By some estimates, an avatar in the virtual game Second Life consumes as much energy as a real-world Brazilian citizen.[9] Then there's the squandering of natural resources. Manufacturing one desktop computer exhausts more than 500 pounds of fossil fuels as well as 50 pounds of chemicals and 3,300 pounds of water—around the same volume of resources used to make an automobile.[10]

E-waste is also a fast-growing concern. Until the 20th century, Americans produced very little consumer waste. Today, discarded electronics alone account for over 3 million tons of trash per year in the US and around 35 million tons worldwide—equivalent to 10,000 elephants per hour.[11] The rapid innovation and turnover rate of computer technologies fosters a culture of disposability that is "clearly problematic," Tomlinson says.[12] He believes that IT can potentially yield benefits greater than its environmental footprint, by making both the industry and society more sustainable.

Sustainability is more than just a buzzword. What exactly does it mean? The word has been used (and overused, and misused) in so many ways that scholars have found more than three hundred definitions.[13] The *Oxford English Dictionary* describes it as "the property of being environmentally sustainable; the degree to which a process or enterprise is able to be maintained or continued while avoiding the long-term depletion of natural resources." In current usage, sustainability has both an ecological and a social dimension. While environmental stewardship has long been central to its meaning, people now incorporate social justice, as well.

Tomlinson's definition exemplifies this evolution: a sustainable global ecosystem is one in which "all defining processes, such as the maintenance of biodiversity (including *Homo sapiens*) at a high quality of life, are able to continue indefinitely."[14] An unsustainable system is one that collapses because, for example, it has depleted natural resources, overproduced waste, undermined biodiversity, or harmed quality of life. My discussion embraces this broader sense of sustainability, one that explicitly includes human well-being. These are some of the questions driving this book: How do people apply sustainability principles to their mediated lives? What alternative practices related to media use and production do they foster? What challenges do they face in trying to change an unsustainable media system? In sum, how can our media culture be transformed in order to promote a more sustainable society?

Sustainable Media and the Popular Imagination

People have begun to recognize that the status quo of digital media production and consumption is insufficiently responsive to human and environmental needs. Books devoted to practical and ethical concerns about digital media resonate with a public grown somewhat wary, sometimes weary, of devices and networks and the companies that make them. Authors who have helped stoke this conversation include Adam Alter (*Irresistible*), Mark Bauerlein (*The Dumbest Generation*), Nicholas Carr (*The Shallows*), Jaron Lanier (*You Are Not a Gadget*), William Powers (*Hamlet's Blackberry*), Douglas Rushkoff (*Throwing Rocks at the Google Bus*), and Sherry Turkle (*Alone Together, Reclaiming Conversation*). A broad swathe of people has decided that their mediated lives are too fast, too exploitative, too digital, too disposable, too dirty, and too distracting. In other words, they consider current patterns of media use to be untenable, and they're seeking viable alternatives.

It's not just a few pensive book lovers from a generation wistful for the paper cuts of its youth, either. Many do come from the ranks of digital immigrants, who remember media habits being less disruptive to daily life in the 20th century. However, in defiance of the "digital native" stereotype, many are young people, for whom media fasts offer a quasi-intercultural experience, as well as much-needed relief from stress. People of all ages have grown concerned about the cumulative effects of unbounded work, unbridled information, and unlimited communication on family life, health, relationships, learning, spirituality, work-life balance, and creativity.

Counter to what one might expect, many of the contrarians are people working in media and technology fields who are disenchanted by the realities of computerized culture, for which they once held high hopes. (Back in 1984, Apple professed a desire to smash Big Brother. Today, the company's ads demand blind faith: "Trust us. It's better.") People apprehensive of technological change have been marginalized and belittled as "Luddite"—a phenomenon that I will explore in depth. It's harder to dismiss such ideas when they come from forward-looking people who are adept with digital technology and hope to harness it for the public good.

In the 21st century, a wide range of creative people are embracing sustainable approaches to using and producing media. Because many of them were inspired directly or indirectly by the Slow Food movement and its allies, I use the phrase

Slow Media to encompass these imaginative responses to mediated life and describe one facet of the broader sustainability alliance. I like to call people who adopt these new principles and practices *Slow Medians*, although it's unlikely that anyone has adopted that moniker. They represent a fertile subset of "cultural creatives," a loosely networked movement that's difficult to recognize because its members often act on sustainability values through culturally innovative practices rather than political action. The cultural-creative phenomenon provides an illustrative example of the movement toward Slow and sustainable media.

Cultural Creativity beneath the Radar

Cultural creatives constitute a large segment of the population that cares deeply about ecology and social justice, yet pursues those causes by effecting cultural change rather than participating in organized politics. Social researchers Paul Ray and Sherry Anderson estimated this group at around 26%, or 50 million people, in the US in 2000, and it has likely grown larger since then. (There are around 80–90 million cultural creatives in the European Union, too.)[15] Members of this group were influenced by post-1960s movements for civil rights, women's rights, peace, and the environment and are interested in globalization, corporate reform, and new forms of spirituality. This creative subculture has a strong affinity with sustainability.

Several hallmarks of cultural creatives correlate with sustainable values: loving nature and being concerned about its destruction; seeking action on planetary problems (biodiversity loss, overpopulation, ecological unsustainability, exploitation of poor people); being willing to pay more taxes or pay more for consumer goods if it helps the environment; wanting governments to spend more on health, education, community improvement, and environmental protection; and being concerned about the negative impact of corporations. Ray and Anderson think this category of people was hitherto unnoticed because it cuts across traditional boundaries and synthesizes perspectives from progressivism, conservatism, traditionalism, and modernism. Sustainability actors defy conventional orientations such as left or right.[16] The movement flew below the radar for a long time precisely because it was so large, diverse, and decentralized.

The sustainability movement has five main characteristics, in Edwards' view. First, it is committed to ecological health, economic viability, and social equity ("the Three Es"; education is sometimes considered the fourth). Second, it has a large and diverse number of groups—he estimates 30,000 groups in the US alone. Third, it has a wide range of issues. Fourth, it has a decentralized leadership. And fifth, it has varying modes of action, both oppositional and alternative. *Oppositional actions* includes protests against habitat destruction and undemocratic globalization, while *alternative actions* include voluntary simplicity and local economies (such as community-supported agriculture and renewable-energy projects).

The sustainability revolution took an innovative step in the 1980s by broadening its scope to include the pursuit of economic and social well-being alongside ecological health. Earlier environmentalists, who had recognized the damage caused by human activity, viewed a dynamic economy and healthy ecosystem as conflicting goals. You had to sacrifice one to get the other, it had been assumed. When sustainability advocates realized that economic viability and social equity could be complementary to ecological heath, a much broader coalition formed.

One influential advocate who underscores the creativity, heterodoxy, and near invisibility of this sustainability network is Paul Hawken. His book *The Ecology of Commerce* was a clarion call for early sustainability innovators in the business community.[17] After years of saving business cards, Hawken began to see a pattern that suggested something important was happening all around him. The cards he collected were from individuals in recurring professions (education, law, architecture, business entrepreneurship) that might have little impact alone but together could become a force for large-scale change.

The movement arose organically from grassroots groups and civil society, giving it an amorphous network structure that makes it stronger. "No one started this worldview, no one is in charge of it, no orthodoxy is restraining it," Hawken said. It is "unrecognizable to the American media because it is not centralized, based on power or led by charismatic white males."[18] Hawken is an environmentalist and entrepreneur (and, yes, a charismatic white male) who promotes a "new type of industrialism" that he believes can be efficient and profitable while also helping the environment and creating jobs. In *Blessed Unrest*, a book about the sustainability revolution, he proposes that this movement grew quickly because members cared more about solutions than ideologies.

The sustainability movement is deeply concerned with issues of speed and time. Economic advisor and social theorist Jeremy Rifkin correlates the emergence in the 1980s of "ecological time" with an "empathetic" orientation shared by diverse activists devoted to feminism, holistic health, organic farming, animal rights, and other progressive causes.[19] Their actions appear apolitical, he says, because they advance nontraditional politics of personal and collective transformation rather than traditional politics of ballots, bills, and referenda. Ecological time pursues harmony and ultimately conflicts with the "efficient time" promoted by computers. The latter pursues economic growth that conforms to artificial rhythms of production and severs human bonds with the environment. Re-orienting ourselves toward ecological time can repair those bonds. Slow Media and sustainability advocates share a goal of slowing down society to align with environmental processes and the sacred rhythms of life.

Sustainability in Media and Communication

I define *sustainable media* as values and practices characteristic of a media culture able to indefinitely maintain biodiversity and a high quality of life while avoiding the long-term depletion of natural and human resources. The term is distinct from *sustainable communication* or *green communication*, although these concepts share some common ground. People usually say "sustainable communication" when they mean communication *about* sustainability, especially about sustainable development, rather than communication or media practices that *are* sustainable in human or environmental terms. Similarly, they often use "green communication" or green media to mean communication *about* green issues and policies in the context of nongovernmental organizations. Many people apply such phrases in business consulting, marketing, public relations and advertising—industries whose commitments to sustainability vary greatly.

By contrast, I conceive of "sustainable media" more broadly. *Sustainable* includes human and environmental well-being, among other values, and *media* includes communication, among other practices. This inclusive definition enables us to make important connections between a variety of scholarly fields, pedagogical areas, and cultural phenomena that otherwise would fly beneath the radar. This book explores an array of new ideals for sustainable engagement with media that have arisen in the public imagination. Many people have begun to envision ways of creating and using media that are slower, fairer, more material, cleaner, greener, and more mindful. This includes ways of using media *less*. From a sustainability perspective, growth is not a criterion for progress and proliferation of digital media cannot be limitless.

As a verb, "sustain" can mean to strengthen or support, to uphold, to continue, to bear without breaking, as well as to undergo or suffer. As an adjective, "sustainable" means bearable, supportable, defensible. In their 2016 anthology *Sustainable Media: Critical Approaches to Media and Environment*, Nicole Starosielski and Janet Walker invited contributors to expose and analyze media's unsustainability. With a focus on adverse physical effects ranging from cellphone tower radiation to excessive water usage in Hollywood, the book might have been called *Unsustainable Media*. "Sustainability discourse has often served the interests of the privileged," the authors contend, noting that corporations use the term to conceal the real environmental impacts of media products and organizations.[20] To complement important studies like these, which spotlight untenable practices, we also need to envision what viable media alternatives look like.

Slow Medians resemble cultural creatives in not having been recognized as a coherent entity—even by themselves. They comprise a large, diverse, decentralized group whose media use is incredibly heterogeneous. Until now, sustainable media practices have been known by different names to different people. For example, various forms of unplugging have been called *digital detox, media fasting, information diet, tech* or *Internet* or *digital* or *secular sabbath, evening laptop shut, no email day, device nap* or *vacation, predictable time off,* and so on.

At first, I thought this movement toward Slow and sustainable media might qualify as a counterculture or subculture. In reality, these alternative values and practices have been adopted by so many people in so many ways that they are almost mainstream. A look at the history of alternative media can help us understand how the Slow Media movement fits within the cultural order. And sustainability ideals can help reinvigorate public conversations about the relevance of alternative media in a digital age.

Slow Media as Alternative Media

From Thomas Paine's *Common Sense* pamphlet to Soviet Russia's dissident *samizdat* publications and beyond, the communities that produce, distribute, and consume alternative media have long antagonized the status quo and sought social change on ecological issues. Proponents of alternative media often highlight failures of the corporate-commercial media structure, a concern shared with Slow advocates. They tend to view corporate media as an unsustainable monoculture and alternative media as a healthier permaculture. And they fault advertisers for consigning media to the role of cheerleader for hyper-consumerism.

In the field-defining book *Alternative Media*, Chris Atton describes environmentalism as a distinguishing feature of the alternative press through the 1970s, 1980s, and 1990s.[21] His analysis of publications promoting radical ecological views and actions found principles such as *opposition, nonconformity, autonomy, creativity, anti-capitalism,* and *communitarianism* woven throughout—echoing many Slow Media values.

In my interviews with alternative-media users, they professed to many ideals that run parallel with cultural creatives and sustainability advocates, including socially progressive values.[22] Three values they cited as "most important" to alternative media were a nonprofit and noncommercial orientation, a commitment to social change through education, and a decentralized or nonhierarchical organization that encourages participation.[23] One environmental activist said alternative media were driven by "the same goal that motivates a lot of activists. Just the desire to get information out there, to get people talking, to create these new models, these new modes of thinking."[24] They agreed that alternative media are propelled by long-term sustainability, not short-term gain. "I think the alternative media are aiming for a more balanced sustainable world, whereas mainstream media is more toward the here and now and 'Let's make money now,'" another told me. Mainstream media are "building toward a vision of our future of monetary prosperity, whereas the future of alternative media is more of a togetherness and a sustainable conservationist" society.[25]

The term *alternative media* retains great currency with media audiences, producers, and scholars who find the contrast with *mainstream* useful.[26] Yet alternative media have long been associated with features that are no longer distinctive: open access, interactive technologies, horizontal organization, and participatory forms. New media developments have smudged the already fuzzy line between what's mainstream and what's alternative. Scholars and activists alike have wondered whether we still need alternative media in a world of digital devices and networks that seem to offer so much empowerment. In *Cyberprotest: Environmental Activism Online*, Jenny Pickerill echoes the common refrain that once-peculiar processes of production are now normalized in Internet practice: "Alternative media are no longer alternative in their form."[27]

If alternative media start to explicitly integrate sustainability values and practices in both their form and content, as I propose, that will no longer be the case. With sustainability issues central to alternative media, and vice versa, our conception of the latter can evolve to better address long-term human and environmental well-being. To be clear: Slow Media *are* alternative media. In this light, questions about the latter's relevance fade.

Using alternative media and being skeptical of mainstream media helps many activists to understand their role in the world and form bonds with like-minded people. Similarly, people could band together by identifying themselves with Slow Media. This identity benefits from an association with other Slow movements, especially the global one that steers agricultural systems and cultural attitudes toward sustainable farming and eating. Slow Food challenged the story put forth by profit-maximizing industrial producers that technology always means progress. "It seems wrong that cultural heritage is discarded due to enthusiasm with false development," wrote Carlo Petrini, one of the movement's founders. "A way of living in the world is vanishing because it is no longer compatible with the rhythm of global capital"—even when those traditional practices are still popular, more beneficial to society, and healthier for the natural environment.[28]

Slow Food effectively told a new story. Its aficionados, akin to Slow Medians and cultural creatives, unite conservative impulses with progressive values in what are called the "three pillars" of sustainability: ecological health, economic viability, and social equity. They have taken action both oppositional and alternative—for instance, developing community-supported agriculture and other networks that bear the Slow Food spirit, if not its name.

Slow Media, like Slow Food, encourages people to reassess consumer culture, to conserve natural resources, to resist commodification, to fight standardization, and to preserve traditional tastes. Slow Media is useful for thinking about long-term sustainability because it foregrounds problems such as mass manufacturing, disposability, planned obsolescence, and superficial measures of efficiency. Print, analog and other nondigital forms of Slow Media provide a glimpse of another culture that was, is, and will be possible—a culture guided by the quality of human lives.

Satisfying, Sustainable, and Smart

Slow Media focuses on the fertility of individual and collective imaginations about mediated life. It describes and analyzes an array of Slow approaches to media culture that creative people have invented, practiced, and promoted since the turn of the millennium. Along with Slow Media, we will look at three other novel concepts that are central to this phenomenon: *green media, mindful media*, and *post-Luddism*. This new vocabulary offers a fresh perspective for assessing digital culture and for understanding complex relationships between everyday media choices, human well-being, and the natural environment. As you will see, Slow Media is not really about slowing down. It's about adopting media practices that allow both people and the planet to replenish themselves. In other words: going Slow can be smart.

This book draws from a number of important sources, including a growing body of research on Slow journalism, sustainability, new media materialism, green media, mindful tech, and ecomedia studies; years of experience of practitioners in these areas; and personal experience. I have spent more than a decade studying alternative and sustainable media phenomena, immersing myself deeply in the ideas of both theorists and practitioners. The evidence given here consists of hundreds of scholarly and popular books, a greater number of articles, and thousands of blogs and posts. The most vital sources are contained in the bibliography at the back of this book.

By looking at movements and manifestos supporting Slow Media, we can see how this new concept fosters environmental sustainability and human agency. **Chapter 2, "Slow Media: Lessons from the Food Revolution,"** considers some values driving the Slow revolution and some practical, collective actions contributing to Slow Food's success. It discusses thriving revivals of print and analog media that help us understand the Slow critique of consumerism. I explain how Slow Media offers an alternative to global, corporate practices that are unresponsive to the situated needs of human communities and natural environments. This chapter dispels myths that Slow Media are elitist, apolitical, conservative, anti-digital, or anti-fast. I explain why Slow Media is not really about speed and why we need to pay closer attention to the politics of time.

Chapter 3, " 'Good, Clean, Fair': A Sustainability Framework for Journalism," explains why publishers are embracing Slow approaches to news reporting, writing, and editing. Slow Journalism challenges mainstream assumptions that news work must be *competitive, commercial,* and *corporate,* as well as *fast.* This chapter describes some quintessential Slow publications that have not only attracted new audiences but also persuaded them to *pay* for content. My analysis shows how Slow Journalism is similar to and different from journalistic forms that came before. Using the Slow Food motto "Good, Clean, Fair," I explain how this movement can produce journalism committed to the well-being of communities, treating sources ethically, pursuing social justice, supporting ecosystems, and

ensuring nonexploitative working conditions. Current Slow practitioners, however, seem more concerned with creating *good* journalism than with making *clean*
or *fair* products, which limits their contribution to sustainability. I consider how
Slow producers could nurture a healthier news ecosystem: by being more transparent and enabling audiences to recognize journalism that comes from cleaner,
fairer sources.

We also dig into the flowering field of Green Media, which focuses on how
digital technologies materially affect the environment and human culture.
**Chapter 4, "Greening Media: New Directions in Environmental Citizenship
and Scholarship,"** looks at burgeoning research and activism on the ecological
footprints of digital media systems, which were long invisible to the public. In this
chapter, we confront the illusion that digital media are eco-friendly. Society has
begun to recognize the significant amounts of energy used, resources depleted,
and pollution created by data centers, device manufacturing, and communication
infrastructures. I offer insight on some persistent obstacles to sustainable media
such as rapid obsolescence, tech fascination, commercial hype, anthropocentrism,
greenwashing, and "business-as-usual" practices. You will learn about individual
and collective actions being taken to "green the media" by promoting sustainable
production and consumption.

In **Chapter 5, "Mind Your Media: From Distraction to Attention,"** we ponder
the eruption of mindful approaches to media use—which respond to concerns
about the physical, emotional, intellectual, and interpersonal effects of information overload and digital addiction. I share wisdom from prominent teachers and
researchers of "mindful tech" who advocate for more contemplation in daily life
and media use. Scholarship has shed light on how multitasking and other media
habits interfere with cognition, breathing, and other basic functions. Innovative
experiments have shown that mindful media use makes people feel more creative, productive, focused, self-aware, and happier. People gain insight to their own
brains, bodies, emotions, and lives when they use media more mindfully—and,
importantly, when they *stop* using media. Brief abstention from digital devices
and networks helps bring their effects to the fore. In this chapter, I convey some
principles and practices of mindful media use through which people renegotiate
mediated experiences at home, school, and office.

It's important to recognize that Slow, mindful, and sustainable approaches
to media do not oppose new technology per se. Yet in popular discourse, critics
of digital culture are routinely and inaccurately called "Luddites." In **Chapter 6,
"We Are All Post-Luddites Now,"** I discuss how the term *Luddite* became syn-
onymous with someone uncomfortable with or unskilled at using technology.
The original Luddites—factory workers in 19th-century England who destroyed
machines in protest against the social-political consequences of early industrial
capitalism—have long been misperceived. As you'll see, their legacy offers a constructive rhetorical stance for modern conversations about digital media. The
nuanced approach that I call *Post-Luddism* reinvigorates this critique by addressing

21st-century concerns about the environment, globalization, and sustainability. Along the way, we explore precursors such as the anti-television, Neo-Luddite, and Technorealism movements. Rebooting Luddism to resonate with the sustainability revolution can inspire creative new attitudes and behaviors toward media.

Lastly, we turn to opportunities for establishing a significant and sustained Slow Media movement, as well as obstacles that remain. **Chapter 7, "Conclusion: Toward a Sustainable Media Future,"** explores visions for a world where more Slow, green, and mindful ideas are adopted. It discusses ways that individuals can take control of their own media rhythms and green their own media use. Society can cultivate collective visions of Slow Media through open-minded dialogue, improved access to information, and policy changes that make sustainable choices easier. To be Post-Luddite, we can demonstrate empathy toward people with differing media attitudes and behaviors, rather than demanding that everyone conform to one standard. I take into account how the "politics of time" (in a nutshell: people are overworked and underpaid), constrains individual choices about media and contributes to social unsustainability, eco-unfriendly consumption, and civic disengagement. This chapter provides insight on the roles that schools, nonprofit groups, religious communities, and legislators could play.

The tensions between these two revolutions of the new millennium—the digital one and the sustainability one—need to be reconciled. We can respond more effectively to the challenges that face human and environmental well-being if (among other things) we embrace new ways of using and producing media, such as those described here. The theories, examples, case studies, and stories featured in this book illustrate the power of human agency and the promise of sustainable change. My hope is that *Slow Media* can help people to better grapple with the risks and rewards of digital life by sharing the creative approaches of Slow Journalists, green cultural citizens, mindful media users, and post-Luddite thinkers. These coinages can inspire new ways of thinking about media use and propel new conversations about sustainable culture. Despite—or, perhaps, because of—rising public anxiety and political cynicism, this is an opportune time for people to band together and nurture Slow visions of a better media system and healthier cultural environment.

2

Slow Media

Lessons from the Food Revolution

We are 24-7, we are always-on, we are status-updated, we are tweet-fed; we are real-time media junkies and everything about our mediascape exists to remind us that we don't have time to slow down.
—Grayson Cooke, *Transformations*[1]

Carl Honoré realized there was a problem when he started quarreling with his two-year-old over bedtime stories. Every night, Honoré would reach for the shortest books and read them as quickly as possible. His son would ask for longer stories, to be read slowly, and beg for more when Dad dashed for the door. "Part of me feels horribly selfish when I accelerate the bedtime ritual, but another part simply cannot resist the itch to hurry on to the next thing on my agenda—supper, emails, reading, bills, more work, the news bulletin on television," said Honoré, a Canadian journalist based in London. "My whole life has turned into an exercise in hurry, in packing more and more into every hour. I am Scrooge with a stop-watch, obsessed with saving every last scrap of time, a minute here, a few seconds there. And I am not alone."[2] Honoré decided to struggle against the speedaholic tendencies that interfere with life's pleasures, and he encouraged others to do likewise.

In the best-selling *In Praise of Slowness: Challenging the Cult of Speed*, Honoré examined the worldwide growth of the Slow Movement as a response to the increasing sense of hurriedness. The 2004 book described the Slow Food phenomenon and analogous attempts to slow down cities, medicine, sex, work, leisure, and parenting. In an extensive academic study of this movement, Wendy Parkins and Geoffrey Craig cited the popularity of *In Praise of Slowness*, the prominence of organizations such as Slow Food, and growing media coverage as evidence that "a space is being carved out in public discourse to question the assumptions of everyday life and to explore alternatives to a multi-tasking, conspicuous consumption version of daily existence."[3]

Here, I pick up the story where *In Praise of Slowness* left off, looking at the rise of Slow Media philosophies and practices in recent years. Honoré didn't consider

Slow Media per se because when he wrote the book, these new cultural ideas hadn't gathered momentum yet. How have people adapted Slow Food values and practices to media use? How do these nascent ideas about media compare and contrast with those for food? What lessons did Slow Media proponents learn from the success of their foodie progenitors, and what challenges do they face going forward? To answer these questions, I draw upon popular discourses about Slow phenomena and scholarly explorations of this burgeoning area of culture.

Readers will note that I use a capital "S" here to distinguish this new conception from plain old slowness, the state of moving or acting at an unhurried or leisurely pace. The Slow movement is often considered a reaction against the sociocultural effects of modernity's massive acceleration of transportation, communication, and production processes. Narrowly focusing on the question of speed's role in modern life, however, misses the point of the Slow movement. We get a fuller understanding of Slow Media by considering it from the dual viewpoints of *agency* and *sustainability*, rather than velocity. One main thrust of this chapter is to demonstrate that, in fact, Slow Media is not really about going slowly. Slow Food has become widespread enough that "Slow" serves as shorthand for leading a balanced life, pursuing quality over quantity, and valuing artisanal skills, natural ingredients, and organic processes. Slow also implies education and contemplation, encouraging people to learn about systems of production and to consciously enact their roles as a consumer or co-producer.

Thanks to Slow Food, many people view food culture from a richer ecological and ethical perspective, instead of a reductive industrial one focusing on speed, cost, and efficiency. Building on the organic movement and other cultural forces, Slow Food has helped recalibrate 21st-century attitudes toward farming, cooking, and dining and promoted "farm-to-table" systems that can yield high-quality, eco-friendly, and fair-trade products. Slow Media has untapped potential to similarly transform our thinking about the use and production of books, film, music, and other mediated forms of culture. This chapter explains the rise of Slow Media not only as a personal lifestyle choice but also as a political, ecological, and ethical commitment.

Lessons from the Food Revolution

Conversations about Slow Food were long anchored in the problem of speed, with good reason. Hence its name. The movement for Slow Food was ignited in the mid-1980s amid opposition to Italy's first McDonald's franchise opening in Rome, where the golden arches were seen as an aesthetic affront to the historic Piazza di Espagna as well as an insult to local culinary traditions. Three years later, Slow Food co-founder Carlo Petrini joined delegates from 15 countries to launch the movement. Its first manifesto began by declaring the acceleration wrought by industrial civilization a threat to human autonomy: "We are enslaved to speed and have all succumbed to the same insidious virus: *Fast Life*, which disrupts our habits, pervades the privacy of our homes and forces us to eat *Fast Foods*."[4] The organization chose the snail as its symbol—a versatile logo that can connote fine gastronomy while denoting, above all, a refusal to be hurried.

Fast food was just one symptom of the cultural problem at the heart of this movement, but it presented a viable and concrete target. Slow Food efforts to preserve regional, artisanal traditions gained traction in the context of a backlash against mass-produced comestibles. Franchises like McDonald's have been derided by many as purveyors of homogeneous, disposable, unhealthy—one might say unsustainable—products. This public mindset was fueled in part by unappetizing depictions of meat-processing facilities, artificial flavor enhancements, and worker exploitation in the bestseller *Fast Food Nation: The Dark Side of the All-American Meal*, by Eric Schlosser. That muckraking book inspired persistent criticism of the global fast-food industry, including widely seen films like *Food, Inc.* and *SuperSize Me!* Worries about society being "McDonaldized" by the spread of fast-food values such as efficiency and standardization were high on that era's agenda.

Against this cultural backdrop, as well as protests against globalization in Seattle and beyond at the turn of the millennium, a wave of local Slow Food chapters—called *convivia*—were quickly founded in France, Germany, the United States, and elsewhere. Slow Food USA opened 70 convivia between 2000 and 2002 in this country alone, compared to 40 in Germany during the previous decade. The global Slow Food network connects more than 100,000 members through 1,300 convivia in 150 countries, including 200 chapters in the US. The organization's activities involve millions of people around the world.

Since its emergence, Slow Food International has embraced a diverse range of projects and mastered the art of publicity. It publishes guides for local gastronomes and food tourists as well as hosting food seminars and festivals around the world. Three characteristic initiatives were the *Ark of Taste*, a directory of endangered foods around the world that members rescue by enjoying them; the *Presidia*, grassroots organizations that Slow Food supports with advice and money as a way of making Ark foods available to the general public; and the *Slow Food Award*, "the Nobel Prize of biodiversity," which brings inspiring artisans and agricultural activists, mostly from underdeveloped nations, to global attention and gives them concrete assistance.[5] Its resources come mainly from membership dues, corporate grants, and sales of its successful guidebooks.

Slow Food excels in building networks. Worldwide, it unites more than 2,000 Terra Madre food communities who practice small-scale and sustainable production of quality foods. At the local level, chapters often work in support of farmers' markets, community-supported agriculture, school, community gardens, and the like. Slow Food has helped to develop direct "farm-to-fork" relationships between urban dwellers and food purveyors so that consumers are invested—in many senses of the word—in the well-being of producers. In less than a generation, the group has forged strong connections between the artistic, political, and agricultural worlds.

At its inception, Slow Food focused on educating people about pleasure, taste, and traditions of food production. Later, the movement transformed itself from a primarily gastronomic organization to a self-proclaimed "eco-gastronomic" one that connects the plate and the planet. Slow Food describes its members as eco-gastronomes devoted to the pleasure that food brings as well as to maintaining respect for nature and preserving the environment. One move in support of this renewed priority was the 2003 inauguration of the Slow Food Foundation for Biodiversity, which provides information, training, and technical assistance to small-scale producers around the world.

The Slow Food, organic, and locavore movements were propelled by many other champions who made a deep impression on public attitudes toward food in the 21st century. Journalist Michael Pollan is known for books such as *The Omnivore's Dilemma, In Defense of Food,* and *Food Rules,* which includes the memorably parsimonious advice to "Eat food. Not too much. Mostly plants." Pollan appeared with Schlosser in the documentary *Food, Inc.*, which shows how an industrialized food supply threatens public health and the environment. Alice Waters, an eminent chef and food activist since the 1970s, developed a network of local farmers and ranchers espousing sustainable agriculture to provide her restaurant Chez Panisse with a steady supply of ingredients.

Waters fosters sustainability education through a foundation that integrates garden experiences and cooking classes into public school curricula. The Edible Schoolyard project employs food systems as a unifying concept to foster greater understanding of how the natural world sustains us and to promote environmental and social well-being. Calling herself an "agent of seduction," she uses the pleasures of food as a catalyst to effect deeper ethical and political changes in how people eat. Waters, a vice president of Slow Food International, credits the movement for making people more aware of fast food's far-ranging human and environmental costs.[6]

A former journalist, Petrini played a major role in building the Slow movement for more than two decades. His numerous books include *Terra Madre: Forging a New Global Network of Sustainable Food Communities; Slow Food Nation: Why Our Food Should be Good, Clean and Fair; Food and Freedom: How the Slow Food Movement is Changing the World through Gastronomy;* and *Slow Food Revolution: A New Culture for Eating and Living.* Notice how these titles consistently connect sustainable food practices with collective social actors: networks, communities, nations, movements, revolutions. Petrini coined the slogan "Good, Clean, Fair" (in Italian: *Buono, Pulito, Giusto*) to capture the breadth of the movement's philosophy. This motto urges society to enjoy healthy and tasty food while protecting the natural environment and appreciating the people who make and distribute food.

When Petrini describes the deleterious effect of speed on food quality, social life, and nature, he blames global capitalism more so than the fast-food industry.

Speed is a symptom, not the root cause. To him, Slow Food is a "critical reaction to the symptoms of incipient globalization."[7] Industrialization has done much good for the world, helping to bring food, clothing, shelter, heat, and cooling to people who lacked it. But, he contends, it produced an unsustainable environment and a technocratic worldview that relies too much on speed as a criteria for judging human activities.

Slowness and hurriedness are equally useful and desirable, according to Petrini. "It's not just a question of opposing slow to fast, but rather of highlighting more important dichotomies, like carefulness and carelessness or attentiveness and haste," he says, touching upon the modern preoccupation with mindfulness. "To be Slow just to be slow would be stupid."[8] He emphasizes that fast and slow rhythms can co-exist harmoniously. One should seek the right speed for any given situation—what Italians call *il tempo giusto*. Slow isn't always better. But fast isn't always better, either.

Scholars like to avoid the simplistic dichotomy of fast/slow in favor of more sophisticated, nuanced explanations of social attitudes. One sociologist found that discussions about Slow Food extolled a wide range of speeds, both slow and fast.[9] Another observed that the movement has made great strides toward redefining and revaluing the word "slow." In modern Western culture, *fast* has long signified desire, plenitude, superiority, efficiency, libidinal energy, performance, and intelligence.[10] Meanwhile, *slow* means frustration, lack, inferiority, deficiency, impotence, and weakness. More people have begun to realize that fast isn't necessarily good (or bad), and neither is slow.

When Parkins and Craig analyzed the Slow Food manifesto, *Slow* magazine, and interviews with Slow Food leaders, they noticed that people described the movement's values by contrasting slow with fast—but in a new way.[11] In the Slow milieu, traits associated with fast included *enslaving, virus, multitude, inauthentic, false progress, absence of taste, homogenized globalization*, and *worse future*. By contrast, slow signified traits such as *liberating, health, antidote, individual, real culture, true progress, taste, international exchange*, and *better future*. In other words, the common valence was reversed to prize Slow principles that have little to do with speed.

While the Slow Food manifesto does lambast fast life and fast food, the remainder of the text calls for "a quiet defense of material pleasure," in "suitable doses," to banish the "degrading effects" of efficiency and productivity, which "threatens our environment and our landscapes," and to guarantee "a better future."[12] Try substituting "media" for "food" in that sentence, and you'll get a taste for how these principles guide Slow Media philosophy. (While providing much food for thought, it bears repeating that the analogy of Slow Food to Slow Media has limits. The systems through which food is produced, distributed, and circulated are subject to cultural, physical, political, social, and economic forces that overlap in many ways with, but also differ substantially from, those for media.)

To see how discussion of Slow Media echoes the sustainability concerns of its foodie counterpart, let's examine a few aspects of this movement in more depth. First up: film.

Cinema: An Early Incarnation of Slow Media

The earliest reference to Slow Media that I know of came from a former director of the National Alliance for Media Arts and Culture, in California. In a 2001 essay, Helen De Michiel proposed adapting Slow Food's community-supported agriculture model as a method of developing audiences for independent media. "I would use the concept of 'slow media' to characterize a practice that all members of the media arts field hold in common: We share the ability to do a lot with a little," she said.[13] Slow Food and Media Arts are similarly "quiet movements built on the ideals of self-determination, community empowerment, and preservation of legacy in a throwaway milieu," she wrote. While neither movement is valued or well understood by the mainstream, they represent significant niches in our cultural landscape that help sustain individuals and communities "with imaginative practices that transform consciousness in a slow and steady flow."[14]

Slow Media should focus on supporting small-scale producers, preserving local traditions, forging community alliances, and providing healthy alternatives, in De Michiel's view. She exemplified Slow values when promoting her documentary *Turn Here Sweet Corn*, which followed a family of organic farmers as they lost their property to developers. She partnered with land stewardship activists to screen the film, lead public discussions, and plan actions for saving endangered farms. Both the content of her film and the form of her filmmaking activities helped to develop local sustainability and agency.

This interpretation of Slow Media deviates slightly from the earlier Slow Cinema associated with the contemplative or minimalist films of European artists like Michelangelo Antonioni, Andrei Tarkovsky, and Bela Tarr. Some landmark films in this genre, which predates the sustainability revolution, are several hours long. Andy Warhol's 1964 movie *Empire*, in which viewers gaze at the Empire State Building for eight hours, is an extreme example. Stanley Kubrick's 1975 film *Barry Lyndon* could arguably be considered an accessible, familiar version of the genre; so could Gus Van Sant's *Gerry* and *Elephant*. While Slow Cinema thrived mainly in the 1960s and 1970s, cultural arbiters have nurtured a revival in recent years, including at the 2012 British AV Festival dubbed "As Slow as Possible" (a John Cage allusion befitting its avant-garde style).

Slow Cinema tends to emphasize aesthetic elements such as long takes, understated narratives, and uncompressed time that demand more patience from audiences than mainstream movies do. It downplays action in favor of "mood, evocativeness, and an intensified sense of temporality," noted one film critic in a 2010 essay that helped restore interest in the genre. "Such films highlight the viewing process itself as a real-time experience in which, ideally, you become acutely aware of every minute, every second spent watching."[15] The rhythm of Slow Cinema contrasts starkly with the pace of visual media in the 21st century. While there are strong cultural differences in how audiences respond to these movies, some modern critics dismiss such work as boring, pretentious, sullen, or contemptuous of viewers' time.

Fans of Slow Film celebrate its power to spark new sensibilities. One connoisseur who sees political value in encouraging audiences to downshift is Scott Macdonald. This film historian has championed a Slow subset called "eco-cinema," movies whose form and content both reflect and foster environmental awareness. In terms of form, eco-filmmakers often use handheld camera, extended run-times, serene pace, time lapse, ambient noise, silence, or an immobile camera. In terms of content, they often document seasonal transitions, tell the history of landscapes, capture collisions of the natural world with industrial technology, or examine controversies about environmental exploitation. Macdonald thinks that noncommercial filmmakers are effectively harnessing such aesthetics to environmentalist causes.

To audiences, Slow techniques offer a respite from the "machine of modern life," consumerism, and conventional media spectatorship, according to MacDonald.[16] Instead of spurning long films as gratuitous time wasters, we could welcome them as opportunities to enhance our perception and create a new state of mind. Such cinema embodies an environmental message: sometimes we must rearrange our lives to focus on pressing issues. As he explains, "If we are to conserve natural beauty, we'll need to develop a persistence and patience for which film experience can be, in a small way, training."[17] MacDonald proposes that a respite from conventional media spectatorship should ultimately aim to slow down consumerism, not just movie viewing.

Other cinema enthusiasts attach the word "Slow" to projects that decelerate the filmmaking process by using analog equipment. For them, Slow practices enhance the pleasures of production while also fostering agency. One example is a nonprofit center in Los Angeles that trains teenagers with little media-making background to capture urban life on 16-millimeter film, inspired by the "city symphony" documentaries of Berlin, Kiev, and Paris in the 1920s. By helping young people "explore communal creative process and contemporary environments," this community group aims to help build a global Slow Film movement.[18]

These examples show the myriad ways in which slowness can be applied to one medium: cinema. Film buffs believe that the Slow movement will benefit media production, consumption, form, content, and activism alike. They want Slow Cinema to nurture sustainability by educating viewers about nature, attuning them to the passage of time, training them to be patient and persistent, and encouraging them to take environmental action. Such discussions about how and why to adopt Slow principles and practices in media use have proliferated beyond cinema—to books, magazines, recorded music, and a spectrum of other forms.

Disenchantment with Digital Life

Media technologies can do astounding things. But what are we *actually* doing with them? "Documenting our lives obsessively, chatting to our friends, trafficking in digitally encoded entertainment, locating restaurants, gossiping about celebrities." That's the lament of rock critic Simon Reynolds, who describes pop-culture inertia in his book *Retromania*.

> None of this is particularly new, culturally speaking, and little of it is especially impressive. The future is supposed to be heroic and grand but the activities (or should that be 'passivities'?) enabled by the new technology are more redolent of the decadent, inward-looking phase of an empire rather than its outward bond, boldly-going-forth phrase.[19]

By contrast, the decades during which slower media reigned felt more fertile and inventive to him. "In the analogue era, everyday life moved slowly (you had to wait for the news, and for new releases) but the culture as a whole felt like it was surging forward," Reynolds writes. "In the digital present, everyday life consists of hyper-acceleration and near-instantaneity (downloading, web pages constantly being refreshed, the impatient skimming of text on screens), but on the macro-cultural level things feel static and stalled. We have this paradoxical combination of speed and standstill."[20] Going faster does not necessarily make culture move forward. We could be just spinning our wheels.

Reynolds indulged his digital disillusionment by joining the Slow Listening movement. He described this activity with a food metaphor: going on a *diet*, not a *fast* (like "No Music Day").[21] From January to November 2009, he restricted himself to downloading only one MP3 at a time; he could not get the next MP3 until he had listened to the first one. "The general principle of intake restriction struck me as not just a cool idea but quite possibly a vital sanity preserving measure," said Reynolds, author of the post-punk history *Rip It Up And Start Again*.[22] This professional critic felt simultaneously overwhelmed by the quantity of digital content available and underwhelmed by its quality, as many cultural connoisseurs do.

Through the first decade of the 21st century, especially in affluent Anglophone parts of the world, people began calling for a Slow Media movement.[23] They hailed Slow philosophy as an important source of new ideas about production and consumption of media, as it had been for food mores.[24] Some conceived of Slow Media as an antidote to speed in daily life. Others saw it as an opportunity for print media to attract new audiences by rebranding newspapers and magazines as high-quality alternatives that preserve local traditions—in other words, as Slow. As the case of cinema demonstrated, popular goals for Slow Media range from the pursuit of aesthetic pleasure and psychological gratification to the potential for effecting social and cultural change.

The Emergence of Slow Media

No one seems to have used the term "Slow Media" before 2001, but the idea definitively entered the public agenda by 2010. A National Public Radio broadcast about Slow Media in November 2009 touched a cultural nerve and earned a spate of attention from the press and the public-at-large. *Marketplace* reporter Sally Herships described Slow Media as a "movement . . . kinda like Slow Food, but without the food. Slowies write letters and, you know, talk to each other, offline. They like to do one thing at a time."[25] The segment featured Nick Jones, the creator of a Facebook group called "Slow Media Movement," as well as three scholars, including yours truly. (This was when I announced my plan to spend six months living like it was 1989—which, for better or worse, obliged me to go through with it.)

This seminal news story captured the prevailing preoccupations of Slow Media at that time. Jones, a computer programmer, had started a Facebook group to locate others who saw Slow Media as a way of coping with multitasking stress by using digital media more mindfully. "Sometimes I would have the British [TV show] *The Office* playing—it would be like, on mute and running and then there's a song playing and then there's me writing code, and it was just too much, it was like trying to drink from a fire hose, it just wasn't—it didn't work," he explained. "Thanks, high-speed Internet!"[26] Gulping from a digital geyser is surely not sustainable behavior for a human being.

The NPR broadcast sparked conversations about Slow Media across three continents, encompassing filmmakers and academics, bloggers and business strategists, computer programmers and copywriters, and others. Journalists began dropping the phrase "Slow Media" into their writing with no attribution and little explanation. News outlets such as the *Philadelphia Inquirer, Boston Globe, Times of London, Forbes*, CNET, and *Huffington Post* referred to Slow Media as a "movement."[27] Cultural commentators of the era also proposed movements for "Slow Communication," "Slow Listening," "Slow Books," "Slow Reading," and other variations on the theme. For me, the term "Slow Media" is a big tent embracing these other ideas.

One example is a former editor of the literary magazine *Granta* who published a Slow Communication manifesto in *The Wall Street Journal* bemoaning constant connection. "This lifestyle of being constantly on causes emotional and physical burnout, workplace meltdowns, and unhappiness," John Freeman said. "How many of our most joyful memories have been created in front of a screen? If we are to step off this hurtling machine, we must reassert principles that have been lost in the blur."[28] He blamed business culture for setting an untenable pace of digital interaction. "We need to uncouple our idea of progress from speed, separate the idea of speed from efficiency, pause, and step back enough to realize that efficiency may be good for business and governments but does not always lead to mindfulness and sustainable, rewarding relationships." Freeman framed Slow Communication as a form of resistance, pushing back against *The Tyranny of Email*—as he titled his 2009 book—and other despotic forces coercing us to stay connected to machines.

Another critic, from *The Atlantic,* imagined Slow Books as a deliberate form of reading. As Maura Kelly wrote, "In our leisure moments, whenever we have down-time, we should turn to literature—to works that took some time to write and will take some time to read, but will also stay with us longer than anything else."[29] Unlike blogs, she said, belletristic works not only entertain but also help readers develop empathy, self-awareness, memory, and cognitive skills by interpreting plot, language, and imagery. Kelly repurposed an indelible phrase from Pollan, replacing *food* with *books* and *plants* with *classics*: "Read books. As often as you can. Mostly classics."

The notion of Slow Reading dates back at least as far as 1887, when Friedrich Nietzsche described himself in 1887 as a "teacher of Slow Reading." He praised contemplation, self-control, and quiet while bemoaning the fact that people find virtue in doing something more quickly than someone else. In *The Genealogy of Morals,* Nietzsche wrote that "the temporary shutting of the doors and windows of consciousness, the relief from the clamant alarums . . . make room again for the new, and above all for the more noble functions." He urged people to exercise their willpower and rise above sheepish masses. One can only imagine what Nietzsche might have said about social media, crowdsourcing, and the hive mind.

Other writers and teachers in the Slow Reading movement believe that preva-lent habits of speed-reading and Web surfing require a counterbalance. Yale pro-fessor Lancelot Fletcher believes that studying philosophy *requires* one to read slowly and to avoid the rush to interpretation and judgment encouraged by some educational practices. John Miedema, the author of *Slow Reading,* said this prac-tice shares with Slow Food such principles as mindfulness, self-determination, and localism.[30]

Values and Practices of Slow Media

Popular thinking about Slow Media draws upon disparate influences beyond Nietzsche. These include Buddhism and other Eastern traditions adopted by Western culture in the recent century (as chapter 5 examines closely). Another is the pursuit of moderate pleasure and serenity originally espoused by Epicurianism in 300 bc. People usually understand an "epicure" to be someone with refined taste who enjoys indulging (or over-indulging) in food and drink, akin to a "gourmet" or "gourmand." The word, however, derives from Greek philosopher Epicurus, who held that the goal of life should be serenity of mind and the enjoyment of mod-erate pleasure—ideals that reverberate in Slow Media.

The 19th-century transcendentalism of Henry David Thoreau, Ralph Waldo Emerson, and Walt Whitman looms large in Slow philosophy, too. These idealists sought to enrich inner life through self-reliance, undistracted contemplation, and immersion in nature. Thoreau, in particular, is venerated for his quest to escape the "whirlpool of time" and live according to his own rhythm by moving to Walden Pond in the 1860s.[31] He expressed a distaste for fast communication (newspaper and telegraph, back then) and a fondness for solitude, idleness, and nonconformity. Thoreau is sometimes mischaracterized as a technophobic Luddite. But he was an engineer and businessperson committed to technology and its role in everyday life. (He also was not an anti-social ruralite, as some imagine; he welcomed frequent visitors to his cabin and often walked the short distance into town.) Stimulated by this turn from mediated to direct experience, his writings about naturalism, voluntary simplicity, and civil disobedience pervade the sustainability movement.

Proponents of Slow Media often commend Thoreauvian qualities related to 1) one's personal disposition, using words such as *serene, moderate, attentive, focused, mindful, careful, self-reliant, disciplined, present,* and *discerning*; 2) the media one uses, with words such as *material, physical, beautiful, local, handmade, traditional, with character, timeless, long-lived, sensuous, tactile, heritage, heirloom, high-quality, eco-friendly,* and *fair-trade* ; and 3) the broader context of one's life and interactions, praising the *human, natural, simple, sustainable,* and *democratic.* These Slow Media values, derived from my research, resemble ones identified by analysts of other Slow iterations.

While it's easy to agree on the Slow Media value system, it's harder to pinpoint a "typical" way of practicing it. I hesitate even to define and delimit Slow Media by its activities. Similarly, Parkins and Craig proposed that Slow living is "as much an attitude or disposition as an action" and "a way of cultivating an ethical approach to the everyday."[32] Flexibility of interpretation accounts for much of the Slow appeal. Nonetheless, it will help you understand this phenomenon if we consider some specific techniques that people have experimented with.

Increasing one's consumption of print and analog forms. In practice, this often means reading, watching, and listening to print and analog media, especially high-quality and longer forms such as books, newspapers, printed magazines, handmade art, film photography, comics, audiocassettes, vinyl records or movies.

Increasing one's production of print and analog forms, by using traditional or vintage tools. This often means writing letters by hand, typing on typewriters, learning calligraphy, sending postcards, using fountain pens, making 16 millimeter or Super 8 films, doing photography with Polaroid and rangefinder cameras, recording with analog equipment, or printing by letterpress.

Using any form of media, whether fast or slow, in moderate ways that can be considered slow. This often means monotasking, reading carefully, paying close attention, checking email less frequently, increasing response time (the gap between receiving a message and replying to it), or turning off alerts and other "push" notifications.

Reducing one's use of fast media, whether temporarily or permanently. This includes a panoply of activities like unplugging, digital detox, media fasts, Internet sabbaths, and more.

Some people who adopt these practices enjoy Slow Media as a way of escaping the negative effects of digital media. Others come from a less critical perspective, simply seeking time to appreciate print and analog media alongside digital ones. Some take a more extreme approach of reducing their use of *all* media, fast and slow, in favor of unmediated activities. In other words, they pursue more first-hand experiences, as if at Walden Pond.

To some degree, the fast/slow binary lingers in such conceptualizations. Speed is seen as the problem with media, and slowness as the corrective measure. While Slow Media questions the desirability of going as fast as possible, it does not argue that people should do everything slow all the time. Rather than prescribing a universally correct tempo, Slow Media appreciates variable speeds and the joy of alternating between them. Like yin and yang, this philosophy contends that you can better understand fast media by recognizing and engaging deliberately with slow counterparts. You might call this *strategic, deliberate,* or *intentional slowness,* wherein slowing down one's media use is a means, not an end.

As we saw with the Slow Food movement, however, speed is just part of the story. In both theory and practice, Slow Media has begun to address sustainability issues in a politically meaningful way.

The Slow Media Manifesto

This emerging movement became more familiar to the press and public in 2010, when a "Slow Media Manifesto" was published at *Slow-Media.net* and widely cited in online forums, including tech venue *Wired.com.* The manifesto declared that Slow Media ("as in 'Slow Food' and not as in 'slow down'") should be integrated to the new technological landscape; that popular desire for easier, faster, cheaper content had subsided; and that Slow and fast media each exist because of the other. It credits accelerated networked life with making "islands of deliberate slowness" possible—and also essential.[33]

The manifesto's authors cited problems with media systems that parallel those Petrini noted in food systems: global inequality, shoddy products, unfair labor practices, environmental degradation, and unsustainable consumption.[34] They ascribed a broad spectrum of social, cultural, and political goals to Slow Media. The movement promotes monotasking ("Slow Media can only be consumed with pleasure in focused alertness," they explain). It attains high standards of quality (that stand out from "short-lived counterparts"). It advances active "prosumers" (rather than passive consumers). It is discursive and dialogic ("'Slow' means to be mindful"). It propagates diversity and respects distinctive local features.[35] All of these ideals coincide with those of the Slow Food movement.

Of a dozen items listed in the Slow Media Manifesto, the first one cites human and ecological sustainability as a guiding principle:

> Slow Media are a contribution to sustainability. Sustainability relates to the raw materials, processes and working conditions, which are the basis for media production. Exploitation and low-wage sectors as well as the unconditional commercialization of user data will not result in sustainable media. At the same time, the term refers to the sustainable consumption of Slow Media.

This precept, linking production to consumption, suggests that some commercial aspects of the current media system are untenable in theory or practice.

Several other items in the manifesto challenge the media status quo and promote alternatives. For instance, Item No. 5 highlights the agency of users, who "actively define what and how they want to consume and produce" media and who are "inspired by their media usage to develop new ideas and take action."[36] Item No. 9 recommends circulating media objects as gifts instead of commodities and publicizing media through personal networks instead of commercial ones. Item No. 10 challenges planned obsolescence and disposability by suggesting that "Slow Media are long-lived. . . . They do not lose their value over time but at best get some patina that can even enhance their value."[37] And Item No. 12 asserts that Slow Media are progressive, contradicting perceptions of Slowness as reactionary, nostalgic, or conservative.[38]

The Slow Media Manifesto was written by a trio of media researchers in Bonn, Germany, who originally described their project as "a blog with a manifesto."[39] In the years since publishing the credo online, their mission has expanded. Jorg Blumtritt, Sabria David, and Benedikt Koehler have frequently written and spoken about Slow Media in academic and public venues. Their Slow Media Institute has conducted applied media research on Slow principles and archetypes. In a survey with a representative sample of 2,500 Germans predisposed to Slow living, they found that people highly valued mindfulness, quality, and monotasking in media consumption.

This study helped to identify eight dominant Slow types: "The Luxurious," who cares about quality, brands, and trends; "The Sustainable," who cares about environmental factors; "The Digital," who adores smartphones and the Internet;, "The Focused," who prefers monotasking and avoids distractions; "The Networker," who cultivates a network of far-flung friends and acquaintances; "The Professional," who sees their work as more than a job; "The Relaxed," who prefers doing nothing or "chilling out" in front of screens; and "The Stressed," who feels overwhelmed by digital communication. The scholars concluded that "Slow" does not signify *slow* or *backwards*, but rather *strong, intelligent, thoughtful, reflective, open-minded, self-confident, balanced*, and *sustainable*.[40]

The Slow Media Institute also collaborated on a project called "Streaming Egos, Digital Identities" with the Goethe Institut as well as on media trends research with the University of Vienna. Yet this Slow Media endeavor is not an "institute" in the rigorous sense. The group does not have a university affiliation, regular funding sources, or a program of instruction. In other words, it does not have the requisite organizational structure or financial support to shepherd a unified Slow Media movement and coordinate a complex network of local and global actors, as Slow Food International has done in its own arena.

Progressive Alternatives, Noncommercial Forms

A crowd of young people bumped elbows in an urban record shop, drinking among racks of music, taking selfies, and celebrating the launch of *The World's First Perfect Zine*. Opinions inevitably vary as to whether the new publication lives up to its self-congratulatory title. Some find it paradoxical that the zine was created by "David Shapiro," the nom de plume of someone known for reviewing *Pitchfork* reviews and writing for the online culture magazine *The Awl*. Why would a prominent blogger resort to lowly pulp as a means of expression?

This endeavor sprang not from irony but from a sincere Slow Media sensibility. "One night last year I was reading the *Cometbus* zine compilation . . . and I thought it was really amazing. It made me want to make a zine of my own," Shapiro told Jenna Wortham of the *New York Times*. "It's satisfying to produce something that people can hold and treasure and value partially for its physicality instead of something [online] that gradually disappears,"[41] the 23-year-old said, noting the "pleasure" of reading zines in print instead of on screens.

With the rise of digital publishing came a resurgence of paper zines: low-budget, low-tech publications devoted to idiosyncratic themes and usually made for fun, not profit. (Some—like hardcore-music stalwart *Maximum RocknRoll*, which has been publishing since the early 1980s—never went away). Production techniques can be sophisticated (desktop publishing, offset printing, binding, specialty stock) or low-tech (handwriting, typewriters, cut-and-paste, office paper). A few notable titles are *Beer Frame, Ben is Dead, Bitch, Craphound, Dishwasher, Eight-Track Mind, Murder Can Be Fun, Pills-a-Go-Go, Temp Slave*, and *Thrift Score*. They continue a long tradition of independent printing that weaves through Riot Grrrls, punk rockers, 60s countercultural types, Dada and Surrealist artists, and sci-fi fans, all the way back to Ben Franklin and Tom Paine. People often associate these DIY publications with democratic ideals of expression, inclusion, and participation.

Some people assume that Slow Media is a nostalgic or conservative reaction against digital culture. My research on the persistence of print and analog media negates that view. Proponents of Slow Media don't feel they need to choose between enjoying digital media and embracing slower forms. Pulling one closer does not perforce mean pushing the other away. Some zines have grown out of blogging communities and some blogs have grown out of zine communities, in a recursive process. These cultural producers see little contradiction in using digital and print media, recognizing their complementary aspects.

Wortham herself presents a prime example of slow-fast reconciliation. A former *Wired* reporter, she has written for *The New York Times'* "Bits" blog and has been named one of the most influential women in technology—along with Arianna Huffington and Sheryl Sandberg—because her ideas are so widely read. (She has also praised analog alarm clocks as an alternative to devices in the bedroom.) Wortham developed a passion for zines in her teens, both making her own and contributing to other people's. After neglecting the hobby for years, she re-discovered a flourishing zine industry. These DIY publications have enjoyed a comeback among the Web-savvy, she explains, partly in reaction to the ubiquity of the Internet.

When I interviewed long-time zine creators in the early aughts, they told me that their interest in self-publishing never waned.[42] Rather, the institutional infrastructure for promoting, distributing, and selling zines eroded in the 1990s. In response to a lack of real-world support for zines, some self-publishers began online ventures and found new technologies attractive, artistically or economically—for a while. Web publishing never replaced or dimmed their enthusiasm for paper publishing but, instead, renewed their re-appreciation of zines' physicality and permanence. Above all, zine creators said, they missed social rituals of interacting face-to-face with people as they distributed publications. Their decisions about making zines, like ours about using media, were not entirely a matter of personal choice, but depended on a web of cultural and structural factors.

The vinyl revival of the early 21st century further illustrates tensions between media structures and popular agency. While digital culture widens the variety of some individual choices, it narrows others. Our media environment is often shaped by what companies want, not what the public desires. Vinyl records were still commercially viable in 1989 and there was little demand for compact discs. Because CDs were more profitable, however, major label distributors pushed merchants to stock the digital format through strategies such as releasing new albums only on CD, deleting vinyl from their back catalogs, and no longer accepting returns of vinyl. Many retailers could not afford the risk of carrying vinyl because if it didn't sell, they would be stuck with it.[43] For the music industry, what mattered about technological change was "less the technology than the change."[44] Record buyers migrated to CD—temporarily, as it happens—not solely because they wanted "shiny, aluminum, plastic and digital" music but because they had less access to the format they preferred.

The market for vinyl rebounded as the CD market collapsed amid competition from online radio, digital downloads, and streaming services. The number of record albums sold increased by 33% in 2013, compared to the previous year, and by another 49% in 2014.[45] Sales of vinyl LPs increased for the 12th consecutive year in 2017, reaching an all-time high of 14.3 million units.[46] People are sometimes coerced by the dominant commercial culture, along with peer pressure and network effects and employer mandates, to adopt new media technologies more energetically than they otherwise might.[47] Slow Media thus highlights how the development and obsolescence of media products are driven by business imperatives, profitability, marginal costs, and market control, not just by social needs or consumer preferences.

Analog came back with a vengeance in the 2010s, wrote David Sax in his 2016 book about real things and why they matter. People began to discover or rediscover the pleasures of typewriters, film cameras, Moleskine journals, ball-point pens, Polaroids, paperback novels, turntables and LPs. *The Revenge of Analog* highlights the recent proliferation of record shops and diversification of vinyl customers. Record buyers today include many young music lovers, lots of them girls, in their teens and twenties, who grew up listening *only* to free digital music. In fact, Sax observed, young people revered and craved analog media: "The younger someone was, the more digitally exposed their generation was, the less enamored I found them of digital technology, and the more wary they were of its effects."[48] It's not just hipsters and nostalgic old guys.

The analog revival is a complex phenomenon that offers "a powerful counternarrative to the techno-utopian belief that we would live in an ever-improving, all-digital world," according to Michiko Kakutani.[49] Contrary to technophile forecasts, print books are outperforming e-books today and the number of independent bookstores has bounced by 35% since 2009, despite enormous pressure from online retailers. Companies like Facebook, Amazon, Apple, Netflix, and Google (known by the acronym FAANG) might be giants, but they are also unicorns. According to Sax, more than 90% of companies are still analog. Analog media are not going away any time soon.

In this revised story, technological innovation is not "a slow march from good to better to best," Sax explains. "It's a series of trials that helps us understand who we are and how we operate."[50] Now that the honeymoon is over, we're ready to recognize when analog tools or approaches simply outperform digital as the best solution. And we're willing to pay for those enhanced media experiences, even if they are less convenient or more costly. The entrepreneurial companies and organizations that he writes about are not driven by "rose-colored nostalgia for an idealized, pre-digital past."[51] They are welcoming the opportunity to make money from a renewed consumer desire for analog products and services.

Slow Media criticism echoes alternative-media scholarship in its attention to corporate-commercial media's influence upon the public sphere.[52] For example, Robert McChesney has shown how the alternative potential of the Internet was thwarted as it became dominated by mainstream commercial messages and profit motives.[53] By contrast, Slow print and analog forms with limited commercial viability might retain more oppositional power. Slow Media are usually produced on a small scale without advertising subsidies, which makes them relatively expensive compared to mass-made and commercially supported alternatives. This niche status has helped insulate Slow Media producers from commercial pressure until now. As Sax confirms, many print and analog forms are moving out of the margins. Such developments could throw into question Slow Media's ability to challenge consumerism.

While media devices made just a few years ago are likely to be out-of-date or unusable, those manufactured decades ago often still work perfectly well. Print and analog fans in the US, Europe, and Australia note that their analog artifacts are of higher-quality and have a longer lifespan than digital ones. "You don't necessarily have to say, 'That's outdated and we can do better now,'" one aficionado said. "There's a kind of resurgence of old technology, people realizing that actually, it does still have something to give, and we don't have to leave it all behind. The two can exist happily alongside each other."[54] The Slow perspective sheds light on the decline of durable media goods in Western society and the rise of planned obsolescence—which contributes significantly to an unsustainable pace of consumption and disposal of resource-intensive products.

Dispelling Myths about Slow Media

The absence of influential leaders and institutions advocating for a Slow Media movement presents one obstacle to its growth. There are also misperceptions about Slow ideals and activities that likely curb their appeal. Top among these myths is that Slow always means slow, as already addressed. In addition, some people perceive Slow phenomena as inaccessible to the average person, because it takes time, money, information, and other resources to make and use them in the proscribed ways. Others mistakenly characterize the Slow Movement as encouraging us to withdraw from mainstream culture instead of engaging with problems, which could limit its real-world impact.

Many aspects of Slow living—being contemplative and deliberative, buying sustainable products, eating or shopping in the "right" places—are "reserved for those who have time to make time" and who have enough money to participate in these activities, notes scholar Sarah Sharma. "Few people are economically or culturally positioned to claim the progressive, political, or sustainable promise of Slowness."[55] Here, Sharma repeats a persistent criticism of Slow Food: that this movement is elitist and effete, too expensive for ordinary people, just a snobbish trend among foodies and gourmands.

Certainly, some Slow products—in food and media alike—are expensive and trendy. Manual typewriters and landline phones, which once piled up in thrift stores and junk shops, can sell for hundreds of dollars, now that celebrities collect them and interior decorators covet them. (Tom Hanks, for one, has hundreds of vintage typewriters, most of them in working order.) However, Slow Media are more than a fringe luxury for those who can afford them. Many print and analog alternatives are financially accessible to almost anyone. The public library is a good place to start: books, magazines, movies, and other materials can be had for free. Libraries: the original sharing economy.

Indeed, the Slow Food movement was founded upon anti-elitism. Petrini spent his early days as a sociology student, radical activist, and founder of the one of the first left-wing independent radio stations in Italy.[56] Slow Food's initial challenge was quite the contrary: trying to sell sensual pleasure to activists who found it too bourgeois and decadent. Much of its work, less visible to consumers and critics, is devoted to aiding small-scale producers and activists. As Slow Food expert Corby Kummer explains, the group aimed from the start to "combat every elitist tendency, every overpriced wine and fancified food."[57] In contrast with high-end restaurants of that era, which turned their backs on traditional foods and looked to France and Asia, Petrini and his comrades combed their own country for home-style trattorias, roadside restaurants, and farmhouse inns—"places serving simple, seasonal, inexpensive food that had long held together village life and helped define local identity."[58] Many Slow Foods are time-tested peasant foods that spring from regional cultures.

The Slow Food co-founder recognized that there was a gulf in the global food community. On the one side, he saw "rich consumers who look for good, genuine products cultivated by poor people who only got poorer by continuing their traditional practices," Kummer says. "On the other, poor people were constrained to buy bad food at cheap prices made possible by immensely potent industrial producers."[59] (Notably, this food is artificially cheap due to corporate farming subsidies and huge social and environmental costs of the industrial food system that are externalized, i.e., not reflected in prices.) Petrini and other Slow leaders aimed to help bridge this economic divide.

Some worry that the Slow movement encourages people to retreat into comfort zones, instead of joining together to build alternatives. Sharma, for one, describes Slow Food in terms of disengagement, using the snail's shell as a metaphor for "protected" and "resistant" spaces (Slow Food restaurants, urban gardens, farms, and so on) that the movement creates.[60] In his analysis of *The Culture of Speed*, John Tomlinson reiterates this concern. Yet he concludes by striking a largely optimistic tone. "To hold oneself away from the cultural mainstream—as a protest, as a route to spiritual fulfillment, or as a personal contribution towards environmental preservation—are marks of a sense of individual moral responsibility," he asserts.[61] Retreating from media offers political possibilities, especially when such actions are temporary.

The solution lies partly in agency: creating an attractive, emotionally compelling narrative that persuades people to make the Slow effort—not through moral exhortation but through the promise of rewards.[62] The visions of Slow Media described in this chapter do just that. People have shared a multitude of stories describing the rich possibilities of adopting Slow Media values and practices. The project of "slowing" media production and consumption requires us to transform culture, not just distance ourselves from its failings. As Slow Food has done, Slow Media is generating alternative modes of positive engagement that could, ideally, be integrated into mainstream culture.

Moving Slow Media Forward

Critical minds are keen when they note the structural and cultural obstacles to participating in Slow practices. Much discourse about Slow Media to date has implied that the adoption of sustainable alternatives is a question of individual responsibility, "as if the problem were a matter of lifestyle choice, while advocating for Slowness as an attainable public good," Sharma argued. "Living slowly will not become a form of radical activism until it acknowledges the truly temporal."[63] In other words, the choice of voluntarily slowing down is a luxury available to relatively few.

I agree that Slowness risks depoliticizing time and "must move beyond the issue of pace and toward what is considered sustainable," as Sharma concluded.[64] She also contended that space and time are not the solution to material inequalities and that the political possibilities of Slowness are not worth rescuing. As you might guess, I diverge on those latter points. To my mind, Slow Media presents an opportunity to engage in conversations about politicizing time and to pursue actions toward making Slow values and principles more accessible.

The first step is to cultivate a deeper awareness of "the politics of time." Social theorist Hartmut Rosa calls it *chronopolitics*. Time scarcity is not an inherent part of life, in his view; it is created by a "circle of acceleration" that includes technological change, social change, and pace of life. These three structural and cultural factors mutually reinforce each other. In modernity, a rush of chaotic change has failed to transform social institutions and, instead, merely weakened them—which leaves people feeling stressed, vertiginous, disoriented, anxious. Modern individuals increasingly have less control over the speed, rhythm, duration, sequencing, and synchronization of their daily activities. This raises important questions of politics and ethics, of domination and free will. To truly live our own lives, we need the power to allocate our own time.[65]

Modern society presents many different modalities of time, but people do not enjoy equal access to these modes. Governments create a regulatory context in which employers require many people to labor long hours (without adequate financial security as recompense), while others are underworked or don't work at all. Individuals live at different tempos, according to their occupations, socioeconomic status, ages, health, spiritual beliefs, families, national cultures, relationships to nature, and much more. Digital devices and networks enter deeply into these rhythms, often increasing the demands made by employers, corporations, or other economic agents. The fact that some groups of people have little control over their own time, while others have a great deal, deserves more attention as a political issue.

One wonders what kinds of people *do* exercise agency by adopting Slow Media lifestyles, especially in light of work commitments. This question offers a promising area for future research. Addressing the problem of overwork, Parkins and Craig see evidence that "a politics of time is emerging across a diverse and proliferating range of social life and which is clearly articulated in the politics of slow living."[66] By contrast, Sharma seems to believe either that Slow movements cannot make any significant political difference or that individual acts of Slowness do not suffice. To me, the latter position is more persuasive. Such reservations underscore the significance of reframing Slow Media as a collective issue and of creating institutions that support sustainable media use and production.

For Slow Media to have a meaningful impact on media culture and time politics, it must resolve some of the issues detailed here. Slow Media advocates could move forward by better communicating their commitment to human and environmental sustainability. They could take political action to help make Slow culture a more realistic choice for everyone. Gaining support from prominent institutions and public figures could help promote those goals. For those who share Slow Media ideals, recognizing the creative and collective aspects of the phenomenon marks an important step. This nascent discussion about mediated ideals and practices brings to light concerns that we will examine in the next chapter: the ethics and politics of Slow production and consumption in journalism.

3

"Good, Clean, Fair"

A Sustainability Framework for Journalism

Are you exhausted by the 24-hour news cycle, never-ending tweets and live blogs
telling you what is happening minute-by-minute but never explaining what it
means? Are you tired of the short attention spans, PR-driven stories, knee-jerk
reactions and churnalism of much of the mainstream media?[1]

So inquire the editors of *Delayed Gratification* (*DG*), a magazine launched in 2011
to offer collectible stories that have simmered for a while, instead of disposable
news that's half-baked. This might sound like a marketing appeal, and it partly is.
But it is also more than that. These publishers believe that journalism can learn
from the Slow movement. Their vision of Slow Journalism means waiting three
months before assessing news events. Each issue examines news of the previous
quarter. For example, the October–December 2016 edition was published in
March 2017 and covered topics such as the election of Donald Trump, the evacua-
tion of Aleppo in Syria, and the standoff at Standing Rock between police, private
security, and people protesting the Dakota Access Pipeline.

By letting three months pass before publishing its stories, *DG* embodies the
slogan "Yesterday's News Tomorrow."[2] Delayed news becomes an asset, not an oxymoron. As a *DG* editor explains, when tragedy strikes, most news organizations
send in crews immediately and give the event blanket coverage for a few days. The
journalism agenda moves on, and reporters quickly leave town. Yet months later,
communities are still struggling to recover, while promises made under the spotlight have evaporated. "When you return to events after the dust has settled, what
you often find is a completely different story," Rob Orchard told *Nieman Reports*.[3]
He sees Slow Journalism as a complement to fast news, not a substitute.

DG editors have "fashioned themselves as ambassadors of Slow Journalism
by educating readers about the basic tenets of the movement as a means of
promoting their brand."[4] Enter "Slow Journalism" into a search engine and
The Slow Journalism Company will likely be a top result. And *DG* is not alone.
The phrase describes a constellation of experiments pursuing alternatives
to journalism-as-usual, a mosaic of changes simmering in the field.[5] Slow

projects, which vary in frequency, scale, technological form, and economic structure, share the conviction that a dose of slowness can rejuvenate the news industry.

A movement toward Slow Journalism—and its siblings Slow Media, Slow News, Slow Writing, Slow Word, Slow Blogging, Slow Storytelling—began percolating in the early aughts. It has gained substantial momentum among practitioners and captured the attention of scholars. In addition to *Delayed Gratification* (UK), some notable examples of start-ups self-identifying as Slow demonstrate the breadth of this global movement:

> Journalists at *De Correspondent* (The Netherlands) highlight "placing less emphasis on what is trending and more on what is truly relevant; taking the time for investigative pieces and creating a space for alternative journalistic formats; ensuring transparency about our own journalistic choices and dilemmas."[6]
>
> The magazine *Jot Down* (Spain) is the lynchpin of a Slow network across Spanish-speaking countries in Europe and Latin America. Described as "an ode to slow production," it is a "paradigmatic example of a sustainable journalistic model built on long-form narrative pieces and in-depth reporting."[7]
>
> *Long Play* (Finland) is a democratic collective that publishes one in-depth story per month, sold online as an e-single. "In the age of big newsroom cuts, investigative journalism is the kind of journalism that suffers and the first to go," one editor said.
>
> The producers of *Narratively* (US) aim to give online stories more space and time. They avoid breaking news in favor of "untold, human-interest stories" conveyed through "rich, intricate narratives."[8] In 2016, *Columbia Journalism Review* called it one of the best experiments in journalism.
>
> Editors of *XXI* (France) think their printed quarterly connects better with readers by exploring slower rhythms, spending more time in the field, and concentrating on "lasting substance, whether the article is 10 lines or 10 pages long."[9]

The Slow moniker has been embraced by journalists working with mainstream organizations, too. Paul Salopek began a seven-year "Out of Eden Walk" in 2013, traveling by foot from Ethiopia to Tierra Del Fuego to recreate the historical journey of human migration for *National Geographic*. Naka Nathaniel's videography for *The New York Times* (alongside reporter Nicholas Kristof) documents genocide, the slave trade, refugee camps, and other human-rights tragedies. In the "Sochi Project," Rob Horstra and Arnold Van Bruggen spent four years in Russia digging up untold, local stories about the 2014 Winter Olympic Games for *The New Yorker*.

Salopek considers his journalism "slow" by virtue of moving at "a human pace of three miles an hour."[10] Nathaniel sees the movement as challenging the pack mentality, which yields redundant coverage while neglecting important topics. "Why do a hundred photographers try to get the same shot of Michael Phelps?" he wondered. "Why not stop competing with each other and share resources? One or two photographers will do the trick. Send the rest out for other stories."[11] As for Horstra and Van Bruggen, they sought to "provide a grassroots analysis of what's going on in [Sochi], an analysis not made by politicians and the usual talking heads, but by slowly composing a new image . . . by doing almost anthropological fieldwork."[12]

The attentive reader will discern here many continuities with well-established traditions such as literary journalism, creative nonfiction, muckraking, and civic journalism. Long-form narratives are so ubiquitous, you might not even notice them anymore. Influential precursors of Slow Journalism include *The New Yorker*, *Vanity Fair*, and *Esquire* in print as well as *Slate* and *Salon* online. Which begs the question: What makes this new genre different from preceding ones? To pinpoint the defining characteristics of Slow Journalism, let's first consider the role played by speed in journalism past and present. Then we will look at lessons that journalists have taken—and, in some cases, not taken—from the Slow Food movement.

The Problem of Fast Journalism

If you ask people about the state of mainstream journalism, they will agree on one thing, regardless of political learning: there's a problem. The editors of *Delayed Gratification* conveyed the sense of crisis in the quote above: endless news updates, hasty reactions, lack of explanatory context, and "churnalism" (a portmanteau bemoaning reliance on press releases and wire stories).[13] A concern with excessive speed unites these complaints.

Journalists' fetish for speed is confirmed by surveys showing that "reporting news quickly" ranks highest among their values.[14] This is not new. For more than a century, the pace of journalism has been fueled by the culture of the scoop and an ethos of competition—which long preceded 24-hour channels and social media newsfeeds. Critics began to believe in the 1990s, if not earlier, that the classic function of journalism was being undermined by Internet-driven speed, as demonstrated in the rush to report on President Clinton's sexual indiscretions and impeachment hearings.

The Internet both helps and hinders reporters in constructing thoughtful, accurate stories and conducting time-intensive investigative work. In *No Time to Think: The Menace of Media Speed and the 24-Hour News Cycle*, Bill Kovach and Tom Rosenstiel explain why they think digital technologies diminish the credibility of journalism.[15] A faster news cycle leads to each story being less comprehensive.

A rising demand for news amid a limited supply of newsmakers gives sources more power over journalists. A proliferation of news outlets diminishes the authority of each and widens the range of standards. A need to fill time and space on news websites induces organizations to churn out inexpensive commentary rather than resource-intensive reporting.

While new technologies contribute to the problem, competition and profit-seeking are important factors, too. Organizations have an economic incentive to put journalism on an assembly line with ever-higher speeds and ever-decreasing numbers of skilled workers.[16] Some compare industrial news to fast food: a standardized, unhealthy product. One critic decried "the era of McNews" as "spatulas of information carelessly splattering the hot grease of half-thoughts and half-truths on camera and online."[17] The emergence of Journatic, an outsourcing company that uses software to systematize production of local news articles—rewritten by English speakers, often in developing countries and paid a few dollars—might epitomize this Taylorization of journalism.[18]

A certain amount of fast journalism is critically necessary to provide breaking news about war, natural disaster, terrorism, and other events of great democratic importance. Society needs a spectrum of journalism ranging from fast to slow. The balance has lately shifted toward the former. The business model for traditional journalism relies on periodicity or planned obsolescence—on selling a commodity that is impermanent and disposable. There is constant tension between the commercial value of news (based on its short shelf life) and the democratic value of news (derived from its longevity and usefulness). Cranking out flimsy news products can generate more revenue faster than asking larger, more profound social and economic questions.

The problem of fast journalism extends far beyond people who produce it—who are not always journalists. As the "fake news" phenomenon demonstrates, many entrepreneurs and ideologues are motivated by political as much as financial gain. And news producers are not the only ones guilty of sometimes going too fast. Stories circulate quickly online and audiences scan them at breakneck speed. They often scan a headline but don't take time to click through to the full story. Science shows that human attention spans are now shorter than those of goldfish, thanks to smartphones.[19] People often fail to evaluate the reliability of their news sources or, indeed, to learn when, where, and by whom their "journalism" was produced.

Many consider fast journalism the equivalent of junk food, getting junkier as it gets faster. And they think Slow principles can make news better. Journalists from media outlets like American Public Radio, *Forbes*, *HuffPost*, *The Observer*, *The Wall Street Journal*, *The Washington Post*, and elsewhere have chimed in to support Slow Journalism.[20] Their conversations demonstrate the Slow movement's growing influence on the production of news. And a growing cadre of scholars has been exploring how journalists put Slow values into practice and how audiences are responding to these new alternatives in the mediascape.

A Quick Definition of Slow Journalism

Slow Journalism has gained currency among media scholars, practitioners, and commentators since 2007, when people like Salopek, Nathaniel, and Susan Greenberg began using it. Greenberg, a scholar and former correspondent for *The Guardian*, defines Slow Journalism as essays, reportage, and other nonfiction forms that offer an alternative to conventional reporting. "The journalistic equivalent of slow food keeps the reader informed about the provenance of the information and how it was gathered," Greenberg explains. "More time is invested in both the production and consumption of the work, to discover things we would not otherwise know, or notice things that have been missed, and communicate that to the highest standards of storytelling craft."[21] The proliferation of Slow publishers marks a new and critical alternative in the mediascape, she said.[22]

Media researchers have studied a panoply of Slow Journalism endeavors, with the lion's share of attention going to the actions and intentions of producers, primarily by analyzing content and interviewing editors. For example, scholars have scrutinized collaborative newswork in post-Katrina New Orleans that shares costs, bylines, and branding; the rejection of traditional objectivity in favor of personalized, transparent, and engaged approaches; publisher interviews about Slow projects such as *6 Mois, Aeon, Help Me Investigate, Mission and State*, and others; the rise in alternative revenue sources such as crowd-funding and micropayments that marginalize advertisers; the aesthetic choice of evoking permanence, scarcity, and finitude through film photography; ethical reporting that encourages sources to tell their own stories; the value of spending long periods or even "wasting time" in the field; and the benefits of adopting Slow approaches in journalism education.

This profusion of Slow enterprises illustrates that journalism practitioners have entered an era of high experimentation and theorization, as Le Masurier observed.[23] If we avoid defining Slow Journalism too narrowly, or viewing it as a simplistic binary opposition to fast practices, the idea can help us make sense of current changes in journalism.[24]

Slow Journalism can have at least seven layers of meaning, one analysis found, including *Slow* (journalism that enacts a critique of live reporting and the culture of speed); *investigative* (it rehabilitates time-consuming legwork and rejects packaged news); *less* (it is more selective and explanatory in its choice of topics, to avoid overload and triviality); *narrative* (it often, though not always, takes a longer form, which requires more time to produce and to consume); *fair* (it pursues equitable relations with producers, who are better paid; attends to the treatment of animals and the earth; gives consumers access to quality content at a fair price; provides transparency about the information sources it uses); *community oriented* (it serves a community and feeds a public sphere); and *participatory* (it invites audiences to contribute content, to become partners in journalism, and to take a stand). The first four criteria are widespread and the final three rarer among Slow projects.[25]

The Slow Journalism category is thought provoking but also fuzzy, as one scholar observes.[26] This interpretive flexibility can be both a strength and a weakness. Any set of criteria ascribed to Slow Journalism could "just as readily fit with New Journalism fifty years ago, the 'intimate' journalism or the 'new-new' journalism of the past twenty years," Erik Neveu said.[27] (New Journalism emphasized intensive reportage and fiction-writing techniques, as pioneered by the likes of Truman Capote, Norman Mailer, Gay Talese, Hunter S. Thompson, and Tom Wolfe.) In his view, it is most fruitful to think of the concept as an "ideal-type" that questions general assumptions about journalism, rather than delineating a specific set of new practices. By avoiding a strict definition that might offer some kind of purity test, we can pay more attention to differences, hybridizations and ambivalences.

I share the concern that Slow Journalism risks appearing like a new label on old practices, since some aspects of Slow Journalism are not especially radical. In defining the genre on his blog, Mark Berkey-Gerard proposed that a Slow reporter "gives up the fetish of beating the competition"; "values accuracy, quality and context, not just being fast and first"; "avoids celebrity, sensation and events covered by a herd of reporters"; and "takes time to find things out out."[28] These Slow Journalism ideals "sound a lot like the advice I received from my journalism teachers and editors," said the educator and former newsman. "It is the kind of work many of my students aspire to, but fear they might never get a chance to do." A careful look at Slow Food principles reveals how Slow Journalism could better distinguish itself from what has come before, by applying Slow Food ethics to media and journalism.

Sustainability Principles for Journalism

While many people enjoy the concrete fruits of Slow Food, fewer have delved into the conceptual framework in which the movement is rooted. One motto that guides Slow Food is "Good, Clean, Fair" (GCF). As explained in Slow Food Nation,[29] the GCF slogan is equated with sustainability, where "clean" more or less means environmentally sustainable and "fair" means socially sustainable.

Good means fresh, flavorful, satisfying to the senses, and connected to local cultures. In Carlo Petrini's view, Good is a subjective quality determined by taste (which is personal and linked to one's senses) and knowledge (which is cultural and linked to one's environment). Human senses suffer today because we have less time to select and perceive stimuli, he says. Training yourself to recognize what's Good is both a cultural and political act. It can bring you more pleasure, freedom of choice, and influence over the decisions of producers. "To reappropriate one's senses is to reappropriate one's own life and cooperate with others in creating a better world," says Petrini, who thinks sustainability and quality go hand in hand.[30]

Clean means produced in ways that protect the environment, animal welfare, and human health. Petrini ties Clean to actions such as deindustrializing agriculture, encouraging biodiversity, and supporting small producers. This latter group includes, among others, chefs who "indicate the provenance of their products in their menus. . . . Let them make their own quest for excellence the driving force behind sustainable development."[31] Petrini proposes that things made and consumed locally are usually cleaner and more sustainable than those produced farther away. For people to know whether a product is clean, they need information enabling them to evaluate its costs and benefits to the environment and to people. While "the clean creates conditions for the good," he says that "a good product is not necessarily clean."[32] And, a product that is Good is not necessarily fair.

Fair means that workers, users, and the public are treated ethically. According to Petrini, "the word 'fair' connotes social justice, respect for workers and their know-how, . . . pay adequate to work, gratification in producing well, and the definitive revaluation of the small farmer."[33] The principle is closely aligned to social sustainability, to "promoting quality of life through dignified jobs that guarantee sustenance and fair remuneration."[34] Petrini believes that we need slower models of investment and more sustainable business practices, which pursue social justice and have a low environmental impact.

The Slow Journalism movement could benefit from borrowing the GCF motto. An early proponent of this perspective was scholar Harold Gess. He envisions *Good* journalism as well produced and committed to the well-being of its community; *Clean* as treating sources ethically, pursuing social justice, and supporting sustainable ecosystems and livelihoods; and *Fair* as making media accessible to the community and ensuring nonexploitative working conditions.[35] Gess explained how GCF could be helpful to complex, slow-developing stories such as climate change that lose their novelty value and require long-term relationships between journalists and local communities.

Some of these conceptions diverge somewhat from Petrini's explanation of GCF. To unite these varied perspectives, I summarize them succinctly thus: Good journalism offers content that's satisfying to one's intellect, emotions, and senses as well as politically engaged and connected to local cultures. Clean journalism is produced in ways that protect environmental health, animal welfare, and human well-being. Fair journalism shows respect to news workers, through satisfactory pay and working conditions, as well as to its readers and the wider community.

The Slow interpretation of fairness, as related to sustainability, has a substantially different meaning to how it is traditionally construed in journalism ethics. (The phrase "fair and balanced" might spring to mind.) To most journalists, fairness is a characteristic of good reporting that necessitates seeking a wide variety of sources and getting multiple viewpoints on a topic. I propose that we must understand "fairness in journalism" in a broader way that recognizes the decisions not just of reporters but also of people who own and manage news organizations.

The journalism industry overlooks many ethical issues related to environmental and social sustainability, as a glance at the profession's foremost declaration of standards will corroborate. According to the *Code of Ethics* of the Society of Professional Journalists (SPJ), "Ethical journalism strives to ensure the free exchange of information that is accurate, fair and thorough."[36] Its principles include:

> *Seek Truth and Report It.* For example, journalists should be honest and coura-
>   geous in gathering, reporting, and interpreting information.
> *Minimize Harm.* For example, journalists should treats sources, subjects,
>   colleagues, and members of the public as human beings deserving of
>   respect.
> *Act Independently.* For example, journalists should avoid conflicts of interest,
>   real or perceived. They should refuse gifts, favors, fees, free travel, and
>   special treatment. They should also deny favored treatment to advertisers,
>   donors, and other special interests, and distinguish news from advertising
>   and prominently label sponsored content.
> *Be Accountable and Transparent.* For example, journalists should explain
>   ethical choices to audiences. They should encourage a civil dialogue with
>   the public about journalistic practices, coverage, and news content.

Setting aside the question of whether contemporary journalism manages to live up to these standards, one cannot help but notice the absence of ecological concerns in the SPJ code. These principles focus on choices made by individual journalists in the course of gathering and reporting news, rather than on decisions made by owners and managers. The Slow standards of Good, Clean, and Fair offer a much-needed corrective to this structural oversight. In current conversations about Slow Journalism, the first word of the GCF triad gets the most attention, whereas the latter ones deserve a closer look.

Being "Good" Is Not Enough

Proponents of Slow Journalism are overwhelmingly interested in making content better, or "Good." Scholarly analyses, publisher interviews, and mission statements reveal a preoccupation with telling better—and, especially, longer—stories, by allowing journalists ample space and time for good reporting, writing, and design. Quality is the primary goal at *Delayed Gratification*, for instance. "We believe that beautiful, considered publications are the future of print," said editor Marcus Webb. "We like products that are crafted, that somebody has labored over—and we hope to have created something that people will treasure. The Internet is fantastic for getting the first word on any story, but we are interested in giving our writers time to think and our designers time to look at the best way of presenting information graphically," he said, explaining their decision to publish on paper.[37]

Speaking of print, two other titles have been lauded as landmark products in Slow Journalism: *The San Francisco Panorama* and *Monocle*. The *Panorama* was a limited-edition newspaper published in 2010 by Dave Eggers and the McSweeney's collective (as an unusual form for Issue 38 of their quarterly literary journal). Quickly selling out at $16 per copy, it featured a 112-page broadsheet as well as a 112-page magazine, 96-page book review section and some pull-out posters. "We at McSweeney's love newspapers. But we love the Internet, too," the editors said, making it clear that they are not "Luddites."[38] "We believe that print newspapers are an invaluable part of the journalism landscape."

London-based *Monocle*, meanwhile, is a monthly magazine designed to be "tactile" and "collectible," according to publisher Tyler Brûlé. The magazine's blend of global affairs, business, and lifestyle stories has attracted a large and growing international paid readership since its 2007 debut, even with a sticker price of $17 per issue. *Monocle* has also diversified into other ventures such as guidebooks, a radio station, TV shows, cafes, and retail shops.

Though Eggers, McSweeney's, and Brûlé did not adopt the Slow sobriquet per se, their projects reverberate with Slow attitudes. An essay for *Forbes* cited *Monocle* and *The San Francisco Panorama* as proof that "the aesthetic pleasure of reading can make people so excited about journalism that they'll buy it—not just conceptually, but in terms of parting with cash"[39] A Slow Media, Slow News, or Slow Word movement could lure audiences by providing "luxuriously produced" media that preserve local print traditions, wrote Trevor Butterworth. He urged journalism businesses to adopt the Slow label as a way of rebranding high-quality newspapers and magazines as "pleasurable," "sustainable," and "local." Some dismissed this call for a Slow marketing strategy, contending that such high prices were commercially nonviable on a broad scale, perhaps even elitist. (Such complaints have likewise been lobbed at Slow Foods' organically grown and artisan-made products, which are sometimes pricey due to small-scale production.)

Worries about the democratic press, as well as the bottom line, have been driving such pleas for Slow News. Echoing Rosenstiel and Kovach, Butterworth recounts how "warp-speed" publishing and "villainous" blogging led to crises of journalism such as the Clinton-Lewinsky scandal.[40] At that time, mainstream journalists had hesitated to report on an alleged (later confirmed) affair between President Bill Clinton and intern Monica Lewinsky—until their hand was forced by a story on the conservative blog *Drudge Report*. The 1993 incident spurred traditional journalists to recognize increased competition for news and to accelerate the pace of their reporting, for fear that online amateurs might scoop the pros. In the post-Lewinsky era, respectable reporters feel pressure to publish allegations before carefully checking them out as thoroughly as they might have in the past.

Rather than complaining about how terrible and "fake" the news has become in the era of social media, Slow Journalism offers a feel-good alternative. Few people are likely to flock toward high-quality journalism merely out of civic duty or a realization that they should eat their cultural vegetables. "The public needs something to believe in rather than rail against, something elegantly simple and bipartisan that has sufficient aesthetic compulsion to sound pleasurable rather than penitential," Butterworth proposes. It is "simply unrealistic to expect the public to read newspapers as a daily personal moral commitment to democracy."[41] Slow Journalism offers one such rallying cry.

Proponents herald Slow as a solution for rebranding Good journalism. They think better content and design could attract new paying audiences for news. Greenberg used a marketing concept called "the end of the middle" to explain how publishers could differentiate their products through Slow approaches that improve quality. On the low end, we get basic news cheaply or for free. In the middle is traditional print journalism, the sector that is losing readers. Slow Journalism could tap the luxury end, according to Greenberg: "There should be a growing market for essays, reportage and other nonfiction writing that takes its time to find things out, notice stories that others miss, and communicates it all to the highest standards."[42]

High-quality, long-form journalism is neither new nor unusual—even if it has not been billed as Slow. Many serious, investigative, and literary US publications such as *Harper's, The New Yorker, Rolling Stone*, and *The Atlantic* have long produced content in accord with the Slow model. Indeed, *Harper's* and *The New Yorker* developed many of the reporting methods commonly associated with Slow Journalism. Such magazines have emerged as vocal supporters of the movement. Many "born-digital" publications also are devoted to this genre, including *The Atavist, Longform, Longreads*, and *Narratively*.

The growing imperative for journalists to meet strenuous quotas and attract clicks detracts from the time spent on original, in-depth reporting. While the public would benefit from more investigative journalism, and better promotion of such work, there is already a decent supply of high-quality, long-form news. Characteristics such as length and quality are not sufficient to distinguish Slow Journalism from previous forms. Otherwise, the line separating Slow Journalism from Amazon's Kindle long-form singles or from *Newsweek*'s print edition (relaunched as a "premium" or "boutique" product featuring longer stories) is blurry, at best. That's why "Good" is not enough.

The Slow pursuit of quality is, at some level, about marketing: attracting new audiences and convincing them to pay more (or simply pay at all) for a product perceived as different from news-as-usual, and thus worth the price. That's all well and good. There's nothing wrong with promoting and profiting from one's ideas or products. Slow Food did so brilliantly through its ubiquitous Snail of Approval and collaboration with Eataly's global network of gourmet emporia.

No matter how good the product is, quality alone does not suffice to make it virtuous. The urge to frame Slowness mainly as a branding tool is morally problematic. To truly be Slow and sustainable, we could address the ways in which news work (1) is unfair to people who create journalism and (2) contributes to ecological degradation.

Slow journalists could be more transparent about the provenance of their information, as Greenberg notes. In her view, provenance is rooted in the provision of Good content through practices such as properly crediting sources, identifying material derived from PR sources, acknowledging subjectivity, and linking to source documents, as *Delayed Gratification* does.[43] Few people have addressed the Clean and Fair dimensions of the Slow triumvirate, including better pay for workers and better treatment of animals and the earth.

One notable exception is David Leigh, in an article about Slow Journalism for *The Guardian*. He feared that in an era of declining budgets, the role of the reporter was endangered by the citizen journalist, the blogger, the commentator, and the "news bunny" who can bash out a story in ten minutes. "Slow Journalism would show greater respect for the reporter as a patient assembler of facts," he said. "A skilled craftsman who is independent and professionally reputable. A disentangler of lies and weasel words. And who is paid rate for the job."[44] Leigh argued that if society values good news stories, it should fairly compensate the people who make it, in part to make journalism a sustainable career choice.

Delayed Gratification has adopted several Fair and Clean practices suitable to calling itself a Slow Journalism company. *DG* editors try to compensate contributors as fairly as possible, providing at least a minimum wage—though one "laments that he is only able to pay writers 32 cents per word, compared to typical word rates in the U.K. of 50 to 65 cents per word."[45] *Narratively*, by comparison, pays a few hundred US dollars per story, versus rates of $1 to $3 per word for national magazines. Writers for *The Atavist* typically get at least $10,000 per story, including revenue shared from subscriptions, single-copy sales, and TV and film rights. Such efforts to pay fairly are meaningful in a news environment where many journalists feel pressured to work for free.

Publishers of *Delayed Gratification* have taken steps to be Cleaner by reducing the magazine's ecological impact, too. Issues are printed on paper approved by the Forest Stewardship Council, which addresses indigenous rights, workers' rights, long-term community well-being, and the environmental impact of forestry practices. They use a printer registered to the ISO 14001 environmental standard, which aims to reduce waste by recycling.[46] And they support sustainability by selling all of their back issues, in contrast with the mainstream practice of pulping most old magazines. The Slow Journalism Company doesn't boast about its strides toward sustainability. Perhaps it should.

A "Fair" Analysis of Journalism

Case in point: *HuffPost* is, in many ways, Good. It has offered pleasurable reading experiences and earned the highest accolades in the journalism profession: a Polk Award and a Pulitzer Prize. Arianna Huffington earned my appreciation by writing about the Slow News movement, the National Day of Unplugging, and *In Praise of Slowness*. Yet under her leadership, the blogging behemoth didn't pay the majority of its contributors.[47] And at *Patch*, the blogging network once owned by AOL-HuffPost, editors were given higher story quotas and asked to recruit more unpaid contributors. "Burnout became a big problem," said one former employee. "Two great editors quit within a year, partially due to stress. It was hard to take a vacation or turn off the phone."[48] (So much for unplugging.)

Complaints about unsustainable working conditions are common in today's news organizations. One blogger likened his profession to "a digital sweatshop." Journalists often create enormous amounts of content while receiving less than minimum wage, no healthcare. and no paid time off, he said. "This is not a sustainable model for people producing content."[49] Another reporter, whose production quota was doubled from 5 to 10 stories per day, compared his workplace to "a galley rowed by slaves and commanded by pirates" that evoked "many of the worst abuses of the old economy's industrial capitalism—the sweatshop, the speedup and piecework; huge profits for the owners; desperation, drudgery and exploitation for the workers."[50] Media scholar and activist Robert McChesney quotes a former *Seattle Times* journalist: "I don't know anybody from my profession who isn't heartbroken, devastated, terrified, scared, enraged, despondent, bereft."[51]

Many established journalists—as well as aspiring ones—feel compelled to work for free in this environment, where people who produce content are undervalued by the market. Some call this donated labor *promotion, publicity, branding*. It's a remarkable subsidy to news organizations (often large, profitable corporations) that comes at the expense of journalists. Sustainable working conditions could enhance news quality by encouraging good reporters to stay in the profession instead of seeking less stressful and more remunerative careers. Instead, a lot of talented journalists opt to leave the field.[52] The current situation also restricts reporters' diversity in terms of race, ethnicity, gender and socio-economic background. Only certain groups of people can afford to work at jobs that don't pay the bills.

According to McChesney and his co-author John Nichols, a living wage for journalists is one of the most pressing concerns for democratic society. Journalism risks being the province of a small group of people—perhaps independently wealthy ones, or those desperate enough to be docile—if it cannot attract people from diverse backgrounds by offering adequate compensation. Meanwhile, as David Leigh anticipated, a "precariat" of freelancers, part-time workers, and unpaid interns has filled the void.[53] Contingent workers lead a precarious existence without benefits, rights, or security, which puts downward pressure on everyone's wages and labor protections. With fewer resources devoted to reporting and editing staff, journalism's ability to monitor public issues and to sustain democracy withers.

If anyone seems amenable to promoting sustainable alternatives, it's Huffington. Upon stepping down from her role at *HuffPost*, she launched an organization devoted to fighting workplace stress and burnout. Its mission is to educate companies about how to nurture employees' well-being, creativity, and productivity.[54] She admires the Slow critique of "turbo capitalism," which uses "natural resources faster than Mother Nature can replace them" and uses people "to serve the economy, rather than the other way around."[55] If Huffington found it difficult to run her publications according to such values, then countless other publishers are clearly in the same boat.

Alternative Economic Models

Regardless of Arianna Huffington's intentions, she did play the journalism game by rules not of her own making. Individual publishers cannot be blamed for systemic shortcomings. Neither can the Internet or social media, since the crisis in journalism precedes them. Rather, the problem springs from corporate control, advertising support, and profit motives, which have increased dramatically since the 1970s. Capitalism, more so than technology, is responsible for slashing reporters' wages and increasing their workloads as well as trivializing content, increasing reliance on press releases, and degrading journalism's public-service function. The nature of huge media companies is to pursue short-term financial gain—to boost the bottom line, quarterly earnings, share prices—not to nurture the long-term good of workers, readers, the environment, and the public. We were lucky, for a while, that the corporate-commercial news structure produced relatively good, fair journalism as a "positive externality."[56] But that era is ending.

Philanthropy, crowdfunding, reader donations, ticketed live events, micropayments, e-singles, "tip jars" to express reader satisfaction. . . . These are some of the strategies adopted by Slow Journalism in search of a sustainable economic model that will bind it more closely to audiences than to advertisers or stockholders. Aiming to immerse readers rather than distract their attention, Slow publishers are turning away from display advertising and instead experimenting with eclectic and *a la carte* revenue streams.[57] Although some Slow projects continue to incorporate commercial ads and other conventional revenue sources, others have been trying new formulas, sometimes ingenious. For example, *Narratively* is funded by a combination of brand sponsorship, crowdfunding, and limited "native advertising" (which integrates ads by mimicking the style of editorial content). It also brokers its contributors to companies in need of content production; in other words, it functions as a talent agency.

De Correspondent was launched by a crowd-funding campaign that raised 1.7 million Euros (most of it in eight days), which established a large base of paid subscribers. The editors pledged that the platform would not strive to maximize profit for shareholders but rather reinvest at least 95% of its revenues in journalism.[58] While donations are welcome from third parties such as universities and research institutes, these partners have no stake in the publication's profits, and editors promise to be fully transparent about the nature and terms of such partnerships.[59] "Economic autonomy and executive transparency thus drive *De Correspondent*'s business plan as a means of generating both real and symbolic capital," Dowling explains.[60]

The financing model developed by *Jot Down* offers additional insight into the potential sustainability of Slow Journalism projects. Inspired by *The New Yorker*, this magazine was launched partly through a fundraising campaign on social media. Its business model is based on maintaining a small permanent staff and a large network of freelancers, who are usually paid around 90 and 150 Euros per article or photograph.[61] Seventy percent of the publication's income derives from sales of its 320-page print quarterly—which contains only a few pages of advertising—with the remaining 30% obtained through promotions, digital advertising, sponsored content, and diverse other means.[62] Another strategy was developing its own distribution network, Soidem, which features more than 100 points of sale and a dozen other magazines and journals throughout Spain and Latin America. This cooperative approach makes *Jot Down* unusual among Slow Journalism projects.[63]

Some organizations have adopted models of community supported journalism, akin to Slow Food's CSAs, in which city dwellers purchase "shares" in a local farm. The successful *Belt* magazine is one example. This independent publication started in Cleveland and expanded to other Rust Belt cities from Chicago to Detroit to Pittsburgh. *Belt* is primarily funded by annual and lifetime "members" who receive free issues of the magazine, thank-you gifts such as t-shirts or books, and discounts at local merchants and events.

Slow publishers are still wrestling with the question of how to sustain their ventures. While some initiatives have thrived, some have not. The print publication *Slake*, featuring long-form journalism about urban culture, made the *Los Angeles Times* bestseller list more than a dozen times. Still, it ran out of money after two years. *Mission and State* was a philanthropically funded website in Santa Barbara, CA that produced deeply reported, multimedia narratives aiming for local, regional, and national impact. It stopped publishing after five years, revealing the limits of philanthropy as a financial model.

In sum: Slow Journalism contrasts starkly with traditional advertiser-dependent models, which overwhelmingly encourage free media content, in its conviction that consumers should and will pay. The overarching purpose of Slow Journalism is "to transform readers from a collective commodity 'delivered' to advertisers to a humanized audience honored for their capacity to delve deeply into long-form stories," as one scholar puts it.[64]

The business philosophy underlying many of these projects is akin to National Public Radio's membership model. They believe that journalism cannot be Good, Clean, and Fair unless its primary responsibility is to readers and viewers. As one manifesto for Slow News urges consumers: "Buy some of your news. . . . When news is free, ask why. Who benefits, and what is their agenda?"[65] When you can get products or services for "free," it usually means that *you* are the product, that advertisers are trying to reach your eyeballs and your wallet. To understand how Slow Journalism might live up to its promise, let's look at the news environment from an audience perspective.

Empowering News Consumers

When Huffington promoted Slowness in one of her columns, she presented it as a consumer issue. "A world of too much data, too many choices, too many possibilities and too little time is forcing us to decide what we really value," she wrote in an editorial about Slow News. "More and more, people and innovative companies are recognizing that we actually have a life beyond our gadgets." Her essay recognizes a "longing to disconnect" from "hyperconnected lives."[66] Yet Huffington proposed not that news be produced or distributed more slowly but that audiences exercise more restraint in consuming news.

The grande dame of blogging gave props to Walter Shapiro (of then-HuffPost-owned *Politics Daily*), who described the Slow News movement as a "form of reader rebellion." Shapiro argued that meaning and context suffer in our faster-faster media culture, where people don't have time to contemplate the information thrown at them. "The news of government, politics and the world is too important to be instantly consumed like a shopaholic racing through a mall," he said. "Our democracy simply cannot survive if we fail to see the forest for the tweets."[67]

Some such calls to slow down news were provoked by the Shirley Sherrod incident. Sherrod was a White House appointee forced to resign in 2010 after mainstream journalists aired stories that portrayed her as racist. Their hasty reporting was based on commentary posted by a conservative blogger, who misrepresented comments that Sherrod had made at an NAACP meeting. (Sherrod sued the blogger, Andrew Breitbart [the now-deceased founder of Brietbart News], for defamation; the two parties reached a confidential settlement in 2015.) The Obama administration apologized to Sherrod and offered her a new position, which she declined.

Like Shapiro, Ruth Marcus of *The Washington Post* cited the Sherrod case in proposing that *journalists*—not (as Huffington said) *readers*—should give Slow News a whirl. She christened it "Slow Blogging." News producers could learn a thing or two from Slow Food about preserving "traditions of excellence and ethical behavior," Marcus wrote. "The Sherrod affair reminds us all that slow, or at least slower, news is often better news."[68] Not always, but often.

To better understand the respective roles of news consumers and producers in Slow Journalism, let's reconsider what we mean by participation or "co-pro-duction." The term means something different in media professions than in Slow Food communities. Journalists tend to think of readers as "co-producers" who post comments, participate as amateur journalists, or contribute stories and photos. (Some call such activities "citizen journalism"; others equate them with unpaid labor.) If they hewed closer to the Slow Food model, journalists would think of readers as co-producers who choose to support, purchase, and consume particular products over others.[69]

In the Slow Food context, co-producers become part of the process by learning how their food is made and supporting local producers, sometimes through community-supported agriculture programs. These co-producers see food con-sumption not as an action separate from production, but as the last link in a vir-tuous supply chain that is good, clean, and fair. Slow Food is not founded on the idea that everyone should be growing their own lettuce or volunteering to help farmers produce (and profit from) those greens—although some people do have gardens or donate their labor. Instead, it advances the idea that people who eat lettuce should know its provenance and that the community will support lettuce producers who adhere to good, clean, fair practices.

The reader-supported business models proliferating in Slow Journalism have learned some lessons from this example. They could go further by offering audiences more information about how clean and fair their production activ-ities are, not just how good their content is. To take Slow Journalism to the next level—becoming more sustainable—publishers could be forthright about showing readers the provenance of their news.

Slow Journalism audiences, for their part, could step up to the plate. This means devoting more time, energy, and money to news consumption, as Slow Food supporters have grown accustomed to doing. Slow readers could get better at critically assessing journalism and, for that matter, all media. Co-production requires "a kind of ethical and critical consumption of not just the text, but of the producers and their media organisations," Megan Le Masurier explains. It demands of audiences "a different level of media literacy beyond interpretation, and a responsibility to learn how the journalism they consume is produced and financed."[70] Slow Journalism co-producers could be green media citizens who know the environmental inputs and outputs of the media technologies they use.[71]

Meanwhile, these rebellious Slow readers need more ammunition. A self-la-beling movement could help recognize and encourage fairer and cleaner practices. Labeling could bring to journalism the type of co-production that empowers Slow Food consumers to influence food systems through collective choices. Readers could judge the people-friendly and eco-friendly provenance of their media, if relevant information were available. Transparency and accountability should come naturally to a field like journalism, although this is a new and different kind of transparency: by management, not by reporters. Slow trailblazers such as *Delayed Gratification* have started the ball rolling.

Publishers who want Slow credibility could post bona fides on their websites. Where are owners, editors, writers, and other staff collectively located? How do journalists engage with local communities? What working conditions do publishers strive to provide? On what basis do they determine compensation for people who contribute to the enterprise's success? How do they evaluate the environmental impact of workspaces, technologies, raw materials, and waste streams? (Audiences would just need some general parameters, not specific details such as addresses or salaries.) If publications are trying to do the right thing, they deserve to brag about it.

Voluntary labeling by Slow producers would not eradicate fast news, click mills, and profit motives. But a commitment to informing the public about GCF practices would enable consumers and workers (both actual and prospective) to recognize organizations that are trying to treat people and the planet well. Through voluntary self-labeling, independent ratings, or other strategies, a movement that promotes informed news consumers could save "Slow" from being co-opted in what I call "Slow-washing," the media equivalent of greenwashing.

Toward Sustainable Journalism

The Slow Food metaphor is a great tool for imagining alternatives for journalism production and consumption. When addressing systemic problems like sustainability in media use, a countercultural framework is available to help change the narrative: Slow Food, which has inspired consumer action to improve the status quo through collective choices. And one of the most important lessons that journalism could learn from Slow Food is how to cultivate fair-traded, community-supported products.

I have used the "Good, Clean, Fair" slogan here to draw a roadmap for moving toward better journalism and to show how fairness and cleanliness—more so than goodness—can promote sustainability in media use. Slow publishers could integrate these ethical values in their business practices not only to distinguish their products from other works of in-depth reporting and long-form narrative but also to cultivate a healthier news ecosystem. Boosting journalism's contribution to social and environmental sustainability is what can separate Slow approaches from fast ones.

To merit the qualifier "Slow," journalism could pursue fair treatment for the people who create news the same way we do for people who grow bird-friendly coffee or raise grass-fed cows. Like the fair-trade movement, Slow Journalism can turn its virtuous conditions of production into a marketing advantage that justifies its higher price. The timing for a discussion about fair pay in journalism might be right, as movements to establish living wages gain ground. In what *The Nation* has called "the unionization of digital media," successful organizing campaigns established collective bargaining in 2015 and 2016 for employees at *Al Jazeera America, Gawker, The Guardian US, HuffPost, Salon,* and *Vice.* News organizations that fail to pay freelancers and interns have also found rebuke on many fronts. nothing, it feels like it would decrease

What does the future hold for Slow Journalism? Some proponents think the genre has great potential for marketing itself as a distinctive brand or anti-brand, "one profoundly resistant to the homogenizing standardization of mass-produced online news according to the Journatic model."[72] Others are more skeptical, considering Slow Journalism a passing fad, nostalgic reaction, or simply too marginal to succeed on a broad scale. People wonder whether Slow Journalism, like Slow Food, preaches mainly to the converted, a small public with high cultural and economic capital. Echoing questions about the politics of time posed in chapter 2, Le Masurier asks, "Who has the time to slow their consumption of journalism and engage with longer, more complex narratives? And do consumers want to?"[73] To some extent, the success of Slow Journalism depends on whether consumers will take financial responsibility for its production—as many now do for public broadcasting.

Audience research offers some clues as to what kind of people support Slow Journalism. According to a study of *Jot Down,* this publication's Spanish audience consists mostly of young, urban, educated, and progressive readers. Their youth suggests that Slow Journalism appeals to new news audiences, not just established ones. Another study found that a third of Dutch college students were interested in qualities associated with Slow Journalism, including in-depth reporting that provides context and helps to solve social problems.[74] Yet most members of this young audience wanted news to be mobile, free, and instantaneous. This popular resistance to paying for journalism will temper prospects for audience-supported models.

Taking a sustainability perspective helps reveal why the agency of both producers *and* co-producers is crucial to the growth of Slow movements, in media as in food. Scholars and practitioners alike could learn a lot by turning their attention from the role of Slow journalists to that of consumers. The attitudes and behaviors of Slow audiences have been largely overlooked—a long-standing tendency of scholarship in alternative media.[75] There remains much for us to learn more about how and why readers engage (or don't engage) with Slow Journalism and what meanings they make (or don't make) from it.

The Slow Journalism movement it most likely to flourish in alternative spaces where fair and clean values are being put into action. Slow News is generally more expensive to produce than its fast alternative, making these practices hard to reconcile with the profit motives of big corporations. Slow and sustainable values provide a counterpoint to "Big Media," a long-standing object of progressive critics such as McChesney, Edward Herman, and Noam Chomsky, who have long argued that the financial motives of large media companies undermine journalism. The plight of overworked reporters illustrates tension between local values and global (read: mainstream, neoliberal, corporate) ones. Local media organizations are arguably more sustainable by virtue of being more responsive to the human communities and natural environments in which they're situated. There's also an economic multiplier effect with locally owned businesses: 48% of each revenue dollar recirculates through their community, versus 14% for corporate-owned businesses.[76]

Small producers who employ fair, clean practices appropriate to their local contexts form the backbone of the Slow Food movement (along with greenmarkets, chefs, restaurateurs, and their patrons). Slow Journalism could develop similar networks of small, local, nonprofit producers and co-producers— while facing some dissimilar challenges. We should be cautious, as Le Masurier warns, about "an overly literal mapping of one movement (food) on to another (journalism)."[77] Journalism is, obviously, not analogous to food. News can travel long distances with little degradation in quality. It can be consumed instantaneously and at no cost, especially through broadcast radio and online media. News circulated through social networks, in particular, gives audiences fewer immediate cues about its provenance.

Locavore behavior requires consumers to be informed about how products are made. In the Slow Food world, this means transparent labeling. If everything is clearly stated on a label, and consumers are aware of environmental costs, many production systems could gradually be relocalized, Petrini said. Such labeling is both "an excellent marketing ploy" and "a service to the community," whose members want to exercise their spending power by choosing products that are as clean and local as possible.[78] Slow Journalists could follow this example by helping to educate consumers about the hidden costs of producing news.

While Slow Journalism might be at a competitive disadvantage in respect to higher wages and prices, the greater constraints might be not economics but rather time and imagination. Many readers neglect to evaluate news sources because media choices have exploded and leisure time in which to choose and consume journalism has stagnated. People are prone to scanning news quickly and multitasking in an attempt to keep pace with multiplying demands. Indeed, the proliferation of choice has become a burden.

Individuals can only do so much to support ethical forms of production, in journalism as in other realms of consumption. Society expects people to act like rational consumers who reward the best suppliers, Justin Lewis observes, but most people don't want to spend their free time researching such intricacies. He calls it "the Catch 22 of consumer capitalism in the 21st century": it is perfectly rational for consumers to give up making rational decisions once they realize that the costs, in time and effort, exceed the benefits of making the right decision.[79] That's why Slow Journalism needs to take collective action, promote industry standards, and foster a cultural environment where consumers find it easier to make informed choices and are motivated to do so.

4

Greening Media

New Directions in Environmental Citizenship and Scholarship

> Cloud, *n.* Visible condensed vapor floating high in the air. Often rhetorically used in plural for 'the sky, the heavens.' The fleeting or unsubstantial.
>
> Cloud, *v.* To render obscure; to dim, obscure, darken. To hide, conceal, veil. To overspread with gloom, cast a shadow over, deprive of brightness; to darken with trouble.
>
> —*Oxford English Dictionary*

Many people born before high-speed Internet remember the days, not long ago, when you went to a video store to pick up movies. You transported yourself to bookstores for fresh reading materials and to record shops for new aural delights. You got paper statements and letters in the mail. You bought stamps. You stuck checks in envelopes when bills were due. Digital devices and networks have brought tremendous conveniences to daily life, transforming how we get entertainment, get informed, and get things done. By doing stuff virtually, we're also saving trees and other planetary resources—or so the rhetoric goes. Streaming that movie is greener than watching it on DVD, right?

Not necessarily. We used to assume that digital media consumed few environmental resources—or, at least, fewer than analog equivalents. Digital technologies appear green because they seem so immaterial and can make some processes more efficient. But appearances can be deceiving. The environmental toll of digital media is greater than we once realized. Some companies portray the cloud as "inherently 'green'" despite their lack of transparency and poor metrics for tracking actual environmental impact, according to Greenpeace.[1] Activists, journalists, and scholars have shone a brighter light onto the material operations of the information-technology sector and cast a long shadow over our media use.

Greenpeace, for instance, launched a "Click Clean" campaign in 2010 to hold Internet companies accountable for their efforts to improve energy efficiency, transparency, and commitment to green alternatives. Tech leaders like Apple, Facebook, and Google earned high marks for taking steps toward 100% renewable energy. The environmental watchdog gave "A" grades in 2017 to services such as iTunes, What'sApp, Instagram, and YouTube.[2] By contrast, behemoths like Amazon Web Services and Digital Realty (whose customers include Amazon. com, Amazon Prime, Equinox, Pinterest, Rackspace, Reddit, and Salesforce) have taken moderate action or lagged in the transition from dirty energy. Greenpeace gave "Ds" and "Fs" to these companies as well as services such as HBO, Netflix, SoundCloud, Spotify, Twitter, and Vimeo.

The Click Clean reports have spurred headlines like "Your Netflix Addiction is Screwing the Climate."[3] Streaming video is the single biggest factor in the cloud's growth, accounting for 63% of all global traffic in 2015 and projected to rise to 80% by 2020.[4] One study, sponsored by an industry group boasting that "the cloud begins with coal,"[5] estimates that a device streaming one hour of video per week uses more power annually than a new refrigerator. The cloud is bound to mushroom due to a "truly mind-blowing" scale of investment that will yield an estimated 50-fold increase in the amount of digital information by 2020, Greenpeace says.[6] While moving our lives online could conserve a significant amount of energy, the surge in digital media use is outstripping those gains.

When we watch movies on our laptops or look at pictures on our phones, we might not take time to ponder where the data comes from or how it gets there. But don't feel guilty about your streaming habit just yet. The operational choices that IT companies make regarding energy use, resource extraction, device manufacturing, waste disposal, and other activities with a massive ecological footprint were largely invisible to the public, until recently. As we shall see, there are great possibilities for making the cloud and the rest of the media system more eco-friendly.

Engineers coined the phrase "cloud computing" in the 1990s, and Steve Jobs helped to popularize it.[7] Cloud computing means processing and storing data across a network of computers, instead of in a single device, which optimizes performance. Metaphorical terms like "the cloud" give the impression that digital media are vaporous, unsubstantial, celestial, almost metaphysical. But the cloud is "hardly floating like mist above our heads—it's a physical infrastructure, its many computers housed in massive warehouses all over the world," in the words of one tech reporter. When you upload something to the cloud, "that file slides across the wire and then lives on a physical server—usually more than one—in some far-flung place."[8] You are actually putting those digital files, photos, profiles, posts, and comments in very real spaces.

The places where the cloud touches down are *data centers*, industrial-scale operations with a significant impact on the offline world. Many of these "server farms" are so large they are visible from space and consume energy equivalent to a small town of 180,000 homes. There are also thousands of smaller, less efficient facilities that together account for 95% of data center energy use. If worldwide data centers were a country, they would have been the globe's 12th largest electricity consumer in 2014, somewhere between Italy and Spain.[9] Greenpeace estimates that data centers alone could account for 13% of global electrical use by 2030.[10] Besides energy consumption, data centers have other environmental impacts. They use water, create pollution, and require hardware whose manufacture generates toxic substances and depletes rare minerals. Data centers are the fastest-growing contributor to emissions, with a larger carbon footprint than digital devices or the airline industry.[11]

And that's the tip of the iceberg. Data centers are one of numerous contributors to media's ecological footprint that are relatively obscure to end-users. In reality, virtual media have very material consequences, just like those paper books and plastic discs do. Want to make your corner of the digital world a little greener? This chapter will help, by presenting new research that reveals fascinating links between media technologies, cultural production, and the environment, in fields like *ecomedia studies, new media materialism, media archaeology*, and *new media ecology*. You will see how language and culture might hinder progress toward greener IT, when phrases like "green media" and "media ecosystem" are devalued as business jargon or marketing ploys, instead of meaningful environmental issues. Scholars, activists, and tech entrepreneurs are transforming "green" into a verb and making it easier for you to use media in Slow and sustainable ways.

The Material Effects of "Virtual" Media

For a long time, most of us did not pause long enough to notice the elaborate industrial systems that fulfill our desire for ubiquitous, instant access to infinite information. People have started paying more attention to the life cycles of digital devices and systems, which have far-reaching implications for global welfare. The complex supply chains, assembly lines, and waste disposal practices of digital media have significant "cradle to grave" effects. Two of the most pressing concerns are *electronic waste* ("e-waste") from device disposal and *industrial waste* from device manufacturing, which adds a tremendous load of toxins to the air, water and ground.

Tremendous is no exaggeration. Americans throw away more than 400 million digital devices every year (*not* including unused gadgets lying around people's homes or toys, microwaves, and other household objects with microchips in them). That's around 1.84 million tons of toxic trash, the equivalent of more than 13 million refrigerators each year in the US alone. Less than 18% of e-waste is recycled or salvaged; the remainder goes into landfills or gets burned.[12] E-waste is the fastest-growing component of municipal waste systems in wealthy nations, even though the vast majority of it is dumped in Latin America, Eastern Europe, Africa, and Asia—countries with lax environmental laws and cheap labor.[13] While much manufacturing has moved overseas, Silicon Valley still has the highest concentration of Superfund sites in the US—pollution stemming not from heavy industry but from the production of seemingly immaterial information technologies.[14]

Recent scholarship in fields like new media materialism and media archaeology is helping us to fully fathom the life cycle effects of electronic devices. People often take for granted or fail to notice the enormous material infrastructures that support our media use: Internet data centers, mobile telephone towers, and underseas cable systems that carry transoceanic communication. Nicole Starosielski is one researcher who has explored how these media structures nourish or harm living creatures.[15] In the anthology *Sustainable Media: Critical Approaches to Media and the Environment*, Starosielski and co-author Janet Walker gather studies that illuminate both the adverse systemic effects of media and the alternative futures that could be "imagined, 'rewritten,' and constructed."[16] Starosielski is based at New York University, where the field of media ecology was first nurtured by cultural critic Neil Postman in the early 1970s—a tradition to which we will return anon.

To really understand modern media, we could stretch our vista by millions of years, to a geological time scale instead of a human one. The material effects of the electronics industry will endure for millennia—long after we and our devices have been forgotten. "In short, media are *of* nature, and return *to* nature," observes Jussi Parikka, a proponent of media archaeology. He urges us to imagine what the fossil record will look like in millions of years. Picture yourself as a future archaeologist digging through the ruins of digital media culture. You will find few traces of media devices, keyboards, touchscreens, headsets, or power cables. Instead, Parikka says, you will discover a range of environmentally hazardous materials that are "the true leftovers of 'dead media'—the residue of our expired industrial equipment and personal devices."[17]

Another approach is ecomedia studies, which examines how media are materially embedded in the use or abuse of nature and how popular media represents or ignores the environment. This field has strong connections to eco-cinema theory, eco-critical film studies, and Slow Cinema, as discussed in chapter 2. Media texts and systems "often don't support 'nature' itself or the ecological thinking necessary to uncover and change humanity's troubling relationship with the planet," according to ecomedia scholar Sean Cubitt.[18] A co-author of the seminal book *EcoMedia*, he dismisses the division of society and nature as a fallacy, since humans cannot exist without the environment which they inhabit and from which they derive. If we understand these webs of connectivity, Cubitt says, we can enrich both our lives and our ability to act in the face of planetary crisis.

This pioneering work in ecomedia studies, media archaeology, new media materialism, and other Green Media fields has revealed much about the scope and scale of technology's concrete effects upon the Earth. These researchers share an urgent interest in motivating us to reorient our use of media and take sociopolitical action to minimize the ecological footprints of media, improve working conditions for people who make devices, and reduce the exportation of e-waste to developing countries (for what is supposed to be "recycling" but often is not).[19] Once we understand the complex interactions between our digital and material lives, they say, we can start transforming our individual relationships with media and nature, and building a political movement to demand more sustainable ways of living.

Considering Culture and Consumption

It goes without saying, but let's acknowledge it anyway: digital technologies are not the only (or the largest) source of planetary damage. Humanity faces a broad spectrum of environmental challenges: population growth, resource depletion, bio-diversity decline, ocean acidification, warmer temperatures, habitat decimation, air and water pollution, and rising sea levels, to name a few. We cannot really understand the crisis by looking only at how media technologies interact with the environment. We need to take human attitudes and behaviors into account.

A mosaic of cultural factors contribute to environmental decline. The public is deeply fascinated by technology and accustomed to buying cheap goods in repetitive cycles of consumption. The capitalist economy is driven by corporations, commercialism, capitalism, and competition—forces that encourage revenue growth, profit maximization, planned obsolescence, and advertising hype. Governments have neglected their duties in long-term planning, curbing overexploitation of shared resources, and responding to the will of the people. Indeed, this is just as much a cultural and political crisis as an ecological or technological one.

One solution is for designers and corporations to lead the way in using technology to both solve environmental problems and address their cultural roots, according to Bill Tomlinson. He is a vocal proponent of the Green IT movement, which urges information technology producers to design for sustainability and longevity, to consider the long-term impact of their decisions, and to collaborate in implementing global eco-standards. The public can play a role by developing new consumption patterns and valuing technologies that last longer.[20] In Tomlinson's view, industry groups and individual consumers can work together to move the whole culture toward greener practices. Green IT alleviates some environmental problems, but only if consumers, activists, and researchers hold the industry accountable for adopting ecologically sound practices.

Some people agree that cultural attitudes towards information technology need to change, but they wonder whether green product design can contribute much to sustainability. They doubt that new devices like energy meters and smart grids will make systems significantly more efficient or influence consumer behaviors. Such gadgets frequently fail to reduce actual energy use. They often rely upon fossil fuels and nonbiodegradable plastic. Even green products leave an ecological footprint through their manufacture, use, and disposal—thus contributing to the very problems they aim to solve. According to Gabrys, Green IT raises questions about what "green technology" really means: "Can a technology be green if it is hazardous in its manufacture, prone to obsolescences, and difficult to dispose; and can a technology be green if it is largely powered by coal energy and contributes to increasing carbon emissions?"[21] For many experts, the answer is "no."

The rise of Green IT and Green Media studies in the past decade indicates a paradigm shift in our awareness of the environmental effects of information and communication technologies. The landmark 2012 book *Greening the Media* notes that the connection "between gadgetry abundance and planetary decline is only beginning to enter the consciousness of technology 'experts'" such as academics, journalists, and bureaucrats.[22] Co-authors Richard Maxwell and Toby Miller observe that such experts are finally catching up with activists, public-health advocates, workers, unionists, policy analysts, and creative artists who were ahead of the environmental curve. All of these groups have been working since the 1980s to "green" media industries and to "imagine the relationship of a sustainable, democratic and pleasurable life" to media technologies.[23]

Greening the Media distills and extends arguments that Maxwell, a political economist, and Miller, an interdisciplinary social scientist, have put forth for years. When they began their research, there was little tradition of ecological media history to draw on. They have written not only scholarly books but also dozens of articles for *HuffPost, Psychology Today,* and other publications that engage the broader public in Green Media issues. Are ebooks more eco-friendly than paper ones? Can green apps effectively tackle climate change? Can shareholder activism influence corporate environmental policies?[24] Does Earth Day really generate much worthwhile ecological action?[25] Maxwell and Miller disagree with such "conventional wisdom" and urge readers to do the same. Greening the world, they say, means greening the media.

Maxwell quips that smartphones should have exhaust pipes, so people realize that digital devices are still connected to the centuries-old industrial system. The word "industrial" might seem quaint to those of us who "appear to live in a world dominated by bits and bytes, not smokestacks and coal mines," said MIT scientist Peter Senge.[26] The last quarter of the 20th century brought the most dramatic increase *ever* in industrial activity—a boom in coal, steel, and automobile production that could mislead us to think that industrialism is an eternal norm, not a fleeting anomaly. The Iron Age didn't end because we ran out of iron, Senge noted. The Industrial Age isn't ending because we're out of industry but because people are realizing its unsustainable side effects. Like the Industrial Revolution, and the Renaissance before it, the Sustainability Revolution marks a shift in how people see the world and define progress.

Media Ecology, Upcycled

> People don't actually read newspapers. They step into them,
> like a warm bath.

So said Marshall McLuhan, the Canadian media theorist and literary critic who became a pop-culture guru during the boom days of the boob tube in the 1960s.

He did not originate the metaphor of media as environments—of newspapers as warm bath, of media as the air we breathe. (That was philosopher John Dewey, who suggested during the Progressive Era of the early 20th century that modern media exerted an *environmental* influence on society.[27] Dewey believed that if our communication environment were more democratic, it would better serve the common good.) However, it was McLuhan who spread the notion that the "media environment" was a prime shaper of modern sensibility. Technologies extend our bodies and capabilities, he explained, but also numb our minds, bodies, and senses. Media come between us and our environment, essentially becoming our new environment.

McLuhan's playful aphorisms earned wide attention from the press and public—even in venues that might seem incongruous with intellectual discourse. "Man remains as unaware of the psychic and social effects of his new technology as a fish of the water it swims in," he told *Playboy* magazine in an extensive 1969 interview.[28] For him, media are "environmental and imperceptible, like all environments."[29] Imperceptible, at least, when viewed from inside.

A parallel idea of "media ecology" emerged in the work of educator Neil Postman. He founded a graduate program at New York University and an organization, the Media Ecology Association, devoted to looking at how media "affect human perception, understanding, feeling, and value" and "how our interaction with media facilitates or impedes our chances of survival."[30] Postman's reputation rests largely upon his critiques of technology and of television's corrosive effect on journalism, education, and culture in books such as *Amusing Ourselves to Death: Public Discourse in the Age of Show Business* (1985) and *Technopoly: The Surrender of Culture to Technology* (1993). Following McLuhan, Postman asserted that technological change is ecological. It doesn't merely add or subtract from our lives. It sends out ripples that transform everything. "In the year 1500, 50 years after the printing press was invented, we did not have old Europe plus the printing press," he observed. "We had a different Europe."[31] He equated media ecology with media environments that are "half concealed by our assumption that what we are dealing with is not an environment but merely a machine."[32] In Postman's day, as in McLuhan's, this meant books, radio, film, television—not digital media (yet).

Words like *environment* and *ecology* are vague allusions that resist clear definition. To modern people, they imply that something is important, something deserves our attention, something is at stake, and some kind of complex interrelationships are involved.[33] Analogizing *media* to an *ecology* or *environment* suggests that culture and technology are related in "organic, interactive and complex" but also "imprecise, apolitical and ahistorical" ways.[34] This flexibility is an asset, enabling people to appropriate the metaphor for many kinds of situations. Yet, these analogies convey little or nothing about how media affects the actual physical environment.

For a long time, people have used phrases such as *media environment, media ecology,* and *media ecosystem* in ways that have little or no reference to living systems. Tech journalists, business people, marketing consultants, and cultural commentators perpetuate the habit. When Cory Doctorow, a digital-rights activist and editor of BoingBoing, described the Internet as an "ecosystem of interruption technologies," he was talking about things that appear on your screen—IMs, emails, RSS alerts—and not how your computer and data impact the physical environment.[35] When a financial analyst told *Forbes* that Amazon was building a "competitive media ecosystem," he meant content consumption on tablets, television, and phones—aimed at fueling sales.[36]

The absence of natural environments in eco-metaphors can be interpreted as a sign of *anthropocentrism*: a cultural bias toward the well-being of people at the expense of other living things. Such biases, enshrined in language, shape and constrain discussions about climate-change action.[37] Anthropocentrism reflects a faulty perception that digital devices, data, and networks are separate from the natural ecosystem. Familiar metaphors like media ecosystem, media ecology and media environment reflect thinking that has been bad for the real environment.[38] Like the figurative cloud, they help to render obscure the material impacts of digital media.

You can plot environmental attitudes along many spectra, from *ecocentrism* to *anthropocentrism*, from *deep ecology* to *shallow ecology*, from *dark green* to *light green*. Anthropocentrism coincides with shallow (or light green) ecology. As Antonio Lopez, author of *The Media Ecosystem* and *Greening Media Education*, explains, shallow ecology will not bring meaningful action toward sustainability because it fails to challenge the main causes of environmental decline: our paradigm of economic growth and our pattern of consumption. This anthropocentric attitude "helps the commodities system greenwash itself without providing a legitimate, sustainable alternative."[39]

By contrast, the philosophy of ecocentrism, associated with deep green or deep ecology, values nature (and, particularly, wilderness) for its own inherent worth, rather than how it serves human interests. We could go even further and question this perceived division between human and nonhuman nature. Mankind is, of course, part of nature. Humans have a self-interest in protecting nonhuman nature, since we cannot exist without natural resources like sun, air, water, and food. Reconciling the imaginary rift between man and nature could enhance our survival as a species.

Maxwell and Miller discuss three kinds of ecological ethics: one that is human centered, another that is Earth centered, and another somewhere in-between. They propose that a *mid-green* or *intermediate* eco-ethics could strike a balance and advance ecologically sound uses of media. This middle way would require people to challenge technophilia and ask themselves how much media technology is socially necessary, not only on an individual or household basis but also on institutional and social scales.[40]

Ah intermediate path helps put the "eco" in *media ecosystems* and *media ecology* by adapting these terms to a distinctly environmental purpose.[41] Recycling and updating these metaphors makes them more useful and relevant. Just as environmentalists address the state of the biosphere, media environmentalists "look at sustainability as a problem of the cultural commons and how corporations have colonized the mediasphere."[42] This fledgling brand of media ecologists is shedding new light on these cultural problems, starting with commercial capitalism.

Green Marketing and Green Realities

Media technologies were taking an environmental toll long before the digital age, when people finally noticed the critical mass of harm taking shape. Since the 15th century, the printing press and successive media have incrementally left physical marks upon the Earth: telegraph wires, utility poles, vacuum and cathode-ray tubes, radio transistors, vinyl records, hardwood consoles, mono and stereo speakers, rolls and reels of emulsified plastic film, magnesium and zirconium flash bulbs, movie projectors and screens, chemical-coated photographic paper, toxic processing chemicals, and so on. For half a millennium, the materials required to manufacture all these items have been extracted from the planet and, eventually, returned to it.

Every media technology has to some extent despoiled ecosystems and exposed workers to unhealthy environments, according to Richard Maxwell, Jon Raundalen, and Nina Lager Vestberg. Powerful people who gain from such technologies have tried to conceal this fact from the public. "Those who benefit from ideas of growth, progress and convergence, who profit from high-tech innovation, and state collusion—the military-industrial-entertainment-academic complex and the multinational commanders of labor—have for too long ripped off the Earth and workers," they wrote.[43] Industrialization has made the ecological processes and human labor upon which it depends invisible, disconnecting consumers from workers, and vice versa.

In an era of growing concern about environmental welfare, many businesses want to persuade the public that they are *not* ripping off the Earth and workers. Since the 1990s, green advertising and green marketing strategies have pervaded commercial media and corporate communications. Sometimes they inform people about legitimately sustainable practices of organizations and eco-friendly features of products. Sometimes, however, these strategies can be misleading—a phenomenon called *greenwashing*. This term, a portmanteau of *green* and *whitewash*, refers to information that presents an environmentally responsible public image for an organization's products or practices that provide little or no ecological benefit. (Some argue that few products can accurately be portrayed as Earth-friendly, because sustainability requires consuming fewer natural resources, which means making and buying less stuff).[44]

If you value environmental preservation, social justice, holistic health, personal fulfillment, and sustainable living—as many cultural creatives do—then you are part of a highly coveted demographic segment. In the early aughts, professional marketers identified a large group of consumers who sought an alternative, green lifestyle: the "Lifestyle of Health and Sustainability" (LOHAS) segment.[45] This group is difficult to market to, because they are suspicious of commercial media sources and corporate advertisers.

Green marketing tries to overcome consumer distrust to evoke positive associations between businesses and the natural environment. Such marketers often make claims that are vague, irrelevant, misleading, or unverifiable. Common techniques include using words that imply sustainability (*clean, clear, natural, pure*), images of nature, brown and green color schemes, and recycled- or organic-looking content. Companies sometimes promote a green image by sponsoring Earth Day events and making donations to ecological charities, or facilitating customers doing so. Some of these practices, aesthetics, and vocabulary were once emblematic of alternative media, many of which are driven by a sincere green ethos.[46] Green marketing has become so suspect that some businesses avoid the term. Instead, they label their activities "sustainability communication," which ideally engages audiences in supporting operational changes that substantially decrease a business's environmental footprint and contribute to solving social problems.[47]

While business leaders are rallying behind sustainability in most industries, the media and entertainment sector is trailing behind. Most global executives consider sustainability activities as "critical" to future competitiveness, but there's a disconnect between thought and action. In an eight-year sustainability study by MIT that concluded in 2017, researchers divided businesses into three groups: "walkers," "talkers," and "on the road."[48] In some sectors, like commodities, energy/utilities, and chemicals, people who "walk the talk" outnumber talkers nearly four to one. Talkers are companies that only somewhat, barely, or don't address sustainability issues. Only one industry has a higher percentage of talkers than walkers: media and entertainment (including print media, television and radio broadcasting, film entertainment, video games, advertising, Internet-based media, and media-technology manufacturers). They're not even on the road. Three percent of media and entertainment executives reported themselves as "fully engaged" with significant environmental issues. The media and entertainment industry, which has the lowest percentage of companies with a sustainability strategy, has shown a relative lack of concern.[49]

Many executives admit that they address sustainability issues mainly to improve their image and meet minimum regulatory requirements. They are more likely to take sustainable actions when they can make a business case for it and reap a profit. For instance, media companies like Comcast encourage customers to sign up for electronic "ecobills," "to be green and clutter-free," while the business itself sends enormous amounts of paper through the mail for direct marketing.

This shifts the burden of taking supposedly "green" actions (email is not environmentally neutral, as we know) to customers—with the pleasant side-effect of saving the company money.

Still, there is a silver lining to this corporate clamor to look green, as Lopez has noted: it signals the intensity of the ecological zeitgeist and of public enthusiasm for sustainable products.

Reclaiming Green Media

When many people use the phrase "green media," they do not mean the kind of eco-friendly goals for media production and consumption that activists and scholars espouse. They are more likely referring to green marketing, advertising, or public relations, as an online search for the term demonstrates. Green-Media. com is a marketing firm in the UK, GreenMedia.us is a marketing agency in the US, GreenMedia.com.pl is a PR firm in Poland, GreenMedia.me is an advertising firm in Egypt, and GreenMedia.tv is a visual communications company in the Dutch West Indies. GreenMediaService.com is an ad agency in the US, and GreenMediaBrand.com is (you guessed it) a branding service.

There are some exceptions to this trend—enterprises that take more substantive actions to communicate green objectives. GreenTechMedia.com is a US firm that offers market research and news about clean energy industries, alongside advertising consultancy and conference services. GreenMedia.com is a UK communications consulting group with clients like Coca-Cola, Ford, Philips, and Unilever. It publishes an annual "Climate Action" report to educate businesses about pursuing carbon neutrality, in partnership with the UN Environment Program, a world leader in sustainability communication. Still, both of these organizations are interested in how media *communicate* and *represent* green issues, not in how the manufacture and use of digital devices and networks affects the natural world.

Two books further exemplify the tendency to treat Green Media as a communication issue. A scholarly text called *Green Media: Exploring Green Media Selection and its Impact on Communication Effectiveness* examines how a company's choice of advertising medium affects consumer perceptions of its commitment to acting responsibly toward nature.[50] An academic book called *Green Media and Popular Culture* introduces students to debates and theories about green interpretations of mainstream media texts. Case studies of music by U2 and Bjork, the animated films of Disney, and video games such as the desert-themed *Journey* reveal complicated relationships between media content and environmentalism.[51] This latter book contributes to the growing area of Green Media education.

Analysts of media content typically conceive of Green Media in ways that vary markedly from the people introduced in this chapter. It is important to interpret the environmental messages that circulate through mass media and advertising, but this is only part of the puzzle. Milestone books such as *Greening the Media* and *Greening Media Education* offer clues for broadening our view. In the first, Maxwell and Miller dispel the myth that digital media are ecologically benign by documenting the degree of physical harm media industries cause to people and the planet. In the second, Lopez argues that media educators have neglected environmental issues and need to better address sustainability in their curricula, to raise students' awareness. These titles invoke *greening* as a process, using *to green* as a verb. Together, they suggest that we cannot understand Green Media without embracing both the human and environmental dimensions of sustainability.

It's nigh impossible to disentangle the effects of digital media on the environment from those on human and social health. Almost all devices contain plastics, lead, aluminum, gallium, nickel, vanadium, beryllium, chromium, cadmium, mercury, arsenic, and silica. These substances are linked with health risks ranging from allergic reactions to various cancers, skeletal problems, asthma, bronchitis, ulcers, liver and kidney damage, and impaired brain functions.[52] The workers who make these technologies and dismantle them as e-waste risk exposure to pathogens that can cause cancer and damage the skin, vital organs, and reproductive and nervous systems, according to Maxwell and Miller.[53] Mining of coltan, an obscure mineral essential to most devices, is implicated in an ongoing civil war in Congo that has killed more than 5 million people and contributed to the endangerment of eastern lowland gorillas as well as elephants. Coltan is considered a conflict resource with dire human-rights consequences, akin to "blood diamonds." If society fails to take Green Media more seriously, the human and nonhuman elements of nature will suffer together.

The time has come to restore the environmental significance of Green Media. Greenwashing threatens to diminish the phrase until it denotes only superficial efforts to throw a coat of green paint on otherwise unsustainable products and services. People have started applying it to sustainability activities: greening the media, greening media studies, greening media education. In this sense, Green Media weaves together strands of new media materialism, media archaeology, new media ecology, and ecomedia studies—as well as sustainability communication, environmental communication, and green communication—into an interdisciplinary field. This new conception provides a framework for uniting media *content* and *products* with the activities of media *owners, workers, scholars,* and *users*.

Green Media *content* generates awareness about the sustainability issues that society faces, the physiological impact of media upon the Earth, the relationship between media and environmental discourses, and the actions that humans can take to bolster the ecosystem's health.

Green Media *products* (made in any physical or "virtual" medium) are extracted, produced, distributed, and disposed/recycled in ways that do the least possible harm to the planet and the people who make/use them.

Green Media *owners* engage in environmentally friendly practices and provide safe working conditions along with fair wages, responsiveness to local needs and cultures, and sustainable schedules that facilitate healthy minds, bodies, and communities.

Green Media *workers*, including everyone from journalists to machinists, have and take time to focus on the quality of their productions, human interactions, and environmental stewardship—not on short-term, quantifiable concerns such as productivity and profitability.

Green Media *scholars* gather, analyze, and disseminate information that helps society understand the relationship between media technologies, the natural world, and human behavior. They educate students as well as the general public how to think critically about those interactions.

Green Media *users*, individually and collectively, engage with and consume media products in sustainable ways, learn about the ecological effects of media use, and participate in public conversations and actions that promote green values and practices.

"Green Media" is not only a modified noun, the objective of pursuing and achieving "media that are green." It is also a verb, a process, a means of pursuing this end. If we are to "green media," we will need to take collective action. Some environmental activists, nonprofit organizations, and device manufacturers are leading the way.

Eco-Friendly Alternatives

Annie Leonard knows about stuff. As an environmental activist and NGO staffer, she spent a couple of decades witnessing the ecological and social impacts of the electronics industry by visiting mines, factories, and dumps in more than 40 countries. Since 2007, Leonard has shared her experiences in an online series telling "The Story of Stuff"—from cosmetics to bottled water to digital devices. Viewed around the world more than 20 million times, these videos have entertained, educated, and engaged many people to struggle for a more sustainable future by changing the way we make, use, and throw away stuff.

The "Story of Electronics" is apropos to the subject at hand. Clocking in at 7:47 minutes, it begins with Leonard as everywoman, telling viewers about not being able to find her phone charger amid a tangle of old ones. "How did I end up with so many of these things?" she wonders aloud. "It's not like I'm always after the latest gadget. My old devices broke or became so obsolete I couldn't use them anymore. And not one of these old chargers fits my computer. Augh. This isn't just bad luck. It's bad design. I call it 'designed for the dump.'"[54]

The video cuts to animation explaining why devices are more expensive to repair than to replace: because manufacturers want products to become obsolete quickly, so people will buy more of them. She peppers the script with statistics (the average tube TV contained five pounds of lead; IBM workers making computer chips had 40% more miscarriages) and catchphrases ("toxics in, toxics out"; "designed to last"). Leonard describes global realities that few consumers ever see. "I've visited a bunch of these so-called recycling operations," she says. "Workers, without protective gear, sit on the ground, smashing open electronics to recover the valuable metals inside and chucking or burning the parts no one will pay them for. So while I'm on to my next gadget, my last gadget is off poisoning families in Guiyu or India or Nigeria."

After describing the problem of e-waste, Leonard turns toward solutions. Producers could design things to last longer. They could make devices without PVC or toxic flame retardants. More lawmakers could insist upon extended producer responsibility or product takeback (as many governments in Europe, Asia, and some US cities and states do). They could hold manufacturers accountable for externalities like harming the environment and human health—which are commonly passed along to customers, suppliers, and vendors. Consumers could take action to demand greener gadgets, stronger regulations, and bans on e-waste exports.

Aggregate pressure from citizens and activists has yielded progress toward sustainable media. The "Click Clean" project is a good example.[55] Amazon Web Services (AWS) is the dominant player in cloud computing, controlling around a quarter of the market and three times the market share of its nearest competitor. Owned by Amazon, it provides much of the digital infrastructure behind well-known online brands, including the bandwidth-hog Netflix. In 2014, Greenpeace shamed AWS by giving it D and F ratings for its energy policies and practices. (AWS was using 28% coal, 27% nuclear, 25% natural-gas, and 15% clean energy.) The company soon announced that it was committing itself to a goal of 100% renewables, investing $150 million in solar power for a major East-Coast data center, and hiring its first sustainability executive.[56] Click Clean's scorecard bestows both shame and pride, rewarding companies who are walking their sustainability talk and "winning the race" to build a renewably powered Internet.

In 2015, Greenpeace bumped up AWS's grade for renewable energy commitment to a C, calling the adoption of a 100% clean energy goal "potentially significant." However, the company still withheld evidence that would support its energy claims, making it one of the last large IT companies to do so. Apple, eBay, Facebook, and Google have shown much greater transparency, earning them A grades. Without such facts being made available, individual and corporate consumers who value sustainability cannot evaluate their options. Influential AWS customers such as Tumblr, Hootsuite, Change.Org, Creative Commons, the Sunlight Foundation, and HuffPost have publicly pressured the company to reveal its "energy and carbon footprints and progress toward renewable energy goals."[57]

This demonstrates that many media businesses will put their greenbacks where their green mouths are if the public persistently demands they take greater responsibility for their environmental impact. One successful strategy is to make companies provide a steady stream of documentation about supply chains and physical processes through which they produce media commodities. Today, we can get a wider range of probing answers to questions about how media technologies are made, by whom, where, and under what conditions, as Maxwell and Miller observe.[58] That's good news.

A positive exemplar is Fairphone, a Dutch device manufacturer founded upon social and environmental values. Their slogan is "ethical, open and built to last." The company established traceable supply chains for four internationally recognized conflict materials: tin, tantalum, tungsten, and gold. Fairphone developed its own open-source version of Android operating software designed to not obsolesce. They also conduct lifecycle assessments to gauge their product's impact on climate change, metal depletion, and human toxicity as well as find ways to reduce its environmental effects. The Fairphone 2, released in 2016, is the world's first phone with modular construction and replaceable parts, designed to be easily repairable and prolong its lifespan. So far, they have sold more than 135,000 Fairphones in Europe; it's not yet available in the US.[59] The company was ranked No. 1 among all electronics manufacturers in Greenpeace's 2017 *Guide to Greener Electronics*.

The manufacturers of Fairphone are uncommon in the Green IT community by virtue of their commitment to addressing one of the largest, and growing, environmental threats of digital media: e-waste. Green-oriented device designers mainly pursue innovations geared toward improving energy efficiency and battery life— a narrow vision that limits progress toward sustainability. Manufacturers keep extracting resources and making devices; consumers keep buying and throwing them away; toxins keep accumulating in our air, water, ground, and bodies. Sustainability means both becoming more energy efficient *and* reducing the frequency with which we replace our gadgets.

That smartphone in your purse or pocket? It probably contains around 17 rare, toxic metals. The vibrator and speaker are often operated by magnets made with neodymium, praseodymium, terbium, and dysprosium. The color screen usually uses europium, yttrium, terbium, lanthanum, dysprosium, praseodymium, and gadolinium. The glass is likely polished with cerium, lanthanum, and praseodymium. The circuit-board electronics might have more neodymium, praseodymium, dysprosium, lanthanum, and gadolinium in them. Enormous aggregate harm comes from depleting supplies of these rare minerals for device production and adding toxic substances and radioactive materials to worldwide waste streams.[60]

When Ted Smith looks at his smartphone, he sees the faces of Indonesian or Ugandan miners who unearthed the raw materials, of Chinese laborers who work long shifts exposed to hazardous chemicals, and of people who handle digital debris in a dump halfway around the world.[61] Smith, who began tracking the consumer electronics industry in California in the early 1970s, banded together with other citizens to fight the industry's lack of transparency about environmental threats, labor rights, and health issues. He co-founded the International Campaign for Responsible Technology (ICRT), a network that promotes corporate and government accountability in the global electronics industry. ICRT wants companies to be required to disclose all of the chemicals used in a product's life cycle as a step toward making nontoxic devices. Smith's organization also supports workers suffering from occupational illnesses.

Greenpeace, ICRT, the GoodElectronics Network (GEN), and others envision a global industry that complies with human rights and sustainability standards. GoodElectronics formulated a list of demands for the sector. Several of them appeal for greater ecological sustainability. For example, producers should comply with the highest internationally recognized environmental standards. They should stop designing for obsolescence and commit to green, toxic-free, and democratic design of electronics products. They should ensure that minerals used in electronics are sourced responsibly. And, they should adhere to the principle of producer responsibility: taking back and responsibly recycling obsolete products.

Some of GoodElectronics' demands appeal for fairness and social sustainability. For example, they want companies to be fully transparent and accountable and to engage stakeholders in decision-making that might affect workers, communities, and the environment. Companies should implement international standards against forced labor and child labor as well as for collective bargaining, living wages, maximum working hours, employment security, and safe working conditions. They should end abuse of migrant labor, eliminate precarious employment that leaves workers vulnerable, provide workers with healthcare, and compensate them for work-related accidents, illnesses, and injuries.[62]

The key to achieving greener media production is to get more people throughout society involved as consumers and citizens, as individuals and as collectives. Green consumption, such as supporting companies committed to renewables or buying products manufactured ethically, can make a difference if enough people join in. Yet green variants of consumerism arouse skepticism among environmentalists, for the same reason that buying a new hybrid SUV does. The planet does not get cleaner when some of the things we buy have a small percentage of recycled content in them. Eco-friendly or not, it's still more stuff.

Worms in Your Apple

Planned obsolescence is vilified widely enough to be a punchline for comedians. "Next time Apple wants to do something truly innovative and really 'think different,' they should try *not* releasing a new phone," said talk-show host Bill Maher, jesting about the minor upgrades made to tech products. "The only people who really need you to get a new phone are the shareholders." After mocking Apple for its obsession with boosting sales and share prices, he appealed to consumers to stop buying the hype: "Somebody has to teach Americans that we don't always need something new or better every year."

Hype has proven profitable. Apple sold over one billion iPhones and earned over $620 billion from the device in less than a decade, from 2007 to 2016. Thanks to the iPhone, Apple was the world's most valuable company for most of those years. The company maintains cash reserves of more than $200 billion—mostly stashed overseas so it doesn't have to pay US taxes. (If this pile of cash were its own company, it would be the 11th largest in the S&P 500.) CEO Tim Cook is one of the world's most richly compensated executives. In 2010 alone, he received stock grants that could be worth around $570 million, at current share prices.

Apple and its co-founder Steve Jobs have earned adoration for technical prowess, innovative designs, minimalist aesthetics, and marketing savvy. Despite its success, the company's commitment to human and environmental sustainability has frequently come under scrutiny. Those billion iPhones—and other rapidly obsolesced devices from Apple and other manufacturers—have contributed substantially to environmental degradation. To some people, the company has become a symbol of much that's unclean and unfair about globalization, with business practices that maximize profit at the expense of customer satisfaction, employee well-being, and environmental health.

Enthusiasts feel betrayed when Apple releases new versions in aggressive upgrade cycles and designs products that customers cannot repair or upgrade themselves.[63] Proprietary software and hardware are ample sources of frustration. "If you can't fix it, you don't own it," as one saying goes. It's hard to judge how device designers balance technical needs with sales goals. When Apple released the first iPad, some noted the device was "better defined by what isn't there": a USB slot, camera, and other features that would prolong its usefulness.[64] People believed the company held back some functions to spur purchases of iPad 2—which had a camera, but whose screen was 3.5 times more likely to break than the original (about 10% broke in the first year).[65] Any such decisions that boost product replacement (good news for shareholders) transform more environmental resources into waste and pollution (sad tidings for other living beings).

Another concern is seeming disregard for people who make and sell its devices. Apple once boasted that its products were made in America; by 2004, it had largely turned to foreign manufacturing. (Not just because workers are cheaper but because they are also more flexible, diligent, and skilled, Apple says.)[66] The company made headlines amid deaths and suicides of workers in Chinese factories that supply Apple. At Foxconn, seventeen workers killed themselves between 2007 and 2011, reportedly due to 12-hour shifts, forced overtime, and unrealistic quotas.[67] A *Wired* reporter described the buildings at one of Foxconn's gated complexes in 2011 as skirted with nets that "drape every precipice, steel poles jutting out 20 feet above the sidewalk, loosely tangled like volleyball nets in winter."[68] After these barriers were installed, the suicide rate slowed to a trickle.

Reports circulated about teenage girls working 15-hour shifts cleaning screens with toxic solvents.[69] At another of Apple's contract facilities in China, some employees were poisoned by toxic chemicals used in device manufacturing. They sent a letter to Jobs informing him of their plight. "We don't know, Mr. C.E.O., whether or not you are aware of, or tolerate the conduct of Lian Jian Technology in using this chemical [n-hexane]. If you have known about it, then this would make us very sad," wrote the workers, who earn around $300 a month:

> If you didn't known [*sic*] about this, then we hope that you can step up and using a fair approach resolve this issue. When someone says that Apple products are produced at the expense of employee's health, what do you think? . . . When you look down at the Apple phone you are using in your hand and you swipe it with your finger is it possible that you can feel as if it is no longer a beautiful screen to show off, but the life and the blood of us employees and victims?"[70]

The missive reportedly got no reply.

Ethical concerns have been raised on behalf of Apple employees in the US, not just its overseas contractors. One might expect workers at Apple Stores to share in the company's success. According to one report, about 30,000 of the 43,000 Apple employees in this country—that's 69.8%—work in its stores.[71] Many earn around $25,000 a year. Although the company boasts of being a job creator, most are service-industry positions with few paths to a long-term career. This phenomenally successful company had around 80,000 employees worldwide in 2011, a tiny fraction of the workforce at other large manufacturers.[72] By contrast, IBM had 434,000 employees in 2013. On the whole, digital companies hire ten times fewer employees than traditional companies, earning 10 times the revenue per employee as traditional companies.[73]

Apple is indifferent to neither public perception nor planetary well-being. Its social responsibility website assures readers that working conditions in its supply chain are safe, that workers are treated with respect and dignity, and that manufacturing processes are environmentally responsible. Factories like Lian Jian offer reliable paychecks to poor migrants from rural China who desperately need income. Suicides aside, FoxConn was considered one of the best places to work in Shenzhen and has improved living conditions for its employees, once the eyes of the world were upon it. Greenpeace gave Apple straight "A's" on its Click Clean scorecard and a B- (ranking second to Fairphone) in its *Guide to Greener Electronics* in 2017. It runs a consumer recycling program that disassembles devices and separates some valuable materials for resale to wholesalers. The company has a "full-destruction" policy, however, that some say protects its own commercial interests by removing functional devices from the market. (The program pulverizes or melts down many gadgets that could be reused.)

Apple illustrates how a media company's business practices are deeply intertwined with environmental and human well-being. Many of its sustainability shortcomings reflect wider problems in the media sector as well as in global business generally. Apple's sustainability track record isn't worse than most media and technology companies, though it is one of the largest and most visible players. This case study demonstrates why going green necessitates being simultaneously clean and fair, to re-invoke Slow Media principles.

Almost everyone in the Western world understands, at some level, that our devices have a cost beyond their price, according to *Wired* writer Joel Johnson, who visited FoxConn. Our mediated lifestyle is made possible by nameless workers producing smartphones and computers, laboring in mines and fields and factories, who are essentially slaves. (When a US State Department official was interviewed about coltan mining in the Democratic Republic of the Congo, he pointed to the reporter's smartphone and said, "The likelihood that one of these was not touched by a slave is pretty low.")[74] We squander millions of human lives and millions of years' worth of stored energy, stored life, from our planet when we invest ever-more resources in devices with negligible dividends to our comfort and happiness.

The upshot is this: Should *you* feel like part of the problem every time you buy a new marvel of technological progress?

"Of course the answer, inevitable and immeasurable as the fluttering silence of our sun, is yes," Johnson says. "Just a little."

A Green Light for Slow Media

Rapid obsolescence is a fact of neither nature nor technology. To be sure, some media equipment is bound to become objectively less useful, if not useless, as time passes—regardless of producers' or users' intentions. Although obsolescence is related to technological aspects, it is not solely determined by technology, as John Davis says in "Going Analog."[75] The pace of obsolescence is routinely accelerated by manufacturers who design products for a short lifespan, or "for the dump" in Leonard's memorable phrase. Through ad campaigns, they encourage consumers to think that old technologies are out-of-date, in order to create more demand for the new generation of stuff.

Many critics of planned obsolescence consider it from the viewpoint of suppliers. In other words, corporations contrive to sell us more widgets by building stuff to break, hyping minor improvements, and making aesthetic updates that give products a superficial gloss of newness. (Some do, of course, do these things.) Yet obsolescence is also shaped by unintended structural effects and cultural forces beyond the short-term decisions of producers. These include press coverage and peer pressure as well as access to product information, manufacturers, distributors, repair people, local support networks, and more. You can't use a typewriter without ribbons, a turntable without needles, or an analog camera without film.

Obsolescence is also partly a demand-side phenomenon—as in the case of mobile phones.[76] The typical American gets a new phone every 18 months because they *want* them, not because the devices don't work anymore. According to one estimate, 82% of the phones collected for recycling work fine and could easily be reused. Most people have the perception, rightly or wrongly, that new products will perform more functions, will be faster, will be better.

An important exception is Slow Media communities, where people don't necessarily equate newer with better. Like cultural creatives and alternative media users, people who enjoy Slow Media are conscious of the environmental and cultural dilemmas posed by corporate and commercial practices.[77] In other work, I have characterized the persistence of print and analog media as a form of cultural resistance.[78] The Slow perspective brings to light how companies are motivated by profit—more so than social needs or consumer preferences—to develop ever-newer products. Although analog media are often deemed "obsolete" in the technological sense of being incompatible with digital forms, the people who buy zines, records, audiocassettes and other physical media find them satisfying, effective, and complementary. Slow Medians are not opposed to speed; rather, they wish to preserve a place for slower media alongside faster ones.

Consider the 21st-century revivals of "antiquated" technologies such as vinyl records, typewriters, watches, film cameras, and synthesizers. A wide range of enthusiasts, including many young people, have discovered or continued to appreciate the craftsmanship and longevity of analog devices from a half-century ago—or older.[79]

"Clocks still tell time 100 or 200 years after they were built," a Brooklyn watchmaker told *New York* magazine.[80] "That is incredible in a digital age where things can be out of date in a year and unusable in five."

"It's not about the era, more the quality of the equipment made," said a 20-year-old music producer in London. "A lot of time and money went into making them. . . . I can hear that in the sound."

"You don't necessarily have to say, 'That's outdated and we can do better now'," said a 25-year-old in Scotland who composes poems by typewriter. "There's kind of a resurgence of old technology, people realizing that actually, it does still have something to give, and we don't have to leave it all behind."

The analog revival is founded on forward-looking values such as economic justice and environmental sustainability alongside traditional values such as longevity and frugality. Physical media objects can be more eco-friendly than "virtual" ones.[81] Some might label old media technologies "out of date," but in fact they are still useful and even beloved. There's a dollop of punk sensibility, too—the thrill of rejecting the status-quo and making your own culture. So-called "advances" in digital media are often inhospitable to hobbyists, who can't access the innards, fix proprietary parts, or even change dead batteries themselves. Technological "progress" tends to remove open-endedness, creativity, and real human agency from the workings of a tool, as Nicholas Carr explains. "In its place, we get an abstraction of human agency that represents the general desires of the masses as deciphered, or imposed, by the manufacturer and the marketer."[82]

The vinyl renaissance offers another great example. When the CD market collapsed in the face of digital file-sharing, many audiophiles returned to records. A minority of music buyers, of course, had never abandoned them.[83] In the US, more new vinyl records were sold in 2016 than in any year since 1991. One bell-wether of this resurgence was the 2008 launch of Record Store Day, celebrated globally every April with in-store performances, DJs, contests, limited releases, and big crowds. In 2016, Record Store Day brought the biggest week for non-Christmas sales of new vinyl—more than half a million records—in more than a quarter century. The majority of records sold today, though, are second-hand vinyl. More than $5 million in used records were sold in 2015 through Discogs, the largest online music marketplace, alone.[84] It lists more than 23 million records, with some releases more than a century old (to wit: "Smiles and Chuckles" by Six Brown Brothers, released in 1917 on the Victor label). Vinyl has an enviable shelf life.

Many authors have pondered the endurance of old media tools in a digital world and examined how people reuse, repair, and recycle artifacts such as telephones, typewriters, letters, player pianos, and the like. Some call these artifacts "residual media" or "legacy media."[85] Neither of these terms effectively conveys the fact that people *choose* to use these media products, among many options; they are not merely inherited or left over. Others more approvingly deem them "heirloom" technologies. Some even apply epithets like "dead media" or "zombie media" to abandoned devices—recognizing the fact that artifacts decay and inhabit the Earth long after their supposed deaths.[86]

I prefer calling them "Slow Media," which connotes both a critique of speedy consumerist culture and a set of alternative practices. As this book details, people are seeking a balance that works for them: some combination of using more print and analog media, using digital media in Slow ways, using less fast media (temporarily or permanently), and reducing all media in favor of unmediated activities. The Slow framework foregrounds how speed drives capitalist media processes that have a profound environmental impact: resource extraction, mass manufacturing, planned obsolescence and quick disposal.

The longevity of all these old print and analog objects offers some solace. Our society has designed devices to last before—and we can do it again.

No Longer Obscured by Clouds?

"The central event of the 20th century is the overthrow of matter," declared a group of prominent techno-utopian writers, investors, and futurists in 1994.[87]

Cyberspace was ushering in a new civilization that would overcome materialism, repeal industrial regulations, and retire "Second Wave" attitudes, according to Esther Dyson, Alvin Toffler, and their co-authors.[88] "In technology, economics and the politics of nations, wealth—in the form of physical resources—has been losing value and significance," they wrote. "The powers of mind are everywhere ascendant over the brute force of things."

Au contraire. Things still have force. In an era of ecological crisis, a new crop of Green Media educators, researchers, and activists is reasserting the power of physical matter over immaterial fantasy. These discussions provide a corrective to ones dominated by media producers, advertisers, and investors, who appropriated the phrase Green Media for marketing products and services that are not perforce ecologically sound. This recent body of work encourages us to question long-held assumptions, misperceptions, and rhetoric about the relationships among people, media, and the planet.

Unlike techno-boosters, ecomedia experts think sustainability will only be achieved once the public realizes that "the Internet is not weightless and information is not immaterial."[89] People mistakenly believed in the 19th century that the oceans were inexhaustible and in the 20th century that markets could grow forever, they say. Society has made a similar error in regards to digital information. We know better now. The people introduced in this chapter are changing how we study, teach, buy, learn, and think about digital media technologies, in light of environmental impacts. Their work shows us that "the cloud" is anything but heavenly, and that we have better alternatives, if we choose to pursue them.

You've surely seen this logo too many times to count: a triangle comprised of three arrows, usually called the "recycling symbol." Only one of those arrows represents recycling, though. There are actually three R's, one for each arrow: Reduce, Reuse, and *then* Recycle. That final verb should be the imperative of last resort. Public discussions about the problem of digital waste tend to focus on how to recycle devices more efficiently, which would make a tiny dent in the problem. Americans own around 3 billion electronic products, with a turnover rate of around 400 million units annually—which leaves countless tons of devices in the waste stream.[90] What if, instead, we reduced the number of widgets that we bought? What if they were built to last longer, to easily upgrade, and to be reused, as enlightened manufacturers have started to do? Moving toward a sustainable society means moving beyond green consumerism to reduce our total level of consumption.

Green consumerism usually involves buying things made and used in eco-friendly ways, while also demanding provisions for recycling or reuse, such as extended producer responsibility or cradle-to-grave design. Such actions sometimes help us justify continued consumption, which can increase quickly enough to overwhelm any benefits yielded by eco-friendly production. There's a rebound effect, in which people buy more than they otherwise might have. Green consumerism also focuses on individual decisions, instead of addressing systemic issues.

Not to mention the problem of greenwashing, which can deceive consumers into thinking that products are better for the environment than they are.

The French call it *decroissance*, the pursuit of "selective degrowth" that reduces our use of material resources in ways that improve quality of life. Our economic lives have long fixated on the idea that more is better. But the sustainability revolution has fundamentally destabilized this *idée fixe*. On the environmental level, the planet cannot provide material resources for or absorb the pollution and detritus from ever-increasing production and disposal. On the human level, growth—as we now create it—is producing "more inequality than prosperity, more insecurity than progress," notes Bill McKibben.[91] Growth is no longer making people in economically developed nations happy.

Less is More

A penchant for nonmaterial values has threaded its way through American culture from the Puritans and Quakers to Transcendentalists like Henry David Thoreau, who famously urged us to "simplify, simplify, simplify." Ideas like voluntary simplicity have long been linked with green living, slowing down, meditating, serving the community, and improving ecology. In the 1960s, the countercultural revolution and the civil-rights movement sowed the seeds of sustainability more broadly. Martin Luther King, Jr., insisted that we must undergo a radical revolution of values and rapidly shift "from a 'thing-oriented society' to a 'person-oriented society'." He believed that our social ills could not be conquered as long as "machines and computers, profit motives and property rights, are considered more important than people" (and the planet, he might have added today).

Plenty of people have learned to be satisfied with less. They have modified their daily habits in ways that substantially reduce their use of planetary resources. There is evidence now of a cultural shift toward sustainable consumption in places like the US, Canada, and Northern Europe. The percentage of Americans who say they are willing to make significant sacrifices—such as giving up time, money, or effort—for the environment climbed by a third from 2000 to 2006 alone.[92] "Low-asset" lifestyles have become not only possible but increasingly popular, in part thanks to digital systems that let us stream and download media instead of buying books, CDs, DVDs, and the like.

Ample evidence suggests that material abundance does not bring real happiness. People in poor countries feel happier when they achieve moderate economic growth and wealth, but beyond that, their perceived well-being levels off or declines slightly.[93] Even in the US, the pleasure derived from day-to-day experiences doesn't improve once a household earns around $75,000 per year. As our material lives improve, this "progress" feels like the new normal and stops making us happier. Gross domestic product (GDP) measures consumption but ignores its consequences for humans and other living things. By contrast, the

Genuine Progress Indicator (GPI) distinguishes between economic transactions that contribute to well-being from those that diminish it. While GDP has risen continually since the 1990s, GPI has gone down. Life satisfaction is not tethered to how much money or stuff we have.

The prospect of having less stuff seems scary to many people, as though we're facing a future of hardship and deprivation. In reality, we need only return to a lifestyle similar to the one Americans had in the 1970s, to live within ecological limits. Sustainable consumption does not mean living in caves. Instead, it could mean making a profitable trade-off. We could give up some speed, growth, work, and ecological degradation. We could get more happiness and well-being, more time with family and friends, healthier minds and bodies and natural environments.

From Green Consumers to Green Citizens

To make progress toward sustainable media use, we need to get better at being "green cultural citizens." That's what Antonio Lopez calls this expanded notion of civic life that encourages sustainable practices and public engagement.[94] To be green citizens, people could learn more about the impact of digital media production and consumption on natural systems as well as human perceptions of time, space, and place. We could start by facilitating self-education and integrating green cultural citizenship into more high-school and college curricula. Many professors, like Lopez, bring sustainability into their classrooms, where young people become aware of how mediated messages promote environmental ideologies (of one kind or another) and how media use affects (for better and for worse) our ability to live in sustainable ways. Classes exploring Green Media can make people mindful of their own media practices and encourage sustainable alternatives.

Beyond formal education, people greening their lives need reliable information about digital media products, services, and life cycles. Companies who have this data are not always transparent about sharing it, as the Click Clean campaign shows. Global supply chains can be complex and difficult for experts to understand, yet alone average users. Putting information about green media products and services at people's fingertips would be a step in the right direction. The GoodGuide app is one possible model; it lets users scan UPC codes when they are shopping to learn about ingredients in food, beverage, personal-care, and cleaning products. Digital devices can help people reduce the environmental impact of their digital devices—no irony intended.

Many challenges to promoting green cultural citizenship remain. Media sustainability watchdogs will need a lot of time, money, and manpower to establish, maintain, and publicize such information. This will probably require institutional support, whether from nonprofit foundations or governmental agencies. And, for consumers to educate themselves about Green Media will take *time*, raising again the politics of time that accompanies all discussion of Slow Media.

Human beings are only part of the natural world, but we have an outsized influence on environmental conditions. Many of us perceive digital media habits as having a detrimental effect on our own physical and psychological well-being, too. In response, a panoply of people recognize that there are not just ecological but also human limits to media use. As the next chapter examines, they are using centuries-old principles and practices of mindfulness to explore and manage media's effects on their daily lives.

5

Mind your Media

From Distraction to Attention

Distraction has always been a human condition. Sages have always been quick to
point out how even a few minutes of meditation prove the jumpy nature of our
consciousness—our monkey minds. But now every force conspires to magnify that
inattentiveness: Technology has made distraction ubiquitous.
—Maggie Jackson, *Distracted: The Erosion of
Attention and the Coming Dark Age*[1]

The easy availability of information can turn into information overload;
the presence of multiple communication sources and devices may lead to
the fragmentation of attention; and the ease of acting and communicating
quickly seems to encourage a pace of interaction that is unsustainable and
counterproductive.
—David Levy, *syllabus for graduate course in
"Information and Contemplation"*

Distracted. Stupefied. Addicted. Shallow. Despite the undeniable boons of digital
media, a wave of best-selling books reflects a deep well of public anxiety about the
cumulative effects of screens and networks on human life.[2] Digital technologies
open up wonderful new possibilities, but not without cost. People sense that
sustained media use creates stress, depression, and anxiety. It drains time, energy, and productivity, crowding out other worthwhile pursuits. It hinders empathy, learning, creativity, self-esteem, and reflective thought. It throws work-life
balance out of kilter. Because the process of mediation is incredibly elaborate
and idiosyncratic, everyone has a unique experience with digital devices and
networks—depending on what kind they use, when, where, how, and why. A wide
swathe of people have concluded that media use, when allowed to bloat, becomes
counterproductive and unsustainable.

Media use has exploded over the course of two generations, in what could be
one of the most significant shifts ever in the human environment. People now
ingest around three times as much information each day as they did in the 1960s.
The average American spends around 12 hours per day with media, compared to 5
hours in 1960. That's 75% of your waking life. Adults check their phones around

30 times a day, while millennials do it more than 150 times daily.[3] Nearly 4 in 10 people under the age of 34 say they interact more with their smartphones than they do with their parents, friends, co-workers, or significant others.[4] When people are using media, they are likely to be using at least four kinds at a time, sometimes six or seven simultaneous streams.[5] It has become a cliché to observe that people spend more time using media than doing anything else.

These statistics aren't inherently bad. However, research shows that intense mediatization undermines human health and well-being in many ways—backing up subjective impressions of being overloaded, distracted, and addicted. Sixty-one percent of respondents in one survey said they canceled social activities as a result of information overload.[6] They blamed overload for enjoying their jobs less.[7] People interrupted by email are more stressed than those who focus, and this cognitive strain reduces short-term memory.[8] Information overload contributes to health problems such as eye strain, headaches, neck and back pain, carpal tunnel syndrome, and other stress-related symptoms. Empathy levels are now around 40% lower than in the 1990s due partly to an increase in mediated communication, which reduces our ability to read nonverbal cues of human emotion.[9] Internet use has created the paradox that although people connect more, many of them feel more alone.[10] Half of Americans say they are dependent on social media sites and that this reliance makes them unhappy.[11]

If you're not convinced yet that excessive media use has become problematic, consider this: half of the US population says they would rather suffer physical injury than damage their phones. (You might be weighing the options right now: What *kind* of injury versus how *much* damage?)

People casually use the word "addicted" to describe how they feel about digital devices and networks. Researchers, psychologists and technologists, however, take tech addiction seriously.[12] When we use digital media, it activates the same brain areas and fuels the same needs that some chemical substances do: mental stimulation, social connection, a sense of greater effectiveness. (Media use triggers chemical reactions, too; we'll get to that momentarily.) In the 2017 book *Irresistible*, Adam Alter explains how using media can become a behavioral addiction through the same biological mechanisms as substance addiction, albeit with a different magnitude and intensity. We like to think that there's a "bright line between addicts and the rest of us," he notes, but we are all susceptible to technology's charms.[13]

If you ever feel like you can't stop checking your device, this compulsive behavior doesn't signal a personal weakness. Digital media are habit-forming by design. "Companies might not be trying to make 'addictive' platforms per se," Alter says. But in competing for our limited time and attention, they focus on making "the most engaging experience possible."[14] Engagement can be addictive. Browsing on a social network is psychologically comparable to gambling: *Will I win something? A like, a message, a comment?* We all carry slot machines in our pockets, devices that exploit our mind's inherent weaknesses, says former

Google designer Tristan Harris. Push notifications, which tell users when they have new messages, are a simple yet insidious form of manipulation, according to Justin Rosenstein, who co-created the Facebook "like" button. These alerts are "just distractions that pull us out of the moment," he says, before turning to addiction analogies. "They get us hooked on pulling our phones out and getting lost in a quick hit of information."[15]

Savvy product designers coax user behavior through sophisticated techniques. They incorporate positive feedback such as likes, shares, comments to make users crave more media use. They take advantage of compulsion loops that make it hard for people to stop using media, like when cliffhangers and autoplay trigger binge streaming. They engineer "beginners' luck" into games, giving early rewards to help get novice users hooked. Using media can put people in a trancelike state called the "machine zone," in which daily worries, social demands, and bodily awareness fade away.[16] Some people are disturbed to learn that tech evangelists like Steve Jobs, Sergey Brin of Google, Chris Anderson of *Wired*, Jonathan Ive of Apple, and others privately discourage their children from spending too much time with the devices that they publicly promote.[17] They know how irresistible their products are. There's a saying in the tech biz: "Don't get high on your own supply."

Many people try to alleviate digital dependence by using media mindfully, which means sometimes *not* using it. They want to reassert control over their own psyches and daily rhythms, while still enjoying the benefits of media use. Unlike drugs, addictive technologies are mainstream and total abstinence is not really an option.[18] Moderation is a more viable course. Mindfulness offers a means of understanding how media habits affect one's own brain, body, and emotions—even to people who don't think that devices detract from quality of life.

Mindful practices have been central to Eastern and Western spiritual traditions for millennia, but the past twenty years have brought a veritable explosion of public and scholarly interest in them.[19] Training in media mindfulness has become commonplace in workplaces, clinics, classrooms, and private homes. A large cadre of educators, researchers, technologists, counselors, and physicians advocates for bringing more contemplation into media use and other daily activities. They present mounting evidence that mindful media use *and* non-use promotes human health and well-being.

These conversations connect with ones about Slow Media, of which mindfulness is a core principle. Mindfulness teaches us to slow down, pay attention to media habits, and find new ways of relating to technology, other people, and ourselves. If we want to create more sustainable lives, a good place to start is by deliberately using media, not letting media use us. The choice is ours: to let digital devices distract us, or to put ourselves back into the moment. Individual adoption of mindful practices is intertwined with social structures that foster mindlessness, distraction, stress, and work-life imbalance—problems that cannot be pinned solely on media use.

In Search of Mindfulness

Let's picture a golden Shiba Inu with upturned tail—like the popular puppy cam or "Doge" Internet meme. (*Much fast. Very amaze! Wow.*) This adorable puppy wanders into the frame with boundless energy. It cavorts around the room. Tussles with a toy. Nibbles on a shoe. Wriggles on its back. The puppy chases its own tail, spinning in circles. It barks at its own reflection in the mirror. When its name is called, the puppy will not come. When given a command, it will not sit or lie down or roll over. We might love this puppy, but it needs to be trained.

In Buddhist philosophy, "puppy mind" or "monkey mind" is a common metaphor for wandering attention. All human minds wander and always did, long before the digital age. According to research, we are thinking about something other than what we are doing almost half (46.5%) of the time.[20] And we are less happy when our minds wander, regardless of what we are doing—even when the thoughts distracting us are positive ones.[21] Usually, our minds ruminate over things that happened in the past or might occur in the future. This constant disengagement from the present moment diminishes our emotional well-being as well as our ability to sleep, remember things, enjoy life, motivate ourselves, communicate with others, and use time productively.

The expression "paying attention" should be taken literally, according to Winifred Gallagher, author of *Rapt: Attention and the Focused Life*. "When you focus, you're spending limited cognitive currency that should be invested wisely, because the stakes are high," she writes.[22] "We must resist the temptation to drift along, reacting to whatever happens to us next, and deliberately select targets, from activities to relationships, that are worth of our finite supplies of time and attention."[23] Learning to manage one's attention is just as important to creating a meaningful life as learning to manage one's time. Mindfulness is a basic human capacity for regulating attention that everyone can improve.

When we act mindfully, we are taking conscious action, as opposed to acting in a habitual or distracted way—what psychologists sometimes call being on "autopilot" or in "default mode." The ability to voluntarily bring back wandering attention over and over again is "the very root of judgment, character, and will," said William James, the father of American psychology. "No one is *compos sui* [a master of themselves] if he have it not."[24] Some of James' best-known axioms emphasize that attention involves conscious choices: *The greatest weapon against stress is our ability to choose one thought over another. [Attention] implies a withdrawal from some things in order to deal effectively with others.*

We are neither products of genetic programming nor creatures of habit, said this pragmatist: "The whole feeling of reality, the whole sting and excitement of our voluntary life, depends on our sense that in it things are *really being decided* from one moment to another, and that it is not the dull rattling of a chain that was forged innumerable ages ago," wrote James (italics in the original). [25] The act of paying attention is intimately bound to free will.

A pioneer of such strategies is Jon Kabat-Zinn, founder of the mindfulness-based stress reduction (MBSR) program at the University of Massachusetts Medical Center. He defines *mindfulness* as "awareness, cultivated by paying attention in a sustained and particular way: on purpose, in the present moment, and nonjudgmentally."[26] Approaches like MBSR, though derived from Buddhist tradition, are typically secular. Modern mindfulness requires living consciously, deepening awareness, and putting it to practical use, according to Kabat-Zinn. It cannot be labeled an exclusively Buddhist value or practice, because it draws upon contemplative traditions common across Christian, Hindu, Taoist, Islamic, and Jewish teachings.[27]

In the digital age, increasing numbers of people use mindfulness training to notice when their attention wanders and to reign it in, like a puppy on a leash.

Meditations on Mediated Life

Mindfulness experts advocate for bringing more awareness to device habits. Kabat-Zinn poses it as a sustainability issue: technology can work 24/7 at top speed, but human bodies, minds, and spirits cannot keep such a pace. Whereas nightfall once forced us to stop the day's activities, slow down, and experience stillness, he said, electronic media erased the deadline. Now that we use media day and night, he says, "We submit ourselves to constant bombardment by sounds and images that come from minds other than our own, that fill our heads with information and trivia, other people's adventures and excitement and desires."[28]

Buddhist teachers attuned to modern Western life share their students' concern about mediated distraction. They instruct people in ways of turning away from distractions (external stimuli over which one has little control) and toward the wandering mind itself (internal factors that one can change through training). This stance requires a nonjudgmental attitude. "The objects of our world are just there, innocently, just being what they are," says one teacher. "Noises are just noises, sights are just sights, objects are just objects, smartphones are just smartphones, computers are just computers."[29] The problem arises from an interaction between media technologies and ourselves. We can take responsibility and learn how to respond more wisely to mediated provocations.

Another prominent Buddhist who frequently addresses mindful media use and non-use is Sharon Salzberg. Her vision for doing "stealth meditation" by changing the way you use media at work reverberates with Slow Media principles.[30] Like me, Salzberg promotes getting away from media for a while as a way to step out of ruts, fight stress, and reduce distraction.[31] Unplugging is not about "shunning our stuff or hating our habits of news consumption or social discourse" but rather "being willing to experiment with our time and attention, which are the core treasures of our lives." When we unplug, we get to enjoy being with ourselves and in the world, which helps us to gain insight and feel refreshed.

Multitasking is one deep rut to avoid. It's not only a bad habit but also an illusion and misnomer. Humans are not capable of simultaneously performing complex input-rich tasks, like having a conversation while texting. We switch back and forth between activities. (A computer processor does not perform multiple tasks at once, either. Like your brain, it switches quickly between those tasks. Most computers have more than one processor, but you, of course, have only one brain.) A half-second lag called an "attentional blink" occurs each time we switch from one task to another. And we do this a lot. Computer users commonly visit at least 40 websites per day and change windows 37 times per hour. When multitasking, we take at least 50% longer—sometimes twice as long—to get things done and make up to 50% more errors.

Multitasking raises stress levels while lowering accuracy and productivity. Salzberg's tip for regaining peace of mind echoes the emerging scholarly consensus: learn to be a monotasker. Buddhist teachers thus display good understanding of current neuroscientific knowledge. For their part, modern researchers have been rigorously examining practitioners' claims about the effectiveness of mindfulness.

Neuroplasticity, Multitasking, and the Default Mode

Rational people might be tempted to dismiss a concept like mindfulness that seems mystical, spiritual, unscientific. Yet a growing body of high-quality research demonstrates concrete benefits of mindfulness training for physical health and psychological well-being. Mindfulness-based programs are effective in treating a range of mental and physical conditions. They can improve attention, cognitive performance, immune function, sleep, and resilience. They can decrease levels of stress, anxiety, fatigue, and depression. They can give people a greater sense of well-being.[32] And they have no reported negative side effects.[33]

How does mindfulness practice improve psychological and physical well-being? By stimulating the parasympathetic nervous system (PNS), which controls many automatic and involuntary actions as well as ones like breathing that can be consciously directed by the mind. The PNS has a "rest and digest" function that promotes a slower heartbeat, slower respiration, and relaxation. It gives a break to the sympathetic nervous system (SNS), which controls the "flight or fight" response that releases adrenaline and impairs digestion, sleep, and mental health. The SNS is like the accelerator pedal on a car, whereas the PNS is the brake.

A well-functioning vehicle needs both, so you can slow down and speed up in roughly equal measures.

The science of mindfulness has investigated cognitive factors such as neuroplasticity, default mode, and executive function. *Neuroplasticity* refers to the brain's property of adapting its structure and operation in response to experiences. Until the 1990s, scientists thought the brain stopped developing after childhood. We now know the adult brain remains malleable. It continues growing new brain cells and neural networks and has the ability to "rewire" itself—for better and for worse.

Neuroplasticity means that the more we engage in activities like using search engines and multitasking that affect our brain circuitry, the easier those tasks become. The chemically triggered synapses that link neurons want us to keep exercising circuits once they have formed. Routine activities are carried out ever more quickly and efficiently, while unused circuits are "pruned away," as Carr explains in *The Shallows*.[34] Neuroscience shows that if we stop using certain mental capacities, we lose them—for example, deep reading, remembering things, navigating by map. By using digital media, we sacrifice mental skills such as these that may be more valuable than the ones we gain, Carr says. His work helped familiarize many people with neuroplasticity as well as the term "dopamine squirt." It also stoked public concern that Google might be making us *stoopid*.

Mindful awareness promotes neuroplasticity. Groundbreaking research by Richard Davidson (with Kabat-Zinn and other collaborators) confirms that meditation alters the brain in beneficial ways.[35] His work shows that mindfulness training produces biological changes such as lower anxiety and better immune function—supporting claims that this ancient practice treats stress and disease. In another study, practicing mindfulness helped the amygdala (part of the brain that responds to negative emotions) return to normal more quickly after stimulation, which could make meditators more resilient against strain and anxiety.[36]

The psychological concept of *default mode* involves states of inattention, lack of judgment, and wandering thoughts. Mindfulness experts describe it as "ingrained mental habits" or "the proverbial water that we are swimming in—the very mental environment in which we function."[37] It's like being on autopilot, mindlessly repeating past behaviors. One researcher warns that people can get "mindlessly seduced" into activities they would not engage in otherwise when they fall into habitual routines instead of making conscious decisions.[38] The default mode is mutually exclusive with a set of cognitive processes called *executive function*.

Executive function involves the brain's abilities to pay attention, tune out irrelevant stimuli, be self-aware, make decisions, inhibit impulses, and control behavior. It can be likened to a control tower that helps you focus and set priorities. Many readers will know the classic experiment in executive function in which children who resisted eating marshmallows, when promised a greater number of the puffs later, grew up to be more successful than children who could not overcome the temptation. Poor executive function is correlated with mindlessness and *multitasking*, which trains attention to jump around instead of staying focused for sustained periods. By contrast, strong executive function is related to mindfulness and monotasking. It could be called *anti-multitasking*.

Well-publicized findings by Stanford University show that heavy multitaskers perform much worse than light ones in three key aspects of cognitive function: filtering, working memory management, and task switching. Multitasking people judge their own performance more highly than monotaskers viewed theirs, despite actually performing worse.[39] People get a chemical rush from doing many things at once, which increases dopamine levels in the brain. This makes you feel so good that you don't notice mistakes. And multitasking releases adrenaline and stress hormones like cortisol that contribute to short-term memory loss and long-term health problems. Dopamine, adrenaline, and cortisol are some of the primary chemical components of technology addiction. (Intense media use can also cause an imbalance of nitric oxide, which affects cognition, depression, and immune functions, as I will explain shortly. And it can deprive the body of melatonin, a hormone that regulates sleep.)

While multitasking makes you feel happy and productive, it actually stimulates mindlessness, makes you less efficient, and ruins your focus. Yet multitasking continues to be viewed positively, despite ample evidence that it reduces performance.[40] (Research suggests that 2.5% of the population consists of "supertaskers" who can more easily juggle multiple streams of information.[41] The other 97.5% of us are not blessed with this ability.) The moral of the story: people who focus on a single task are more effective, regardless of whether they feel that way. Anyone can improve their ability to monotask, if they try. People who received three months of intensive meditation training, by comparison to a nonmeditating control group, achieved a focused state of attention with less effort, optimized their attention, and minimized attentional blinks.[42]

Of course, "distraction" has many meanings. Occasional task switching can be good for you. Brief interruptions of an intense focal task, such as studying before a final exam or doing your taxes, can improve concentration. There's a difference between allowing your mind to be diverted by its own thoughts and letting it be hijacked by external stimuli (courtesy of digital devices, networks, content, and sponsors who are gunning for your attention). Your wandering mind might rehash yesterday or fret about tomorrow, but it also might generate creative thoughts and solve problems. Being mindful about media use means learning when distraction is harmful and when it is not.

Experiments in Minding Your Media

Much scholarship explores multitasking, usually defined as performing multiple tasks *with media*—as opposed to combined actions like walking and chewing gum at the same time (unless also texting on a smartphone). Research consistently confirms that media multitasking harms cognitive functions and processes.[43] Some experts think multitasking could even represent a mental-health risk. In one extensive study, media use was negatively associated with social-emotional well-being while face-to-face communication was positively correlated.[44] Research found that when young girls communicated face-to-face, they felt more valued, successful, safer, accepted, and comfortable. By contrast, when they used digital media (watching videos; playing games; sending emails, texts and chats; posting comments) they felt more stressed, judged, rejected, and hurt—even more so when they used multiple streams at once.

Relatively little research has directly looked at the effects of mindfully *not* using media. Some unusual studies, which I'll share here, examine what happens when people are required or compelled to use media in mindful ways. I know of few, however, conducted on people who willingly abstained from media.[45] (Some scholars report having a hard time finding volunteers to avoid email for a few days, because people are intimidated by the prospect of having to catch up on missed messages.)[46]

In an early experiment in mindfulness, social psychologist Ellen Langer found correlations between health, mindful behavior, and context control. That unconventional 1979 study immersed senior citizens in a novel situation to see whether a new state of mind would trick their bodies into reverting to a more youthful state. It did not manipulate media consumption per se but enhanced mindfulness by creating a new experience in which media played a key role. (Unlike many mindfulness studies, people were not training to meditate.) The research team took men over age 70 on a retreat that recreated a complete environment from the year 1959, including appropriate media forms and content.[47] For a week, the experimental group listened to oldies music and radio commercials from the 1950s, watched TV shows like "I Love Lucy" and "The Honeymooners," and evaluated movies like "Auntie Mame" and "Cat on a Hot Tin Roof." A control group read, listened to, and watched whatever media they wanted.

The findings? Vital measurements, photographs, and video recorded before, during, and after the retreat found improvements in vision, hearing, memory, intelligence, joint flexibility, sitting height, manual dexterity, weight, and strength—with greater differences in the experimental group than in a control group (indicating that these positive effects were not due simply to being on vacation). The men as a whole looked younger by about three years after the experiment, according to independent judges. The study gave a "stunning demonstration of the power of mind over matter," one analyst said. "After a week of focusing on their salad days, the old men grew visibly younger—not just in their frisky attitude, but even in their physiology."[48]

Any intensely mindful activity could have achieved those results, Langer said. Actively breaking habits can free you from automatic behaviors—the default mode—and enhance your creativity, she said.[49] People are likely to be more creative when they free themselves of old mindsets, "open themselves to new information and surprise, play with perspective and context, and focus on process rather than outcome," whether they are scientists, artists, or cooks.

One of the world's largest technology companies conducted a similarly bold experiment. In 2009, Intel tried reducing the amount of time people spent using media on the job because managers thought that information overload interfered with employees' ability to make decisions, process information, and prioritize tasks. They wanted to nurture more productivity, focus, reflection, and creativity among workers by curtailing interruptions—above all, email (and, to a lesser extent, meetings, face-to-face conversations, instant messaging, and phone calls). At the time, Intel employees were receiving 50–100 emails per day, with executives getting up to 300 messages daily. On average, 30% of those emails were deemed unnecessary.[50] Company data indicated that the average employee wasted around 20 hours per week, a productivity cost of around $1 billion per year.[51]

Previous Intel experiments in coping with information overload had tried to modify individual behavior through training, but employees quickly slipped back into old habits. This time, the research focused on organizational policies. For seven months, engineers and managers were assigned to one of three different conditions. "Quiet Time" was a four-hour period each week devoted to reflection, during which employees could not have meetings or receive incoming emails, chats, or phone calls. "No E-mail Day" discouraged, but did not prohibit, internal email messages on Fridays. "E-mail Service Level Agreement" encouraged workers to check email two or three times per day and to wait up to 24 hours before replying to messages.

Quiet Time, which notably improved focus and productivity, was most popular with employees overall. People with different job roles responded to the study in vastly different ways. Before the experiment, managers had perceived email as a much bigger threat to effectiveness than engineers did. After the experiment, managers greatly reduced the number of emails they sent and increased their expectations for email reply time, while engineers did not. Around half of managers felt the constraints on media use helped them to innovate and finish important tasks, while only a quarter of engineers did. Fifty-three percent of managers recommended extending the Quiet Time initiative, compared to 34% of engineers.

The Intel pilot found that people appreciated the chance to think and work without mediated distractions. Even those who saw the program as having little impact viewed the experience positively. Some suggested that media restrictions needed more flexibility, such as establishing "legitimate interruptions" of Quiet Time. (Most participants recommended not continuing the other initiatives, No E-mail Day and E-mail Service Level Agreement, unless significant changes were made.) Others cited the community-level prohibition as essential to the program's success. They felt empowered to reduce their communication only when other people did, too.

Other research confirms findings of this study. Reading and processing email can take up half of a worker's time, at a cost of almost $1 trillion to the US economy. In 2010, the majority of employees reported that most work-related emails were irrelevant to getting their job done. According to one study, being forbidden to use work email for blocks of time lets employees be more productive, unshackles them from their desks, and greatly reduces stress, including cortisol levels and heart rates.[52] (Contrary to stereotypes about older people and technology, workers over age 55 were less stressed using technology and better at using multiple devices on the job than their younger colleagues.)[53]

Another experiment, by Harvard Business School, documented more benefits to using media mindfully in the workplace.[54] Researcher Leslie Perlow looked for ways to improve work-life balance in management teams with a 24/7 culture. Employees of Boston Consulting Group (BCG) wanted the advantages of being connected with their colleagues without sacrificing too much personal time. Perlow and her team guided BCG in adopting a new practice of "predictable time off" (PTO).[55] In a nutshell, PTO allows a group to talk about communication needs in a structured way and to schedule time when no one is expected to be available through digital media. People get permission from supervisors to unplug from work on a regular basis (say, on certain evenings every week, or after 8 p.m.) to recharge and tend to their private lives.

PTO is a modest goal that yields major results. Some teams realized that they spent all night checking email to exchange a flurry of minutiae that could quickly be handled in person the next morning. Some partners who sent late-night or early-morning emails learned that others were staying up late or rising early just to respond to those messages, which they said they had not known. "The value of PTO is we didn't have a choice," one executive told Perlow. "Because I was forced to . . . I could really check out and that made a huge difference."[56] Having predictable time off helped people come back to work refreshed and ready to go. Added a project leader: "I know I was more effective on the day after my night off, because my head was clear, I was rested, and I felt so excited to be back at work."

Young people derive similar benefits from media time-outs, research suggests. An ambitious experiment recruited almost 1,000 college students around the world to give up digital devices for a day and share their reactions. In "The World Unplugged," led by researchers at the International Center for Media and the Public Agenda (ICMPA) and the University of Maryland in 2010, young people from Argentina, Chile, China, Mexico, and other countries spared no melodrama in reporting how they felt while offline: *anxious, crazy, dead, empty, helpless, incomplete, insecure, irritable, isolated, lonely, lost, like a drug addict, numb, paralyzed, pathetic, totally desperate.* [57]These college students on five continents found it extremely difficult to unplug—but once they did, they gained a lot of self-awareness.

Here's a sample of the responses from students in the US, UK, Slovakia and Uganda. "I went into absolute panic mode." "Emptiness. Emptiness overwhelms me." "I felt as though everything I had ever known was taken away from me."

"Halfway through the day I felt I could not handle it any more." "I felt as though I was being tortured." "Unplugging my ethernet cable felt like turning off a life support system." "I hope that I never have such a day again in my life." "I realized my addiction to media." "My dependence on the media is absolutely sickening." "I feel like a slave to media." "Maybe [my media habit] is unhealthy." Yet many of these young people reported benefits such as feeling more peaceful, invigorated, happy, liberated, focused and creative once they grew accustomed to disconnection.

This body of research shows that being more mindful about how you use— and don't use—media can make people healthier, more productive, and happier.[58] For people who feel addicted to devices and networks, it might require substantial time and effort to break old habits and adjust to the media-lite lifestyle. You don't need to go cold turkey, though. And you don't need to do it alone. A host of training programs, books, products, apps and collective projects have sprung up that integrate mindfulness and digital media by applying concepts like *mindful emailing, mindful tech, e-mindfulness, contemplative computing, conscious computing, positive computing,* and *unplugging.*

Bringing Mindfulness into Media Practice

Like many other organizations, Google has been trying to encourage mindful use of media among its employees to improve productivity, accuracy, and retention. Until recently, the company had a position titled "Jolly Good Fellow" whose official role was to "enlighten minds, open hearts, create world peace." Those duties were carried out by Chade-Meng Tan, a long-time engineer and Buddhist. Working with contemplation advocate Mirabai Bush, Tan designed and launched the popular program "Search Inside Yourself" to develop mindfulness-based emotional intelligence. Thousands of workers at Google and other tech companies worldwide have taken the course.

One approach to developing emotional intelligence through media is *mindful emailing,* which Bush has taught to employees at Microsoft and Monsanto as well as to activists, judges, and soldiers. The technique is simple: take three breaths before you hit "send." In that gap, practice empathy and re-read the message from the perspective of the person you are emailing. Some people, after taking such a pause, pick up the phone to deliver news personally instead of by email. Bush acknowledges that companies like Google are motivated to bring mindfulness into the workplace for practical reasons. She thinks that spiritual awakening could be an unintentional side effect.[59]

Then there's David Levy, who holds a PhD in computer science and artificial intelligence from Stanford University and did research for 15 years at Xerox's famed Palo Alto Research Center, the think tank that developed graphical user interface (GUI) and other lynchpins of modern computing. Now a professor in the University of Washington's Information School, he advises students and

tech workers on how to enhance their work and their lives by being contemplative about media use. In his book *Mindful Tech*, Levy describes four principles for
staying focused: establish and monitor your goals for using media; use breath and
body awareness to focus and relax; slow down (my favorite); and establish physical and temporal boundaries to your media use.

People who tried these techniques told him they felt calmer and more focused.[60] One graduate student, who often felt tired in the afternoon, said that
mindfulness aided concentration: "I have started to do thirty-to-sixty-second
[breath] meditations prior to opening my inbox in the afternoons and it is a huge
help. Taking that short amount of time to pause the ceaseless racket in my brain
before attempting to focus makes all the difference in my productivity and my
emotional state."

Another said that checking email began to resemble meditating: "It requires
concentration and active filtering to do it right. With email, you have to make a
conscious decision to remain focused and in the present. This exercise forced me
to reflect on ways in which I can challenge myself to live in the present and there-
fore, improve my ability to focus."

A third said by reading each email slowly, she felt much calmer than
usual: "Usually I rush through the email's contents, just scanning through the
words as fast as I can, making quick judgments about its value and whether
I should invest time into it. Strangely enough, emails that I regularly would delete
or find irritation with suddenly seemed kind of interesting. They seemed to have
value."

One of the most common reactions to these exercises in using tech mindfully was surprise. People hadn't realized that their emotional and physiological
responses to media were so intense.[61]

In addition to mindful emailing and mindful tech, specialists in this area have
proposed cultivating more mindful and sustainable media interactions through e-
mindfulness, contemplative computing, conscious computing, and positive computing. For example, *e-mindfulness* suggests that people try to breathe fully and
consciously when they are online, while paying close attention to how their bodies
are feeling and what their minds are doing. This kind of awareness can help you
learn where and how you hold physical tension, how you are sitting, whether your
attention is scattered, and whether you are holding your breath, as many people
tend to do when tense or concentrating.[62]

Many of us know the feeling, described in a *HuffPost* story:[63] "I've just opened
my email and there's nothing out of the ordinary there. It's the usual daily flood of
schedule, project, travel, information and junk mail. Then I notice. . . . I'm holding
my breath. As the email spills onto my screen, as my mind races with thoughts
of what I'll answer first, what can wait, who I should call, what should have been
done two days ago; I've stopped the steady breathing I was doing only moments
earlier in a morning meditation and now, I'm holding my breath. And here's the
deal. You're probably holding your breath, too."

The author, Linda Stone, calls this phenomenon *email apnea* or—more accurately, since it can happen with any online activity—*screen apnea*: shallow breathing or breath-holding when using digital media.[64] Up to 80% of computer users experience this apnea.[65] Breath holding contributes to stress-related diseases by disturbing the body's balance of oxygen, carbon dioxide, and nitric oxide.[66] Not to be confused with nitrous oxide, the laughing gas used by dentists, nitric oxide is 1) associated with processes of learning, memory, sleeping, depression, and feeling pain; 2) used by the immune system in fighting tumors and viral, bacterial, and parasitic infections; and 3) a mediator of inflammation and rheumatism.[67] Breath holding and shallow breathing trigger the "flight or fight" response, whereas deep diaphragmatic breathing stimulates relaxation.

Stone, who worked at high-tech companies like Apple and Microsoft for almost two decades, also coined the phrase *continuous partial attention* to describe the state of semi-distraction in which modern people spend much of their time.[68] Continuous partial attention and screen apnea both produce an artificial sense of crisis in the body. Intense media use can put our bodies in an almost constant low-level state of fight-or-flight, Stone explains.[69] "This is great when we're being chased by tigers," she says. "But how many of those 500 emails a day is a TIGER? How many are flies? Is everything an emergency? Our way of using the current set of technologies would have us believe it is."

You should not be surprised at this point to learn that breathing is a main focus of Alex Pang's book *The Distraction Addiction*. He enumerates several steps to overcoming distraction: breathing, simplifying, meditating, deprogramming, experimenting, refocusing, and resting. People can experiment with these techniques until they find a formula that works for them. It might involve a combination of unsubscribing from email lists, switching off alerts, sending fewer digital messages, or checking email on a fixed schedule (instead of continually). "We all have different capacities for attention, different things that distract us, and different things that help us concentrate," notes Pang, who has been a research fellow at Microsoft and visiting scholar at Stanford. "It's important to tinker thoughtfully with your technologies, usage practices, and work habits in order to learn what combinations support contemplative practices."[70] He uses the phrase *contemplative computing* to describe this approach to media use.[71]

By contrast, *conscious computing* is a term floated by Stone for using personal technologies to increase awareness and reduce stress.[72] She cites tools such as the HeartMath emWave2 or GPS for the Soul for helping people take control of media use. The first is a handheld device that gives users heart-rhythm feedback to help manage mental and physical strain. The second is an app that measures heart rate and prompts users to start mindful practices of their choice when stress indicators rise. The latter tool was launched by a team working with Arianna Huffington (yes, she does realize the paradox of using an app to avoid overusing media). Some popular fitness bracelets offer similar functions, like guided breathing sessions. Stone thinks devices can enhance well-being by helping people attune to their bodies and nervous systems and realize when they are stressed or engaged.

Unlike ideas that focus on how people employ digital media, *positive computing* (or "positive technology") is fostered by tech designers who want to contribute to human well-being, akin to how Green IT engineers pursue environmental sustainability. This design movement finds inspiration in humanistic values also driving the growth of "positive psychology" and "happiness studies."[73] Prime examples of positive computing are apps that guide people in meditation, such as Headspace, Calm, Buddhify, and Smiling Mind. There are also mindfulness devices like Spire, which reminds users to meditate; it looks like a stone and clips to your belt.

In an age of ubiquitous computing, some designers and developers think that turning a blind eye to the detrimental influence of technology on human health and well-being is "to accept a kind of convenient ignorance" of the real impact of their work.[74] One example is Harris, who left Google to lead a nonprofit group that creates better design practices and gives technologists more incentives to help users spend their time well. The current business model that aligns media companies with advertisers' and clients' needs instead of human lives might be too entrenched and profitable to dislodge, according to Alter. In the meantime, people can try exerting more control over their own media behavior.

Your Brain on Speed

Mindfulness is a vital virtue of Slow living in its sundry forms.[75] When you are mindful, you actually slow down your perception of time, expand your subjective experience, and increase the density of information that you perceive and remember.[76] Simply put: being mindful means *slowing down your mind*.

Mindful media unsettles the assumption that fast is good and slow is bad. Our default mode for using media has become what Levy calls "more-faster-better," a lopsided habit that is not desirable or sustainable. Sometimes less is more; sometimes slower is better. When it comes to information, your mind has a speed limit of sorts.[77] The human brain operates at a relatively low bandwidth of 120 bits per second. That's 5,000 times slower than a standard Internet connection. It takes around 60 bits per second to pay attention to one person speaking. That's why multitasking doesn't work. In the tech realm, people tend to associate *slowness* with infirmity or incompetence and *speed* with high energy or performance, according to Pang.[78] But in the human realm, slowness is often a sign of skill, mastery, and experience.

Reading is a great example of an activity that improves when you slow down. It has become commonplace for people to mourn their lost ability to concentrate on a text for long periods of time, be it David Sedaris or Margaret Atwood yet alone Marcel Proust or Henry James. Digital media habits contribute to this sense of restlessness with prolonged reading experiences. When skimming texts on screens becomes your default mode of "reading," it weakens your brain's capacity for deep reading, for interpreting texts and making rich mental connections. Partly in response to such concerns, people have gravitated toward movements for Slow Reading and Slow Books.

Many reading experts advise us to go slower.[79] According to Maryanne Wolf, the developmental psychologist and author of *Proust and the Squid: The Story and Science of the Reading Brain*, deep reading is indistinguishable from deep thinking. The corollary is that superficial reading engenders shallow thoughts. To be sure, scanning texts quickly without sacrificing comprehension is an essential skill. (I'm forever grateful for having learned speed-reading in middle school.) The smart choice is to flex both sets of muscles, fast and slow, exercising the latter instead of letting it atrophy.

Mindful media use means finding ways to strike a better balance between two seemingly contradictory states of mind that are, in truth, complementary. It's not that using media in fast or mindless ways is bad, but that a well-rounded mind requires a slow counterbalance. We need both "an ability to find and quickly parse a wide range of information and a capacity for open-ended reflection," as Carr says. "There needs to be time for efficient data collection and time for inefficient contemplation, time to operate the machine and time to sit idly in the garden."[80] Likewise, Levy argues that fast and slow, high-tech and contemplative, are not separate and incompatible but rather "two threads" from which we weave our lives, which we can bring into dialogue with each other.[81]

Adopting slower, mindful approaches to media use can improve personal well-being and team performance, as this chapter has shown. Society writ large can also gain from nurturing calm, attentive minds attuned to nobler instincts such as empathy, compassion, and moral decision-making that are "inherently slow."[82] So, the question remains: if workers, employers and the social collective benefit from slowing down, why do things get faster? Who gains the most from acceleration? Sure, many of us enjoy the thrill of speed—especially when we are blissfully unaware of, or turn a blind eye to, its consequences.

Commercial forces hold great power to determine how fast things go, and media industries have a financial stake in speeding up our media use. "The faster we surf, the more links we click and pages we view, the more opportunities (they) gain to collect information about us and to feed us advertisements," Carr explains.[83] "The last thing these companies want is to encourage leisurely reading or slow, concentrated thought. It's in their economic interest to drive us to distraction." Digital platforms, content providers, and advertisers often measure success with metrics like "time spent on page" or "time spent on site." (Casinos gauge the effectiveness of slot machines with a similar term: "time spent on device.") They have a strong incentive to get people using *more* media, except they've hit an immovable limit: the number of waking hours available.

Thanks to speed and multitasking, we can cram more page views into a fixed day length, a fixed lifespan. Media companies compete so fiercely for eyeballs that mandarins consider attention the true "currency" of the digital economy. An ever-growing number of sources, platforms, devices, and apps are clamoring for it. Yet human attention remains a scarce commodity, a precious resource. And it is *yours*. Before giving your attention to media, be mindful of what you are getting and losing in the bargain.

Lessons Learned from Mindful Media

To bring mindful media practices into your life, find a few moments when you can play with slow approaches, as a way of creating critical detachment from your default mode. Here are some techniques to try.

First, *conscious breathing*, which can cultivate attention and reduce stress. Throughout time, contemplatives have relied on breath as an internal cue and focal point for the mind's attention. Modern research confirms its effectiveness. Breathing has convenient attributes like being necessary, always available, within our control, and monotonous enough that you can simultaneously focus on your body, your mind, or the task at hand. Get into the habit of deliberate, deep breathing when using computers, watching TV, reading books, or consuming media of any kind. While you're at it, you could practice breathing intentionally when doing anything else, too: standing in line, driving in a car, sitting on the bus.

Second, *monotasking*. Being mindful means doing, or trying to do, one thing at a time. This does not come naturally to people accustomed to doing many things at once, including yours truly. Yet the effort to retrain oneself is worthwhile. Abundant evidence supports the idea that multitasking is counterproductive. Although people are increasingly familiar with such research, "in practice, you still see (multitasking) everywhere," observes MIT sociologist Sherry Turkle. She says it's time for people to think of monotasking as "the next big thing" and "the key to productivity and creativity." Some ideas that might work for you: Turn off nonessential alerts and "push" notifications on devices and networks. Practice Slow reading of books and other long-form writing. (I recommend printed bound media artifacts, but e-books are fine.) Slow listening to music is an appealing option. Play a favorite record and absorb every note, tone, and pause. Wean yourself from the deceptive chemical rush that you're used to getting from doing many things at once.

Third, *stopping*. Even God stopped on the seventh day. It's smart to pause occasionally during and between mediated activities. Take occasional breaks away from screens in order to stretch, rehydrate, move, and get fresh air. Make a point of spending time in real-world activities: conversing with people face to face, going to live events, visiting cultural sites, being in natural settings. There's more to life, and to work, than communicating digitally. Knowing when to stop—and making yourself do it—can help you pace yourself to avoid sloppy errors, poor decisions, physical exhaustion, and emotional burnout. What's more: letting your mind wander, staring into space, and getting bored can make you more creative and more productive.[84]

Fourth, an extension of the imperative to rest, is *unplugging*. People who block out times and spaces for not using media are effectively protecting themselves from unnecessary distractions. Untethering yourself from media leaves you freer to pursue your own agenda, instead of other people's priorities. You could banish devices from the dinner table, bathroom, bedroom, or all three. (Added bonus: you'll sleep better. Buy a stand-alone alarm clock, if you don't have one.) You could try a media-free commute, if your life accommodates it. Or choose a time of day to put away your device, and stick with it. Use that "off" button. Constant connection might have been a fad or a necessary stage in cultural evolution, but it has outlasted its novelty and usefulness.

Fifth, *meditating*, which can reinforce and deepen all the aforementioned efforts to breathe better, monotask more, slow down, and get some rest. Think of it as simply *reflecting* or *contemplating*, if the idea of meditating bothers you. Incorporate a short session or two into each day. Ten minutes could make a difference, if you persist daily. For inspiration, read a book about mindfulness or join a session at a local Buddhist center, yoga, studio or gym. Use a meditation app or website to get guidance in a solo setting.

Just as meditating detaches one's self from monkey or puppy mind, detaching from media use creates critical distance that aids reflection, contemplation, and problem solving. Marshall McLuhan often recounted the story of Poe's *A Descent into the Maelstrom,* wherein a sailor stuck in a whirlpool begins to watch, with curiosity, the numerous things that spiral downward with him. "I must have been delirious—for I even sought amusement in speculating upon the relative velocities of their several descents toward the foam below," Poe wrote. "It was not a new terror that thus affected me, but the dawn of a more exciting hope. This hope arose partly from memory, and partly from present observation."[85]

For McLuhan, this reaction is a metaphor for a critical media awareness, where people survive by choosing to observe their environment rationally instead of emotionally. Poe's protagonist spies a barrel, notices that it is staying afloat, lashes himself to it, and stays afloat himself. By not getting carried away, he resists being swept up. People who use media mindfully can go one better than the sailor: withdrawing from the maelstrom momentarily to reflect on their predicament before jumping back into the waters.

Let's Treat Causes, Not Symptoms

A wise Buddhist scholar once said of mindful eating that the arrow goes both ways. "Mindful eating is a route to better eating; eating is a route to better mindfulness," Jeff Wilson observed in *Mindful America: The Mutual Transformation of Buddhist Meditation and American Culture.*[86] The same is true of mindful media use. Being more mindful of media teaches you about life, and being more mindful of life teaches you about media.

Mindful media offers a promising path toward a sustainable and healthy society, if we tread it wisely. Many of us are seeking more time, focus, creativity, productivity, and peace of mind—and mediated distractions stand in the way of those goals. People who constantly check their devices have higher stress levels (by around 20%) than people who don't use them frequently, according to the American Psychological Association.[87] Contrary to generational stereotypes, adults under age 38 reported the highest stress levels (around 20% higher than older people) related to technology and were most worried about the negative effects of social media on their physical and mental health.

These realities have helped fuel a booming mindfulness industry. It's easy to find cause for both hope and cynicism in the skyrocketing popularity of, say, mindfulness coloring books for adults, which promise relaxation, stress relief, and creativity. In 2015, US sales of coloring books rose from 1 million to 12 million units. This pastime offers burned-out adults an escape from screens and devices, as Thu-Huong Ha wrote in *Quartz*. "Americans today will take anything they can get to escape the hum of their perceived hyper-connectivity and overwork," she said. "That demand has created a sort of mindfulness industrial complex, a sprawling lucrative industry that pedals DIY relaxation of all kinds, from calming crafts to downloadable guided meditation, week-long silent retreats and a $150 'calmness' tracker."[88]

To some extent, mindfulness has become a commodity in our capitalistic milieu. Since it is an abstract "product" that one cannot actually sell, people instead promote auxiliary items: bells, cushions, apps, CDs, heart-rate monitors, and so on.[89] (Breathing, of course, is still free.) One risk of mindfulness devices is that people might buy products that they would not otherwise purchase under the guise of "enlightened" consumption. Mindful media use could conflict with environmental sustainability if it leads to the manufacture and disposal of unnecessary gadgets. Supporters of mindful media are concerned about possible exploitation of the phenomenon, or "well-washing," akin to the greenwashing that began when public interest in sustainable living grew.[90] Instead of selling us more stuff, mindfulness could help us reconnect with nature and detach from mediated anxieties.

The idea of mindfulness has migrated from a Buddhist context that emphasizes transcendence and renunciation of worldly pleasures to a secular one where people seek practical insight, therapeutic benefit, and pleasurable engagement. As Wilson observed, "Buddhism has been creatively transformed, adapted, appropriated, domesticated, modified and integrated" in the US, where meditation easily fits into prevailing scientific worldviews.[91] The movement today is a far cry from the bohemian Buddhism of the 1970s that attracted people like Bush, Davidson, Kabat-Zinn, and Salzberg. That counterculture was driven by a search for alternative ways of being, whereas today's mainstream mindfulness mainly seeks ways of coping with the status quo rather than changing it.

Mindful media training is often treated as a tool for making people happier and more effective in their work—as Google's "Search Inside Yourself" program exemplifies. This IT giant is one of many corporations that have promoted stress reduction in their office culture by offering mindfulness workshops and amenities such as meditation rooms and yoga classes. Organizations that connect employees with opportunities to enhance well-being are doing good, but they could do better to address more root causes, not just mitigate symptoms.

Some companies, realizing that employees are overwrought, take significant efforts to build a culture of media mindfulness. Turkle describes an organization (pseudonymously called "HeartTech") whose managers encourage face-to-face conversation, send out emails in batches at times convenient to their subordinates, and resist the expectation that employees should always be online. HeartTech even observes a daily company-wide pause during which employees are asked to relax and breathe. While employees value these efforts, they told Turkle, the message of mindfulness programs feels at odds with their jobs because "they are, after all, not being paid to be calm." These cultural issues transcend lone workplaces.

Mindfulness is not a panacea for information overload, mediated distraction, and device addiction. To build a sustainable society in which media use exhausts fewer human resources (as well as natural ones), we could pursue more collective approaches. The obsession with mindfulness is—as Ha said of the adult coloring craze—a "cry for help" for which self-care does not suffice.[92] Elected officials could play a role, although there are limits to what government could or should do. Some technologists are taking responsibility for the equivocal social effects of media devices and networks that they design. In *Irresistible*, Alter urges the public to encourage this trend by demanding more ethical design from companies, just as we petition them for ethical environmental practices. Consumers and industry, citizens and government, employees and executives could work together toward sustainable media if they realize they have common cause.

As we move toward a mindful culture, the bias toward "more-faster-better" remains an obstacle. Talking about Slow Media creates an opportunity for reflecting on and challenging our assumptions about the relationship between technology, society, and the planet. Mindful media advocates share a commitment to techniques like breathing, monotasking, slowing down, stopping, and even unplugging. Another thing that most of them hold in common: a background of deep immersion in technophiliac culture—at places like Apple, Google, Microsoft, Stanford, and Xerox PARC. This helps to inoculate their criticism against public accusations of Luddism, as the next chapter explores. One of the biggest challenges faced by sustainable culture could be overcoming binary attitudes— that you must be for speed or against it, for technology or against it, for change or against it—which have long hobbled conversations about digital media.

6

We are All Post-Luddites Now

I regard it as stupid to be anti-technology. That would be something like being anti-food. We need technology to live, as we need food to live. But, of course, if we eat too much food, or eat food that has no nutritional value, or eat food that is infected with disease, we turn a means of survival into its opposite.
—Neil Postman, *Technopoly: The Surrender of Culture to Technology*[1]

If you haven't guessed it already, I should probably admit it now: I use digital media. Yes, I own a desktop computer, a laptop, a tablet, a smartphone, a digital projector, an Internet radio, an MP3 player, and a host of other devices. I almost always enjoy using them. Especially my writing software—I am *in love* with Scrivener. I cut the cord on cable years ago and stream all my TV and films, when I'm not watching BluRay. And I use social media, too. My Klout score was above 60 for a while! That put me in the top 10% of the influencers ranked on that site, at the time. I have published blogs solo on various platforms and know some HTML code. I am savvy enough about technology to teach courses in blogging and social media. Now that you know I like digital media and use them competently, will you take my ideas seriously?

In other words, I am not a Luddite.

For decades, people who dared to express healthy skepticism about digital media have taken pains to avoid being seen as Luddite, or "against technology." This term refers to the oft-maligned uprising in early 19th-century England when textile workers smashed expensive machines that threatened their livelihoods. The original Luddites' grievance, importantly, was not with machinery per se but with its social and economic consequences. Employers of that era frequently adopted machines to increase output, lower wages, eliminate jobs, and discipline their workforce—as in our own times.

After fading from view for a while, the word *Luddite* crept back in the 1960s and its successor *Neo-Luddite* took off in the 1990s, as digital technologies emerged. Whenever you express apprehension about social and political implications of media choices, you risk being compared to those saboteurs of yore. An accusation of Luddism implies that someone is a combination of backwards, fearful, inept, angry, provincial, primitive, and dangerous. It's a bit like being derided as a socialist in the US—and similarly based upon misconceptions of what the word means. The label has long been used as rhetorical intimidation to squelch serious debate about digital media and stack the deck with people who profit from boosting technology. Anti-Luddites portray technology as preordained, critics as irrational, and resistance as futile. Once the specter of Luddism has been invoked against you, your ideas lose credibility.

In anticipation of this name-calling, knowledgeable critics of digital devices, networks, automation, and other technologies preemptively resist the label. They give the ritual disavowal "I'm no Luddite, but . . ." in an attempt to inoculate themselves against mockery and dismissal. In an essay questioning advances in robotics, genetic engineering, and nanotechnology, Bill Joy stated bluntly, "I trust it is clear that I am not a Luddite."[2] In a book about human-focused computing, Dorian Peters declared herself "far from a Luddite" as she acknowledged that technology has social costs. In discussing the Internet's cognitive detriments, Nicholas Carr devoted a full page to affirming his belief that the Web is a "godsend." I could cite dozens, if not hundreds, of other examples. It would seem there is no fate worse than being labeled a Luddite.[3]

Exceptions to this rule are rare, when someone defiantly claims this identity rather than refuses it. For instance, Paulina Borsook is uncommon to have declared herself a Luddite in the true sense of the word. "I'm so glad that I live in an era of photocopiers, laptops, call-waiting, Telfa pads, Advil, and narrow-spectrum antibiotics," she assured readers, before turning to her concern that technological advances tend disproportionately to favor a small group of elites. "Like the Luddites, I am not so sure most change benefits most people."[4]

For the record: Joy was a coding prodigy who invented the version of Unix that became the backbone of the Internet, co-founded Sun Microsystems, and created the Java and MySQL programming languages. Peters is an expert in UX (user experience) who has published with MIT Press and designed Web graphics, information architecture, and digital content for more than 15 years. Carr is an award-winning reporter whose research on information technology and business culture has appeared in *The New York Times, Wired*, and *MIT Technology Review*. Borsook has worked in Silicon Valley since the 1980s and written about tech culture for early online magazines like *Feed* and *Salon* as well as *Whole Earth Review, Wired*, and *Yale Journal of Law and Technology*. (She has been described as *Wired's* only regular feminist, humanist, Luddite, skeptic contributor.) It stretches the bounds of logic to depict such well-informed, tech-engaged people as backwards, inept, or afraid of computers.

How did the Luddites, who were highly skilled machine operators, get saddled with a reputation as crazy technology haters? Why does their struggle still strike such a powerful chord? How does the 19th-century idea of Luddism help us understand public attitudes toward media technologies in the 21st century? What do people with qualms about digital culture have in common—or not—with those mechanical vandals of the early industrial era?

Public perceptions of the Luddite movement have gone through many stages between 1811 and the present. They have been viewed successively as local heroes, public menaces, enemies of the state, noble revolutionaries, and early archetypes of environmental and anti-globalization activists. In my view, it's time for a new stage.

For Slow, green, mindful, and sustainable approaches to media to flourish, we need to defang the rhetorical bogeyman who haunts conversations about technology use. We need to take a *Post-Luddite* turn. The critical approach that I call Post-Luddism can help uproot some of the simplistic thinking that has, to date, narrowed the range of public and policy debate about devices. This term captures the complex, diverse, and nuanced attitudes that people have toward digital culture, in contrast with the binary oppositions that we have relied upon so far: technophile vs. technophobe, techno-utopian vs. techno-dystopian, techno-optimist vs. techno-pessimist. Let's overcome the impasse with language that better conveys alternative ways of understanding how technology and society interact with each other.

I'm a Post-Luddite. You might not know it yet, but chances are excellent that you're one, too.

Luddism in the 19th Century

Sherwood Forest, 1811. The location conjures up visions of a certain mythical outlaw who championed social justice. But this is a few centuries after Robin Hood. From this same region sprang stories of another rebellious leader: Ned Ludd. The *Oxford English Dictionary* recounts a popular story—lacking confirmation—about a "person of weak intellect" named Ned Ludd (or Lud) who lived in Leicestershire around 1779. He was said to have destroyed two stocking-frames in a "fit of insane rage." Hosiery makers began using the expression "Ludd must have been here" whenever they found broken machinery. A generation later, participants in a regional labor movement adopted this persona, which was probably a collective invention that amalgamated oral legends of Ludd and Hood with real people. The spontaneous, semi-organized rebellion spread quickly across the North of England, with Luddite protestors proclaiming Sherwood Forest their base camp.

During the uprising, many people played the role of "Ned Ludd," alternately referred to as a captain, a general, and a king. A single person bearing this name likely never existed. Protestors wrote letters under the Ludd pseudonym to government officials and factory owners, marched in women's clothing as "Ludd's wives," composed ballads about his victories, and led attacks on textile mills throughout Leicestershire, Lancashire, Manchester, and Yorkshire under his banner. The Luddites seemed to be everywhere and gave the impression of being a disciplined organization, although they were neither. Yet they were colorful actors engaging in dramatic activities with a great deal of style and swagger, which gave their cause personality and attracted attention.[5]

These knitters and weavers were also destructive, of property more so than persons. Over a span of 15 months, the Luddite rebels smashed at least 500 stocking frames, spinning frames, power looms, and lacemaking machines in 44 separate guerilla-style sorties—often wearing masks or blackface. They destroyed mostly devices belonging to people whose business practices they opposed. The sabotage was initially disciplined; within the same room, machines would be smashed or spared with regard to the actions, policies, and attitudes of the particular manufacturer who owned them.[6] Within months, however, the use of violence by some Luddites escalated to the point of burning factories and threatening to kill local judges.

The British Parliament was so worried about the spread of Luddism that it passed a bill making industrial sabotage a capital crime. Authorities sent more than 13,000 soldiers to protect property and put down the uprising—more British troops than Lord Wellington had under his command in the Napoleonic Wars of that era. It was the first time the British government resorted to such a measure against domestic protestors, as well as the first time state power was mobilized to defend labor-savoring technologies.[7] In truth, the Luddites might have inflicted less violence than they encountered. Many protestors were killed by soldiers and factory owners during the attacks. Seventeen were sentenced to the gallows for their part in Luddite activities, while others were exiled to penal colonies in Australia.

The *Oxford English Dictionary* defines a Luddite as "one who opposes the introduction of new technology, especially into a place of work." Yet Luddism was not a struggle against technology. These English weavers were highly skilled machine operators, neither hostile toward technology nor inept at using it. And the devices they destroyed were not necessarily new.[8] Invented in Nottingham in 1589 and demonstrated to Queen Elizabeth I, the stocking frame had been in use for well over two centuries before the Luddite disturbances.

What's more: the idea of smashing machines did not begin or end with them, either. Destruction of employer property had been a negotiating technique of labor organizations since the 17th century. The Luddites themselves "were totally fine with machines," says scholar Kevin Binfield, in *Writings of the Luddites*.[9] "They just wanted machines that made high-quality goods, and they wanted these machines to be run by workers who had gone through an apprenticeship and got paid decent wages. Those were their only concerns." Their 19th-century response to industrial production presages 21st-century Slow values like Good and Fair.

Like the Slow movement is today, Luddism was a struggle against industrial capitalism. They fought against not machinery in general but a specific kind: "all Machinery hurtful to Commonality," as stated in a letter written by Luddites in 1812. "If the workmen dislike certain machines," explained *The Nottingham Review* in 1811, "it was because of the use to which they were being put, not because they were machines or because they were new."[10] The source of their resentment was an incipient socio-economic structure dominated by capitalist owners who used technology for their own benefit, while workers paid a steep price. Behind the Luddite rhetoric lies a more sophisticated understanding of the relationship between technology and society than many give them credit for.[11]

The conflict was not simply between pro-technology capitalism and anti-technology socialism. People of various political tendencies have pinned high hopes on technology. Early socialists viewed machines in a positive light, as a means of liberation from capitalism and as the basis of future prosperity under socialism. For Marx, technology was capitalism's contribution to human progress. Many socialists then, as now, believed that technological development would— "moving behind the backs of capitalists, without their knowledge and in defiance of their intentions"—create conditions for the eclipse of capitalism and the dawn of a new social structure.[12] They imagined that technology would work as a double agent, against its supposed masters.

Essentially, the historical Luddites were not "Luddites." Machines were just rational targets—concrete and nonhuman objects that could, for practical and moral reasons, be attacked. The Luddite objective was to resist changes in social relations and production practices—reflected and reinforced by technology— that came at workers' expense. They fought against unemployment, wage cuts, the elimination of skilled work, the lowering of product quality, and "the factory system itself, which entailed an intensification of work discipline and a loss of autonomy and control over their own labour."[13] It was a daunting challenge for a small group of artisan workers.

Heroes or Villains?

The period 1811–1816 was a time of great uncertainty in England, amid a war with France, widespread poverty, and sharp rises in the cost of food. The enclosures acts were turning huge swathes of open field that had been used for common grazing and crop rotation into inaccessible private property. Many peasants were relocating from countryside to cities, where they became factory workers in the "dark Satanic mills" of verse. (The blackening of England's skies by those mills was, incidentally, a milestone on the road to climate change.) The Luddites seem to have enjoyed sympathy from their communities at the beginning of the rebellion. Despite the government's efforts to detect Luddite activists through the use of spies and rewards for informers, few were identified.[14] A likely explanation is that people generally supported Luddism, if only through silence.

After violence increased, so did the perception that Luddites were fanatics and ruffians. Popular approval gave way over time to the official view that the movement was a mindless mob—or even terrorists.[15] Industrial managers and government officials inscribed Luddism in the public memory as destructive, naïve, and retrograde.[16] Then and since, many people have invoked a negative image of Luddism to discourage public support for labor actions. The term "Luddite" became an epithet, "a convenient device for disparaging and isolating the occasional opponent to progress and a charge to be avoided at all costs by thoughtful people."[17] "Playing the Luddite card" persists as a management strategy to delegitimize trade unions, opponents of automation, and other people concerned about jobs being deskilled or eliminated.[18] Luddism, it has been erroneously maintained, offers society little beyond social violence and cultural stagnation.

People continue to wrangle over what Luddism meant. Had the government prevented mayhem, or thwarted a movement for social change? The mid-20th century brought reappraisals of Luddites that helped revive their reputation. The rebellion was reinterpreted as a form of "collective bargaining by riot," one of the most effective means of action available to workers at the time, before the age of unionization.[19] In his landmark history *The Making of the English Working Classes*, E. P. Thompson portrays Luddites as noble, if imperfect, fighters of oppression. He concludes that the movement "was driven steadily in a more insurrectionary direction and eventually 'trembled on the edge of ulterior revolutionary objectives.'"[20] Luddism was neither a series of isolated protests nor an industrial rebellion. It was more than that: a movement for political reform that united socioeconomic critique with direct action and an alternative way of understanding technological change.

Despite losing the rebellion, the Luddites succeeded in several regards. They dared to challenge powerful forces and try to steer the course of technological change. They managed to delay the adoption of some machines, which bought the movement time to reflect and strategize. They garnered public support and awakened a political consciousness among workers, which continued to develop over the course of the 19th century. What the historical Luddites are perhaps best remembered for is *that they resisted*. They were not passive subjects of history but storytellers and myth makers. The Luddites created their own subcultural rituals of street theater, folk music, and symbolic protest—a rich legacy that persists in contemporary political activism and culture jamming. And we're still talking about them more than two centuries later.

The Rise and Fall of Neo-Luddism

Fast forward to the 1990s. People are living in a technological world very different to that of the Luddites. The Victorian era had brought the invention of lightbulbs, photography, recorded music, motion pictures, and telephones. Since the 1920s and 1930s, radio, sound movies, and television were widely popularized. By the end of the millennium, many people had adopted computers, cable and satellite TV, email, mobile phones, the Internet, and the World Wide Web. In quick succession we get webcams, instant messaging, blogs, MP3 players, smartphones, tablets along with a spectacular cascade of e-commerce and social media: Yahoo, eBay, Amazon, Napster, Google, Wikipedia, LinkedIn, Myspace, Skype, Facebook, Flickr, YouTube, Tumblr, Instagram, Spotify, and Twitter.

These media innovations might seem innocuous by comparison to other technologies of the late 20th century. The decades leading up to the 1990s were accompanied by grave concerns about nuclear power, due to recent World War II atrocities in Japan and accidents such as those at Three Mile Island (1979, US) and Chernobyl (1986, Ukraine). Rapid advances in the fields of genetic engineering, stem cell research, cloning, robotics, and nanotechnology added fuel to the techno-skeptical fire. Such developments raised deep ethical questions and posed far-reaching consequences that were (and are), to the public mind, pretty scary.

The growing malaise about technology was expressed by a psychotherapist from New Mexico in "Notes toward a Neo-Luddite Manifesto." In this 1990 article, Chellis Glendinning wrote that technology had begun "desecrating the fragile fabric of life on Earth."[21] People might think of technology as just machinery, she said, but it actually reflects a whole worldview that promotes rational thinking, efficiency, utilitarianism, scientific detachment, and the belief that humans have the right to own and dominate nature. She urged people—be they activists, workers, social critics or scholars—to challenge technological development by adopting a new way of thinking about humanity and its place in the world: Neo-Luddism.

According to Glendinning, Neo-Luddites recognize that technologies are historically embedded, politically structured, and socially constructed—not simply "the way things are." They pursue technology scaled and structured to benefit people and the planet—reflecting the "Small is Beautiful" philosophy popularized in the 1970s by E. F. Schumacher, an influential Oxford economist inspired by Gandhian ideas about self-sufficiency.[22] Through such principles, she said, new Luddites could guide society's transition toward a more sustainable future.

Neo-Luddites acknowledge both the positive and negative impacts of technology on individuals, society, and the environment, Glendinning said. Like the Old Luddites, this new variety opposes only those technologies harmful to human lives and communities. Some tools that passed muster with her vision were renewable solar, wind, and water energies. Also kosher were organic agriculture, engineering, architecture, art, medicine, and transportation. Decentralized social technologies that encourage participation, responsibility, and empowerment were also groovy. As for potentially harmful examples, she cited genetic engineering, nuclear and electromagnetic technologies, television, and computers.

Television and computers! The Neo-Luddite call for eliminating electronic media seems less drastic when you consider the cultural context of the time. Glendinning's philosophy was shaped amid vociferous debates about the influence of the boob tube, especially on children. An author named Marie Winn (known later for her chronicle of red-tail hawks living in Central Park) spurred a TV-turnoff movement among parents and educators with her popular 1977 book *The Plug-in Drug*. That year, a former advertising executive named Jerry Mander also published the seminal *Four Arguments for the Elimination of Television*, which blamed the medium for separating people from natural environments, depriving viewers of bodily senses beyond sight and sound, misrepresenting reality, centralizing knowledge, and suppressing human imagination, among other harms. He thought television was a tool of tyranny.

Another influential voice of the time was media ecologist Neil Postman. He argued eloquently that televised infotainment was debasing education, journalism, and democracy in widely read works like 1985's *Amusing Ourselves to Death*. (The title spun off into its own subgenre. Postman also proposed that we are *Informing Ourselves to Death* while writers following his example worried that we might be fatally amazing, entertaining, distracting, and mediating ourselves.) This book was a precursor to Nicholas Carr's *The Shallows* and Mark Bauerlein's *The Dumbest Generation* in claiming that new technology was reneging on its promise of making people smarter or better informed. That television and the Internet might be "programming" us, not vice versa.

Even Marshall McLuhan, the public intellectual often seen as a proselytizer for new technologies, suggested that the US should get rid of television for at least a few years, to better understand its influence. His early hope that electronic media would enlighten humanity faded as he became convinced that people are "not designed to live at the speed of light." McLuhan imagined that receiving high-speed data from around the world through an Internet-like system would make one "schizophrenic." "Without the countervailing balance of natural and physical laws, the new video-related media will make man implode upon himself," he said. "His body will remain in one place but his mind will float out into the electronic void, being everywhere at once in the data bank."[23] He foresaw not only the World Wide Web but also the possibility of information overload and the importance of a Slow, mindful ballast.

Contrary to popular misconceptions that he adored new technology, McLuhan might have been the original Neo-Luddite. In 1966 he said, "I am resolutely opposed to all innovation, all change, but I am determined to understand what's happening because I don't choose just to sit and let the juggernaut roll over me." Many people thought that he talked about new media forms because he was in favor of them. The opposite was true, in his case. The best way of opposing something is "to understand it, and then you know where to turn off the button," McLuhan explained.[24] He insisted that he had never approved of the "global village," which television allegedly created, but merely observed that we live in one.

The Neo-Luddite manifesto lamented that television gave corporations too much power to expand markets and control socio-political ideas while also breaking down family communications, narrowing life experience, and shortening attention spans.[25] A 1990 episode of *The Simpsons* reflected the era's concerns about TV's influence on children, families, and social life. When Marge Simpson leads a successful campaign to ban cartoon violence, kids stop watching "The Itchy and Scratchy Show." Instead of plopping down in front of the idiot box after school, the children of Springfield frolic outside and build go-carts and excitedly share the day's activities with their parents at dinner time. Alas, this golden age is ended by concerns about censorship (a critique that confuses television's content with its form). The status quo is restored—as sitcoms are wont to do. Such critiques of television continue to infuse public discourse about the impact of other screens on daily life.

The Neo-Luddite movement gained momentum through the 1990s. Provocative ideas flowed from an expanding network that included Mander and Postman as well as early leaders of the sustainability movement. Among them were environmental activist Bill McKibben, science historian David Noble, literary critic Sven Birkets, farmer and essayist Wendell Berry, countercultural scholar Theodore Roszak, and social theorist Langdon Winner. Postman's classic work of that era was *Technopoly: The Surrender of Culture to Technology*, which proposed that technology monopolizes our culture. In societies with a democratic ethos, relatively weak traditions, and high regard for new technologies—like in the US—people are inclined to be enthusiastic about technological change, according to Postman. Entrepreneurs, following their own economic interests, take advantage of this "native optimism" and conceal the cultural sacrifices entailed by adopting new technologies. He urged readers to refuse efficiency and speed as the preeminent goals of human relations. We have to negotiate with technology, to strike a balance between what it giveth and what it taketh away.

The role of Neo-Luddite spokesperson was assumed by Kirkpatrick Sale, author of the book *Rebels Against the Future: The Luddites and Their War Against the Industrial Revolution*. Sale's conception of new Luddism was rooted in a deep-ecology credo that people should subordinate themselves to nature and live in self-sustainable bioregions.[26] He offered a somewhat simplistic diagnosis of what ailed society (hint: it's industrial modernity) along with a primitive remedy (e.g., a return to pre-industrial communities, as epitomized by Old Order Amish groups and Native American tribes).[27]

Neo-Luddite detractors vilified these ideas. *Wired* writer Jon Katz dismissed Sale's views on technology on the basis that Sale did not own a computer (it being 1995, that wasn't so strange).[28] Katz mocked the notion that computers could have an alienating influence on people (an effect that some research supports).[29] He characterized Luddism as "a universal synonym for opposition to technology and the damage it supposedly does."[30] While admitting that the planet might be in environmental peril, he proposed that technology could just as easily save the Earth as destroy it. (One might hope that the odds of those two outcomes are not even.) Katz depicted Neo-Luddites as "xenophobes" working in mainstream media who were fighting not for their lives, as the original Luddites were, but for cultural dominance, to which digital media posed a threat. "The choice after all, is narrow: stasis versus change," he said, repeating the false dilemma commonly posed by anti-Luddites.

In a 1995 interview with Sale, *Wired* editor and co-founder Kevin Kelly also challenged Neo-Luddite theories and methods. The two disagreed on many fundamental points, including the purpose of new technologies. For Kelly (and many technophiles), it is to make higher-quality and more diverse products than can be made by hand. For Sale (and many technoskeptics), it is to save on labor costs and the attendant inconveniences associated with real people. Sale declared civilization a "catastrophe" that would end by destroying itself and the natural environment if we did not abandon all technology—an extreme view shared by a vocal minority of Neo-Luddites. He lauded the possibility of returning to oral, tribal society with virtues like comradeship and harmony—a romantic view shared by a prominent few.

Such responses to *Rebels against the Future* exemplify some of the cultural obstacles that Neo-Luddism faced in the 1990s. First, there remained a perception that Luddites were against technology—which most people familiar with Luddism know to be untrue—rather than against a socio-political structure indifferent toward their well-being. Second, there was a false polarization: you're either a (crazy) Luddite who dislikes technology or a (normal) person who blindly follows technology wherever it goes. No middle ground here. Third, there was a conflation of progress with change. The words do not have equivalent meanings, of course. Change is indeterminate and open-ended, potentially for the better or for the worse. Progress implies a certain kind of change: in a positive direction, an enlightened way forward—not just change for the sake of change. A rational person would not want to stop *all* change but would certainly steer toward positive change and avoid negative change. Fourth, the equation of technology with progress diminishes the very idea of progress; technology does not always represent progress, just as progress does not always come through technology. Fifth, technological change was viewed as a given, not as a choice that's determined by social, political, and economic forces. This proposes that human agency lies only in accepting or rejecting whatever "progress" "naturally" develops—when, in reality, the change is often a particular agenda staunchly promoted by elites.

We could, instead, define progress in ways that far exceed technological innovation. One idea: progress could be equated with nonmaterialism. On the basis of a sweeping historical analysis, Alfred Toynbee declared a "Law of Progressive Simplification," whereby civilization advances through the transfer of energy and attention from material life to nonmaterial: personal growth, relationships, music, arts, meditation, community life, personal expression, democracy. The idea of progress might even pose a danger: by telling us that the future will be better, it might create dissatisfaction with the present. It might diminish the ability of people in materially prosperous countries to enjoy everything that they already have and do, to realize that their lives are already pretty good.

Of Methods and Madmen

When Kelly interviewed Sale for *Wired*, the conversation inevitably turned to destruction as a Luddite protest tactic. Sale described how much he had enjoyed smashing a computer screen and keyboard during a recent lecture—one of his common stunts. He often pummeled computers for theatrical purposes, dressed as an 18th-century laborer. "It felt wonderful," he said. "The sound it made, the spewing of the undoubtedly poisonous insides into the spotlight, the dust that hung in the air."[31] Kelly prompted, "Violence is very powerful, isn't it?" Sale replied, "And remarkably satisfying when it is injurious to property, not people."

This dialogue offered some ominous hints about the future of the movement. "We modern-day Luddites are not, *or at least not yet*, taking up the sledgehammer and the torch and gun to resist the new machinery, but rather taking up the book and the lecture and organizing people to raise these issues," he told Kelly (emphases mine).[32] "Most of the people who would today call themselves Luddites confine their resistance, *so far at any rate*, to a kind of intellectual and political resistance." Alas. A persistent association between violence and Neo-Luddism would contribute to the movement's decline.

Yet in 1996, a new Neo-Luddite manifesto explicitly rejected violence. A "Second Luddite Congress" was convened in Ohio by the editors of *Plain*, a quarterly publication with essays by Quakers, Amish, and others about their experiences living close to the land with minimal modern technology. (The magazine's pages were hand-set and printed on an antique cylinder press running on solar power.) The meeting was intended as a symbolic descendent of an apocryphal congress held by the original Luddites. Around four hundred people attended the convention— including lots of professional activists and journalists. Some reportage focused on the beards and sandals sported by participants of the hippy, beatnik, or farmer persuasion. The gathering also attracted a wide range of rather ordinary people: college students, bankers, and grandmothers. Sale, McKibben, and astronomer/spy-tracker Clifford Stoll were there, too.

So was the shadow of the Unabomber. Ted Kaczynski was not physically present at the convocation of new Luddites, because he was in federal custody. A week before the Second Luddite Congress took place, Kaczynski had been arrested by the FBI at his remote cabin in Montana. (He later pled guilty to charges related to a 1978–1995 mail-bombing campaign, in which 16 attacks killed 3 people and injured 26 more.) Yet he exerted a grim influence on press coverage of the Neo-Luddite event and in public reception of their ideas.

Kaczynski's 35,000-word essay lamenting technology's influence on society had been printed in major newspapers shortly before his arrest.[33] In it, he argued that continued development of technology would "certainly subject human beings to greater indignities and inflict greater damage on the natural world." Industrial society was on the verge of entering "a long and very painful period of adjustment and only at the cost of permanently reducing human beings and many other living organisms to engineered products and mere cogs in the social machine." Because he saw no hope of reforming or modifying the system, he advocated a revolution—which "may or may not make use of violence"—to overthrow not governments but the economic and technological bases of society.

The concurrence of the Second Luddite Congress with Kaczynski's arrest helped sound the death knoll for Neo-Luddism. People saw parallels between the Luddite critique and the Unabomber Manifesto. Sale further raised hostility toward Neo-Luddites when he announced "the Unabomber and I share a great many views" and defended the criminal as sane and reasonable—albeit with a disclaimer that he did not approve of terrorist acts against people. (Sale was not alone in finding some validity in the Unabomber Manifesto. Kevin Kelly of *Wired* called it "one of the most astute analyses" of technological systems he had ever read, though he disagreed, as Sale did, with the conclusion.) An impression lingered that Neo-Luddites who publicly agreed with Kaczynski's concerns about technology might privately condone his violent methods of attracting publicity to the cause.

Turning toward the Environment and Globalization

Still, the dream of Neo-Luddism persisted into the 21st century. While inspired by the courageous defiance of their historical kin, the ideology of this new generation of Luddites diverged from the old one in several ways. Three major developments in Neo-Luddite philosophy that deserve close consideration are an opposition to violent action (especially against people), an embrace of environmental issues, and an alignment with the democratic-globalization movement.

As regards interpersonal violence, Kaczynski acted alone in targeting people and his actions were broadly rejected by the Neo-Luddite community. However, the Luddite tradition of violence against property was emulated by various tech critics through the 1990s. Some deep ecologists in groups like Earth First! and the Earth Liberation Front supported the destruction of property as a form of civil disobedience or "eco-sabotage." That stream of radical thought and direct action was promoted in the 1970s by people like Edward Abbey, author of *The Monkeywrench Gang*, a novel about eco-saboteurs who want to blow up a dam. Activist Dave Foreman wrote a book called *Ecodefense: A Field Guide to Monkeywrenching* that describes how to destroy billboards, sabotage computers, and disable machines used to harm the environment. (The practice of eco-sabotage has largely fallen out of favor.) Then there's Green anarchist John Zerzan, who struck up a correspondence with Kaczyinski and shared some of his views about technology, while criticizing his methods. Foreman and Zerzan both linked themselves to the Neo-Luddite cause.

Environmentalism has taken center stage in the Neo-Luddite critique. The historical Luddites have sometimes been portrayed as proto-environmentalists, but there's no evidence that they were concerned about ecological degradation— despite living in the same time and place as Romantic poets who lauded green and pleasant lands. The new Luddite protest "against technology" arose in the wake of the 1960s counterculture, back-to-the-land philosophies, the rise of organic practices, reappraisals of indigenous cultures, and the growth of environmental movements. This eco-zeitgeist was memorably captured in commercials from 1971, launched to coincide with Earth Day. Many adults will recall the image of an "Indian chief" with tears streaming down his cheeks as he looked upon roadside litter. The ads were part of a nonprofit campaign to beautify the US by discouraging people from throwing trash out their car windows and encouraging community clean-ups and something called "recycling"—which was a novel idea then.[34]

Neo-Luddism arose at the end of the 20th century, when people were becoming more acutely aware of ecological threats like pollution as well as the cumulative effects of automobiles, factories, and fossil fuels. The 1980s brought discussions about a newly discovered hole in the ozone layer that makes Earth habitable and about the growing problem of acid rain, which harms plants and fish while also corroding bridges and buildings. In this era, terms like "greenhouse gas" and "global warming" entered public discourse and climate change went mainstream. Environmentalists are often called "Luddites" as well as socialists and Marxists.[35] (Green has been deemed not only "the new black," signifying that it's fashionable or trendy, but also "the new red," meaning socialist or communist.)

Accordingly, new Luddites paid closer attention to the relationship between technology and the ecosystem than their forebears had. Glendinning's manifesto employed phrases like *ecological balance, planetary biology, the benefit of life on Earth*, and *nature's wholeness*. Capitalist societies had heretofore taken advantage of nature and viewed the earth's treasures as a bountiful resource. An economy not grounded in an understanding of the natural world will wreak havoc "in indiscriminate and ultimately unsustainable ways," Sale said.[36] Neo-Luddism proposed that principles of social justice, ecological harmony, and personal dignity—which are associated today with sustainability and Slow values like Clean and Fair— should guide technological change, not efficiency and profit.

The increasingly interdependent world of the 1990s differed in significant political-economic ways to pre-industrial England: the outsourcing and offshoring of jobs, the seeming decline of state sovereignty vis-a-vis multinational corporations, the persistence of military actions driven by oil dependency. Alliances grew between Neo-Luddites and the anti-free trade and democratic-globalization (a.k.a. anti-globalization or global-justice) movements. Many activists reframed their enemy as neoliberalism or laissez-faire capitalism more so than new technology. The Internet's usefulness as a means of communicating and organizing dissent might have softened their criticism. Yet they remained concerned that globalization gave too much power over tech decision-making to unaccountable institutions. The 1999 "Battle in Seattle" protesting the World Trade Organization echoed the Luddite legacy of direct action, street theater and, to a lesser extent, property destruction.

Jerry Mander, the former adman-turned-TV-opponent, bolstered Neo-Luddism when he founded the International Forum on Globalization (IFG), in response to passage of the North American Free Trade Agreement in 1994. One serious problem with computers, according to Mander, is that they enable multinational corporations to operate.[37] IFG urges public discussion of policies that support local economies and ecological stability. The group has held events featuring writers and activists like McKibben, Jeremy Rifkin, Ralph Nader, Winona La Duke, Langdon Winner, and Vandana Shiva (an IFG board member) that bring together people from the environmental, civil rights, labor, peace, indigenous, and anti-globalization movements. These groups share concerns about many issues, including the risk of letting a small number of corporations use the Internet to consolidate economic and political power.

According to one conservative correspondent, a 2001 IFG teach-in in New York City marked the birth of an organized Neo-Luddite movement. Anti-globalization activism lost a lot of its energy after September 11 of that same year, however, as protestors were increasingly marginalized as potential "terrorists." The power of international agencies like the World Bank and International Monetary Fund, which had been major targets of globalization critics, also began to wane in the new millennium. The IFG and its sympathizers drew closer to the sustainability movement and stopped flying the Neo-Luddite flag. The Occupy Wall Street protests of 2011 gave new voice to many issues from the Neo-Luddite agenda, but the days in which people eagerly identified themselves as Luddites were drawing to a close.

Beyond Redemption?

Whatever the historical Luddites might have achieved, their revolt had a decidedly mixed effect on public discussions about technology. This ambiguous influence has lasted. One failure of Luddism, some say, was that it did not spark a true debate.[38] "The Luddite strategy in the 19th century was not debated and found lacking," the historian Noble explains in *Progress Without People*.[39] "Rather, it was condemned as dangerous and demented, as were all those who identified themselves with it. So too with latter-day Luddites." Their besmirched reputation has impeded meaningful discussion about their goals and actions. To participate in this conversation and be taken seriously, one is now expected to demonstrate allegiance to technological progress wherever it might lead.

The Luddite banner deserves to be hoisted anew, and I hope this book makes a contribution to doing so. Yet the meanings of Luddite and Neo-Luddite might be muddied beyond redemption. The negative connotations are perhaps too entrenched, the misperceptions too pervasive. People use these words now to describe anyone who is inept or ignorant in realms of life beyond technology, who fails to keep up with fads and fashion. People have poked fun at themselves for being "Luddite" because they don't understand what "infused drinks" are or cannot walk in high heels.[40] A Luddite or Neo-Luddite label remains a badge of honor for very few. It is more often considered an insult or a joke.

Exhibit A: "The Luddite Awards," which deride people who resist change. They are meant to dishonor recipients, not commend them—akin to the Darwin Awards, which ridicule people who have killed or maimed themselves by doing stupid things. Awardees include Stephen Hawking, Elon Musk, and Steve Wozniak, for supporting a ban on "killer robots"—autonomous weapons that select and destroy targets without human intervention—that was proposed by a large community of artificial-intelligence researchers. Other nominees have included governments that regulate the so-called sharing economy; that mandate labeling of genetically modified foods; that restrict the use of license-plate readers and red-light cameras; and that oppose putting RFIDs in driver's licenses. People who support Net Neutrality and privacy protections for online health records have also been singled out for opprobrium.

The Luddite Awards are a PR stunt, launched by a think tank advocating for neoliberal economic policies, the Information Technology and Innovation Foundation (ITIF). The group cloaks its free-market ideology in terms with positive connotations such as *innovation, progress*, and *freedom*.[41] These awards perpetuate fallacies that Luddites were "against technology" and that people who question the socio-economic consequences of technical innovations are trying to "block progress." ITIF makes the sweeping, erroneous claim that all Luddism is driven by "the general longing for a simpler life from the past—a life with fewer electronics, chemicals, molecules, machines, etc."[42] It claims that Luddites have gone mainstream, "infecting" public discourse with tech-related concerns about job losses or environmental damage. The awards try to publicly shame intelligent people with legitimate objections to technological development.

There's another way to interpret the Luddite Awards, though. It doesn't need to be taken as an insult. Recipients could salute the heroic dimension of Luddism. Great minds like Hawking, Musk, and Wozniak could take pride in being tagged as rational, influential resisters of technology "harmful to the commonality." We could attempt to re-valorize the word, to give it a positive connotation.

Is it too late for that? Like it or not, the rhetorical offense against Luddism has effectively trapped the opposition and blocked meaningful discussion. Stereotypes do not die easily. Here we find ourselves in a new millennium, reassuring the world that we are "not Luddite" even when expressing relatively tepid criticisms of media technology. People widely agree that we need a new critical perspective on the complex relationship between social structure and technologies—especially of media and communication—that can provide the basis for effective intervention.

I'm not entirely ready to give up on the old perspective.

Going Post-Luddite

The quest for alternatives to commercial capitalism loomed large in Neo-Luddite criticism. For many sustainability thinkers, the idealistic society depicted in the 1975 novel *Ecotopia* served as a touchstone. In Ernest Callenbach's sci-fi tale, residents of the Pacific Northwest secede from the US and build a new nation where humans live in harmony with nature and individuals are encouraged to realize their full creative potential. In doing so, they are guided by an amalgam of Green, anarcho-syndicalist, and libertarian principles (with echoes of the "free" Anarresti society in Ursula LeGuin's 1974 novel *The Dispossessed*). Notably, the inhabitants of this utopia accept and use technology, so long as it supports human and environmental well-being. *Ecotopia* proposed not a return to wilderness but a new type of enlightened consumerism that accommodated environmental concerns, social politics, and individual creativity.

Another Neo-Luddite classic that influenced the movement was Mander's book *In the Absence of the Sacred: The Failure of Technology and the Survival of Indian Nations*. To him, the subtitular themes logically follow one another. To other people, it might sound like a nonsequitur. What does technology's failure have to do with Native Americans' survival? Some Neo-Luddites believed that the way of the future was small-scale and self-sufficient societies resembling indigenous tribes, "bioregions" like Ecotopia, or Amish and Mennonite societies.

While this vision might have some appeal, it has not been widely welcomed. Most people view such alternative prospects as unrealistic or undesirable and such ideals as nostalgic, clichéd, or simplistic. Many indigenous peoples enjoy the blessings of modernity and tolerate its burdens, like the rest of us, just as many Old Order communities choose to use mobile phones and other technologies that benefit their communities. A vigorous discussion about Luddism featuring more diverse voices might yield, instead, visions for a hybridized culture that infuses modernity with sustainable values—low-carbon lifestyles, deeper relationships with nature, stewardship of local ecosystems.

The future proposed by some Neo-Luddites and early sustainability activists skewed anti-urban. Many modern people who might otherwise sympathize with Luddism do not share this dream of returning to rural life or pre-industrial society. The majority might not want to live (at least not permanently) in a yurt, farmhouse, or cabin in the woods. I grew up in Pennsylvania Amish country, accustomed to the sight of horses and buggies. I admire the decision to live plainly and hope that alternative remains feasible. But it's not the choice for me. Many sustainability-minded people are working to realize the potential of well-scaled urban environments, which offer opportunities to use natural resources efficiently as well as strengthen human communities.

In sum: early iterations of the Neo-Luddite project were deeply conservative and fundamentalist—what Kevin Robins and Frank Webster call "a fossilized Luddism."[43] In reality, most people sympathetic toward Luddism "just want to reduce or control the technology that is all around us and to question its utility, to force us not to take digital media for the water in which we swim," they say. This analysis of the 1990s movement is instructive about what a resuscitated Luddism could become. Twenty-first century Luddites deserve a more constructive, sophisticated, and progressive vision for society.

Some facets of Luddism could be recovered to help people critically respond to their post-industrial gadgets, as Richard Byrne proposes. He thinks that repressed Luddite principles of mass rebellion and economic justice could be unleashed to promote a new set of values. Judging by "the ferocity of Luddism's hold on the imagination of the tech class, there may be yet some organizing principle and power in the concept," opined the journalist, poet, and playwright.[44] It's true that people with political, economic, and cultural power seem a bit afraid of Luddism, if only because they make such a point of disdaining it. It makes you think that even a watered-down version could have great power to inspire people and provoke change.

Sensible people have for too long accepted the terms of debate set by those who distort Luddism to suit their own interests. Instead, we could dump the historical baggage and change those terms by adopting new rhetoric inspired by Luddite courage and imagination. A moderate Luddite movement could be unquestionably, unapologetically forward-looking. No romanticization of noble savages and happy peasants here. We could reclaim a middle ground between unbridled acceptance of technology and the unpopular fantasy of rejecting it. I hazard to guess that Neo-Luddites and anti-Luddites represent the extreme fringes of public sentiment. The true and heretofore silent majority is *Post-Luddite*.

Luddism and Neo-Luddism tend to be defined by negatives, by what they stand against (to wit: technology, capitalism, progress, modernity, industrial civilization). This emphasizes their *criticism*, which has a primary meaning of "expressing disapproval or finding fault" that sounds more pessimistic than its secondary one: "evaluating or making careful judgements." Tech critics are more often viewed as faultfinders, not careful evaluators. Neo-Luddite discussion also focused on *resistance*—which can mean "a refusal to accept something new or different"; it can also mean, more hopefully, "an effort made to prevent something from having an effect." (We can all agree that the French resistance was a good thing.) Not to mention *skepticism*, which in common usage tends to imply negation, "an attitude of doubting the truth of a claim or statement" whereas technology critics often use it in a more open-ended way, meaning "a doctrine or method of suspending judgment" until the case is made and evidence is presented. The vocabulary of criticism, resistance, and skepticism amplifies a public perception that Luddites are grumpy, stubborn whiners.

It's instructive to look at the language used by Postman, who was frequently labeled a Luddite. In *Technopoly*, he encouraged readers to become "loving resistance fighters" through oppositional actions such as *refusing, being suspicious, not confusing, not regarding*. Refuse to accept efficiency as the pre-eminent goal of human relations, Postman advised. Be suspicious of the idea of progress. Do not confuse information with understanding. Do not regard the aged as irrelevant. Some rare permissive language sneaks into his rules: *Free yourself* from the belief in the magical power of numbers. *Take religion seriously*, not just science. *Admire technological ingenuity* but do not think it represents the highest possible form of human achievement.

By contrast, Post-Luddism could be characterized by positives, optimism, and flexibility. By what it stands *for*, not against. I propose laying ground rules for a more productive and inclusive conversation with the following nine principles, which resound with Slow and sustainable values:

1. Post-Luddites are progressive: learning from the past, acting in the present, looking toward the future.
2. Post-Luddites ask questions that show healthy ambivalence toward technological change.
3. Post-Luddites encourage nonviolent activism that seeks purposeful uses of technology.
4. Post-Luddites employ technologies to promote human well-being, community health, economic justice, political freedom, individual dignity, and the public interest.
5. Post-Luddites support technological development guided by a sense of stewardship toward and respect for plants, animals, and the natural environment.
6. Post-Luddites recognize that people control technological change and seek wider participation in deciding its direction.
7. Post-Luddites understand that diversity, contradiction, and complexity are essential features of social life and technology use.
8. Post-Luddites foster open-minded discussion about the social, cultural, economic, and political consequences of technologies.
9. Post-Luddites advance ecological and social sustainability based on long-term principles of stability and cooperation.

These general principles are intended to create common ground from which to launch discussion. It's up to us to determine the content of conversations, which goals to pursue, and which strategies to deploy. What machinery today is "hurtful to commonality"? What changes in social relations and production practices wrought by technology are primarily benefitting the few? How can we use technology for broader public benefit? As a society, are we willing to say "no" to some technologies? If so: which ones, and how do we constrain them? Should we adopt some of Wendell Berry's criteria: that new technologies be cheaper and better than the ones they replace, use less energy, support local economies, be repairable (or at least durable), and sustain existing community relationships? Maybe. Let's talk about it.

Getting Real about Technology Criticism

Confession to make: this isn't the first time that someone has proposed a Post-Luddite movement. Except then, it wasn't called Post-Luddism. In 1998, a trio of tech experts penned a manifesto to call attention to the consequences of new technologies and generate a conversation not polarized or paralyzed by extremist voices. The three authors—David Shenk, Andrew Shapiro, and Steve Johnson—had credentials as a tech journalist, cyberlaw pioneer, and online publisher, respectively. Their declaration was endorsed by more than a thousand people, including experts in digital culture like Borsook, Douglas Rushkoff, Simson Garfinkel, Howard Rheingold, Steve Silberman, and Mitch Kapor. This ensemble had been involved with *Wired* in its mid-90s heyday, worked at the Xerox Palo Alto Research Center, hung out with cyberpunks, edited *Whole Earth Review* and *Feed*, studied at MIT Media Lab, contributed to *MIT Technology Review*, created the software program Lotus 1-2-3, and cofounded the Electronic Frontier Foundation. One would be at pains to characterize them as against technology.

They dubbed this stance "Technorealism" and positioned it smack-dab in the middle of dichotomies like techno-utopianism/-dystopianism, techno-optimism/-pessimism and techno-philia/-phobia. "We can be passionately optimistic about some technologies, skeptical and disdainful of others," read the Technorealism Document. "Our goal is neither to champion nor dismiss technology, but rather to understand it and apply it in a manner more consistent with basic human values."[45] Society should assess the implications of technologies, they asserted, "so that we might all have more control over the shape of our future." Technorealists aimed to foster a shift in dialogue away from loud voices at the extremes and toward a deeper, more nuanced understanding of the role technologies play in society. They believed that the silent majority could reach a consensus if noisy "pundits, politicians and self-appointed visionaries" stopped dominating the discussion.

Technorealism never quite coalesced into a movement. The eight-point statement got lots of press coverage, resulting partly from a high-profile launch event at Harvard Law School. It also garnered criticism, focusing on the supposed obviousness of Technorealistic principles, which included that the Internet is revolutionary, but not utopian. Information is not knowledge. Cyberspace is not a separate jurisdiction from Earth. Wiring the schools will not save them. Government has a role to play on the electronic frontier. To the layperson, these ideas might sound like common sense, especially with the benefit of hindsight. Those principles were not so apparent at the time, however—especially in light of the prevailing Silicon Valley attitude of techno-libertarianism. (Even today, groups like the Luddite Award-bestowing ITIF insist that the government should play no role in developing or regulating new technologies—ignoring the fact that it always has and still does.) In online discussions about Technorealism, "the libertarians came out in force, monopolizing the discussion, pounding their shoes on the table as they have been in the habit of doing for so long," Borsook explains.[46] The loudest speakers clung to their microphones.

The idea of Technorealism found a small, welcoming audience among the converted but failed to take off with the broader public. Maybe critics were correct to consider its principles bland or uninspiring. The very name seems uncontroversial. It's hard to argue either for or against realism. A better question might be: Why do we need Post-Luddism, if we already have Technorealism? First, Post-Luddism and Technorealism are circles on a Venn diagram. They overlap, but they don't occupy the same space. Second, the latter—which never managed to capture the popular imagination— is unlikely to start doing so any time soon. Identifying oneself with the cause of techno-realism lacks romantic appeal. Indeed, "realism" hardly sounds like a cause at all.

On the other hand, try saying "I'm a Post-Luddite." By declaring this affinity, you are likely to at least start a conversation, if not spark a little controversy. In adopting Post-Luddism, you can imagine placing yourself in the lineage of a bold movement that stood up for its own interests, that put words into action. None of the first-wave Technorealists have described themselves as Post-Luddites, as far as I know. Several of them have already—perhaps unwittingly—supported this unrealized philosophy through their words and deeds. Here's a roster of media educators, researchers, and commentators who would make ideal envoys of Post-Luddism, not to mention Slow Media.

Paragons of Post-Luddism

First, there's Douglas Rushkoff. The best-selling author and media theorist built his reputation in the 1990s as a cyberpunk evangelizing for the Internet's liberating power. His enthusiasm seemed so boundless, he was even branded a "techno-hustler."[47] Now Rushkoff thinks digital media have begun to oppress human lives. On the podcast "Team Human," he interviews people like Richard Maxwell (*Greening the Media*), David Sax (*The Revenge of Analog*), Micah Sifry (co-founder of the Personal Democracy Forum), and Micah White (former *Adbusters* editor who co-launched the Occupy movement while shunning social media) who share a vision of optimizing technology for human prosperity and values, not for economic growth in a speculative marketplace.

A proponent of coding literacy, Rushkoff worries that people don't understand or thinking critically enough about digital technologies. In *Program or Be Programmed*, he advises readers to "Live in person" and "Do not always be on." He has also espoused secular Sabbaths as a way of reclaiming time from work and commerce. You don't have to "retreat to the backwoods, purchase generators, and live off the land," he said. Just don't answer the phone, go online, or spend money for a while. Rushkoff also participated in a 2014 IFG teach-in on the theme of "Techno-Utopianism and the Fate of the Earth," which signals a promising alliance between the tech team and the sustainability crew.

Another signatory of the Technorealism credo was Howard Rheingold. An educator and long-time proponent of social networking, he once hoped virtual communities and smart mobs would revolutionize society. He even disclaims "I don't want anyone to mistake this for an orthodox Neo-Luddite rant," in a blog post describing his "seduction by high-tech tools."[48] Yet Rheingold glimpses a Faustian bargain through the cracks of his technophiliac worldview. In 2012 he found himself questioning so-called progress: "Where are we going? Do we want to go there? Is there anything we can do about it?"[49] He wonders, when reaching for his smartphone, "Why not stay disconnected for just a minute and see what happens?" (Just one minute? Well, it's a start.) He, too, thinks people could be more critical of technology "without running off to the woods." Rheingold recommends that people get "net smart" and use digital media more mindfully.

Add to this list Sherry Turkle, who upholds an attitude akin to Post-Luddism and Technorealism: a state of mind called *realtechnik*. She describes it as a balanced perspective that avoids triumphalist or apocalyptic visions of technology, that reflects skepticism about progress, and that cherishes "the things we hold inviolate." In the well-regarded book *Alone Together: Why We Expect More of Technology and Less from Each Other*, the MIT professor observed that "We have to find a way to live with seductive technology and make it work to our purposes. . . . Simple love of technology is not going to help. Nor is a Luddite impulse."[50] We must love our technology enough to describe it accurately, and we must love ourselves enough to confront technology's true effects on us. She urges people to reject the pace that machines suggest to us, create space for face-to-face conversations, protect ourselves against media interruptions, and avoid walking into every situation with a device in hand.

There's also Jaron Lanier, a Silicon Valley veteran who urged people to distance themselves from devices in the book-cum-manifesto *You Are Not a Gadget: A Manifesto*. Lanier considers the Luddite label a red herring. "The colleagues I disagree with often conceive our discussions as being a contest between a Luddite (who, me?) and the future," wrote the virtual-reality pioneer.[51] "The debate should be about how to best identify and act on whatever freedoms of choice we still have, not about who's the Luddite." Lanier, who has been described as a hippy "sans the technophobia and back-to-the-land nostalgia," offers proof that being a tech insider gives one a useful rhetorical position in this debate.[52] Analysts deemed him "hardly a Luddite" and found his critique intriguing precisely because he is not "your ordinary Luddite crank."[53] Being "not a Luddite" works.

Public intellectuals with credentials like these are perfectly situated to steer the conversation about Post-Luddism. Plenty of other people could add their voices to the chorus, too. You don't have to be in the tech vanguard to join the Post-Luddite ranks. As I have demonstrated throughout this book, a wide spectrum of people who work intensely with digital media have similar viewpoints: authors, actors, bloggers, filmmakers, journalists, artists, marketers, and more. What makes this phenomenon so robust is the fact that many people who appreciate the power and promise of digital technology are independently arriving at the conclusion: we should use it more Slowly, more sustainably, more wisely.

Moving the Conversation Forward

When I created my Slow Media blogging project, people thought it endlessly ironic that I was using a digital form to explore the prospects of a less-mediated life. If so, then it's also ironic that the Slow Media, Slow Books, and Sabbath manifestos were originally proposed online. It's paradoxical that I'm doing Internet research about people trying to get away from the Internet. It's incongruous that #unplug and #deleteFacebook trended in the Twitterverse. When you take a Post-Luddite viewpoint, this interpretation shifts. The response is no longer "How ironic!" but "Obviously."

The lens of Post-Luddism offers refreshing perceptual payoffs. The choice we face is not declaring ourselves for or against some monolithic, all-powerful enemy called "technology." The old love-it-or-leave-it framework assumed that it was disingenuous for anyone with the slightest complaint about technology to admit using it. There's also a big catch-22 here. If people with misgivings about technology fail to sufficiently demonstrate their allegiance to technological "progress," their ideas are rejected as "Luddite." Yet once they do establish their bona fides, their ideas are still subject to dismissal on the basis of inconsistency. If you have such a problem with technology, someone inevitably argues, then you are a hypocrite for using it.

One of my main goals in this book is to help subvert false or binary choices about digital media use. However, the larger problem is whether individuals still have any choice. Generation X might have been the last for whom decisions about how, when, or if to use digital media remained a matter of personal preference. Our choices regarding technology have narrowed decisively: do we opt to use digital devices *all* of the time, or *most* of the time? At the individual level, many Post-Luddites are just looking for a dimmer switch on technology; they don't want to leave the light on full-blast. (Much the same is true of Slow Media advocates; they just don't want to go full-speed all the time.) At the collective level, Post-Luddites ponder why that light shines on certain things instead of others and whether the light should be powered by new sources—not only renewable energy, but also democratic decision-making.

This middle ground can be incredibly fertile. I struggled over whether to put some individuals on this dream team of Post-Luddites because they had shown little skepticism in past musings about the digital revolution. Rushkoff, Rheingold, Lanier, Turkle . . . they have sometimes sounded like true believers. Maybe they still are. Maybe their stance is not quite apprehensive or ambivalent enough. Maybe their analyses are less reliable by virtue of having changed over time. For not making it entirely clear which side they're on. In fact, these are exactly the qualities that got them on the list. That make their analyses *more* reliable. Post-Luddites are willing to change their minds in response to new subjective experiences and new external realities.

Rheingold, for one, describes how his outlook on digital media evolved over the years. "The online culture has changed. I've changed," he says. "While still a devotee, I'm now aware and wary of the rat holes, hidden biases, unwholesome interchanges, and delusions of grandeur that can plague online culture."[54] He believes that people can temper their ardor for technology with critical thinking, that they can make nuanced choices beyond complete support or total skepticism. Like him, Post-Luddites can hold two opposing thoughts in their minds, sequentially and simultaneously. Media technologies do good, and media technologies do harm. As Malcolm Gladwell says, "If you don't contradict yourself on a regular basis, you're not thinking."[55] The post-Luddite mind not only tolerates a little contradictory thinking, it welcomes it.

7

Conclusion

Toward a Sustainable Future

> In order to bring about social change, we must change ourselves; but we cannot change ourselves without promoting changes in others and in our institutions. At stake for this personal/public politics is time—how we spend our brief passage on earth, not hurriedly but with heart.
> —Ben Agger, *Speeding Up Fast Capitalism*[1]

Few could have predicted two decades ago that Slow Food visions of the good life would inspire such innovative thinking about how our media choices affect fellow human beings and the planet that we share.

It's remarkable that food theory captured the public imagination at a time when many other critical approaches fell short, as Ben Agger observed. Like me, he visualized a new stage of civilization where media could be used to slow down our lives, redefine human progress, and pursue greater harmony with nature. In advocating for what he called "slowmodernity," he refused to make the false choice between a Luddite retreat (slow) and a digitized utopia (fast). Instead, we should be free to move at variable paces, "going back and moving forward, mastering time so that it serves us, not the other way around," he said. "We must break the clocks, resisting and refusing the quickening of our lives. We must not allow ourselves to be overscheduled, hurried, hassled; we must take our sweet time, dawdling in order to slow down the flow."[2] Political protest and cultural reform emerge together from a theoretical understanding of fast capitalism.

The word "Slow" describes a complex range of responses to our media-saturated world. As this book has described, seven principles of media use and production could guide us toward greater human well-being and ecological health: Slow Media are *good, clean, fair, mindful, post-Luddite, progressive, collective,* and *democratic.* Slow reform does not call for universal slowdown; it contends only that we need a meaningful counterpoint to speed. People can, and do, use fast digital technologies in the service of Slow culture. With environmental crises demanding urgent action, any media are fair play if they foster deliberation, build movements, organize alternative communities, and enable sustainable lifestyles.

For more than a decade, people have been calling for a Slow Media movement. When Carl Honoré was doing research for *In Praise of Slowness* in 2003, a Google search for "slow movement" yielded no results. In 2018, there were millions. "Every week I get an e-mail from a student wanting to write his or her thesis on slow cities or slow design," he told *The New York Times*. However, a sustained movement for Slow Media has yet to coalesce. That's one reason why I've written this book.

Slow Food qualifies as a bona fide social movement, because it is informed by a coherent political philosophy and led by a multifaceted organization. However, Slow Media and the broader Slow phenomenon are typically described as "alternative lifestyles" and an "interestingly mixed bag of (generally local) initiatives across mostly Western societies."[3] Efforts to make media more sustainable and to reassert individual control over pace of life get an enormous boost from being rhetorically associated with an established movement like Slow Food. Going against the grain is not easy, as Slow scholars Maggie Berg and Barbara Seeber point out. Using the language of Slow is important, they say, because "knowing that there is a global movement for slowing down can fuel us."[4] It creates a like-minded community and gives people the sense that we're part of something big and important.

The question remains: Is Slow Media a counterculture or subculture? Is it the dawning of a real movement? A paradigm shift? A passing fad? A pleasant fantasy? The short answer is that Slow Media qualifies as a movement in the popular sense of the word: a series of actions and endeavors by people working toward a shared goal. Countless people perceive Slow Media as either a de facto movement, or an embryonic one that they hope will grow. The long answer is that it needs to develop in several regards to become a movement of consequence.

Like cultural creatives and other participants in the sustainability movement, Slow Medians represent a broad, decentralized coalition pursuing a wide range of goals through a variety of actions—which makes it hard to see. There is no voice or face associated with Slow Media that's as recognizable as Carlo Petrini or Alice Waters are with Slow Food. The movement promotes a subtle, complex form of political activity that lies beyond conventional party affiliation or protest action. Slow Media has no formal organization, no defined objectives, or a distinct collective identity—yet.

This presents a problem and an opportunity. To solidify into a meaningful movement, Slow Media needs to progress on four fronts: individual social sustainability (as explored in chapter 5), individual environmental sustainability (as discussed in chapter 4), collective social sustainability (as touched upon in chapter 2), and collective environmental sustainability (as introduced in chapter 3). Personal choices related to media use are a sensible place to start.

What can *you* do to further the cause of Slow Media, as a citizen, student, colleague, and consumer? Good news: you don't have to go live in the woods (unless, of course, you want to). Just make time for enjoying print and analog media, as well as unmediated experiences. Experiment with vintage techniques that will stretch and exercise your brain, like Slow Reading, Slow Listening, keeping a paper journal, or navigating by map. Be mindful about the email you send, check messages less frequently, and turn off alerts to the extent possible. Develop habits like breathing, monotasking, and taking breaks whenever you use fast media. Set some parameters for building Slow intervals into your schedule, even for a few hours. You could also practice empathy for people whose media habits, schedules, lifestyles, and tempos might differ from your own.

That's the easy part. Then there's becoming a green media consumer and citizen, which means recognizing that media use and production involves limits and that planetary resources are finite. Resist buying media that you don't need and reuse what you can. Consume media products and services from companies that follow sustainable practices. Support people who produce magazines, journalism, films, websites, and other media products in ethical ways. Dispose of digital devices responsibly. To do all this, learn some basics of environmental science and become comfortable with a new vocabulary of consumption.[5] Get familiar with processes that take place invisibly behind your screens. Do some research (using resources like Greenpeace's Click Clean Reports and GoodElectronics' website, as well as references listed at the end of this book).

The Slow perspective encourages us to challenge our assumptions about media choices, to look beyond speed, and to imagine alternatives that enhance both sustainability and free will. Small changes in everyday practices can make a difference, when enough of us make them in unison. Yet media use is more than a matter of personal choice. People will find it difficult to change their own media habits without advocating for changes in other people and institutions. Individual actions are necessary but insufficient to solve what is fundamentally a systemic problem. Getting to a new level of civilization will require comprehensive social and cultural changes—particularly ones that give people more control over their own time and pace. Slow Media has great potential to transform everyday lives if its advocates start taking the politics of time seriously.

Ain't Nobody Got Time for That

In the 1950s, theorists of post-industrial society predicted that as technology advanced, people would spend less time working. By 2000, Americans worked longer hours than they had in the 1960s *despite* an 80% increase in labor productivity that could have reduced work hours by at least half. "Advanced" economies like the US require families to have two earners, working longer hours, to pay the bills. On top of this, information technologies enable people to take their work home. Instead of freeing us from labor, technology gave companies new opportunities for making money. There's a paradox here: people who live surrounded by supposedly time-saving technologies frequently feel that they do not have enough time.

Ruth Schwartz Cowan writes about such ironies in *More Work for Mother,* a classic work of women's history. She examines how household tasks expanded over the course of the 20th century, alongside industrialization. As new technologies like electrical wiring, indoor plumbing, vacuum cleaners, and laundry machines spread, it became possible to keep houses, bodies, and clothing cleaner. Social standards rose, and people began washing things more frequently. Of course, "people" usually means "women."[6] Households began to need two incomes to pay for all the modern conveniences to which people had become accustomed. Voila, the Superwoman Syndrome. As Cowan observes, home computing added to this repertoire.

Networked technology has also created "shadow work," things that used to be done for us that we now do ourselves—booking flights, scanning groceries, pumping gas, managing retirement funds. People used to get paid to do these things; now we do them ourselves for free. Performing these tasks purportedly makes them more effective and cheaper (at least, for service and product providers who can operate with fewer employees and less overhead by adopting new technologies), while shifting the cost of labor—*time*—to you and me. By some estimates, we spend five hours a week doing things that used to be done for us.[7]

While we enjoy the benefits of technologies, we don't need to "succumb entirely to the work processes that they have ordained for us," Cowan argued. We can extricate ourselves from those processes not "by destroying the technological systems with which (this work is) associated but by revising the unwritten rules that govern the system." Our rising standards of perpetual cleanliness prefigured our heightened expectations of constant mediation. Maybe we don't need our lives to be so sterile or so connected. Maybe we could rewrite the unwritten rules.

Many women and men find great fulfillment in their work. They enjoy having a haven from home and family. Yet the degree of satisfaction that people get from their jobs varies widely—depending on what kind of work they do, under what conditions, for how many hours, with what compensation. So it is with media use, which can feel like work or play or both. Likewise, the quality and quantity of gratification that people get from using digital media is incredibly personal and contextual.

Because everyone lives in an idiosyncratic media matrix, we should be wary of projecting our own experiences onto others. Your media choices—among an enormous range of apps, programs, platforms, devices, networks—depend on your life circumstances: how old you are, the nature of your job, whether you have a family, how old your kids are, your friends' and parents' and employers' and kids' communications preferences, whether you live in an urban or suburban or rural area, and much more. Just as we respect differing beliefs about politics or religion, we could appreciate and accommodate various stances toward media technologies, including both fast and Slow ones.[8]

On the whole, it would be a boon to social and environmental sustainability if people worked less, including on nights and weekends through digital mediation. It would benefit humans by creating more jobs, by spreading work more evenly across society. Many stressed-out professionals bemoan changes in the Fair Labor Standards Act that redefined low-level supervisors as "exempt" employees who no longer qualify for overtime pay. This reclassification erased the 40-hour work week for millions of US workers and required them to work more hours without receiving more pay. Sixty-hour work weeks are pervasive, especially among knowledge workers (and professors, like me). It also squashed opportunities for people to make extra money by moonlighting. Who has the time and energy for a second job, when the first one is so demanding?[9]

Just as importantly, it would benefit the environment if working hours, both mediated and unmediated, were shorter. When we work more hours, we have a bigger ecological footprint. We spend more money, and we spend it more carelessly. Overworked people have less time to engage in low-consumption activities like gardening and cooking. When we can't find time to grow our own food, go to the farmer's market, or make dinner from scratch, we instead get food delivered, drive to a restaurant, or eat packaged, processed meals.[10] We buy things on the Internet because we can't get to local stores, whose owners might be more connected with their neighborhoods and whose resources might be directed toward community well-being.

As labor productivity goes up, societies have to choose between consuming more and working less. If the income gains from productivity growth were more broadly shared, living standards could remain the same. (In the U.S., however, two-thirds of the gains from 1973 to 2007 went to the top 1% of households). Research shows that working longer hours does not improve the economy, the environment, or quality of life. In fact, countries with shorter workweeks have smaller carbon footprints.[11] By one estimate, reducing work hours by an annual average of 0.5% over the rest of the century could eliminate 25% to 50% of the global warming that is not already "locked in" to the atmosphere.[12] By another, if Americans simply adopting the work patterns of Western Europeans, they would find themselves with seven more weeks of time off each year while also reducing energy use by 20%.[13]

When one US state experimented with shortening the workweek to four days for public employees, they were more productive and asked to keep the new schedule, citing benefits to their relationships, families, and general well-being.[14] The state also saved $4 million in overtime and absenteeism while reducing carbon emissions by 4000,000 metric tons per year. In another state, some workers opted to trade a 20% reduction in work hours for a 10% cut in pay. The New Economics Foundation proposes that a 30-hour workweek could help "solve a lot of connected problems: overwork, unemployment, overconsumption, high carbon emissions, low well-being, entrenched inequalities and the lack of time to live sustainably, to care for each other and simply to enjoy life."[15]

For people to make wise decisions about media and other spheres of life, they need time to become educated users, consumers, and citizens. They need time to look for better, fairer, cleaner products. They need time to spend offline and, occasionally, away from media. They need sufficient financial security that they can afford to pay a bit more for products that will last longer. As citizens, they need time to learn about political issues and participate meaningfully in civic life. In the wake of the 2016 presidential election, one conservative voter regretted that she did not have a deeper grasp of public affairs. "No one that's voting knows all the facts," said a female construction worker from Ohio. "It's a shame. They keep us so f***ing busy and poor that we don't have the time."[16] We often assume that the world's problems could be solved if only people had more data—neglecting the fact that people also need time to gather, evaluate, and act upon information.

Satisfying and Satisficing

Much of the time, we keep *ourselves* busy—often with media, and often with little to show for all the busyness. Some of us have noticed the media knob turned up to 11 and dialed it down. People from diverse walks of life are intentionally reducing the amount of time that they spend with screens, networks, and devices in order to shift some ballast toward friends, families, hobbies, and physical activities. They are challenging the assumption that the more connected you are, the better off you are. As William Powers notes in *Hamlet's Blackberry*, many Westerners have been living as "digital maximalists," with a belief that we should avoid ever being disconnected.[17]

The new breed of Slow Medians are "digital satisficers." (Note that I'm not calling them "digital minimalists.") This draws upon the concept of "satisficing" that Barry Schwartz employed persuasively in *The Paradox of Choice: Why More is Less*.[18] He blamed an overabundance of choices—many of them mediated—for massive increases in stress, anxiety, and dissatisfaction. We are tyrannized by small decisions: always looking at one more X, doing research on one more Y. This foraging behavior wastes time and incurs opportunity costs. Schwartz explained why the sense of having/not having or doing/not doing "enough" is *systemic*. That's why we need a Slow Media movement to promote public action and education about sustainable alternatives.

One Slow strategy is to make fast media consumption uncool, like fast food has become in many circles. That's what Kalle Lasn, who helped foment the Occupy Movement, had tried to do. He calls it "culture jamming."[19] Lasn cannily scheduled a collective event called "Buy Nothing Day" for Black Friday, the day on which US buyers run amok. The founder of *Adbusters* magazine, he also promoted "TV Turnoff Week," a social ritual every April where citizens reclaim a little time and tranquility by staying away from screens for a week. (It later evolved into "Screen Free Week.") The narrower goal was to get enough abstainers on board to depress the Nielsen ratings for that week, as a gesture of consumer sovereignty. The broader goal was to transform culture in ways that improve the quality of people's lives.

Other movement toward sustainable mediation includes the National Day of Unplugging and Sabbath Manifesto, led by the artists, writers, filmmakers, and media professionals of Reboot. The Sabbath might be the oldest and most effective institutionalized rebellion in Western experience.[20] Through it, Jewish people rekindle their communal identity and preserve their shared vision of the future, even when living in the midst of alien cultures wedded to different values. Slow Medians, green cultural citizens, Post-Luddites, and other sustainability advocates can do the same.

Many people crave a secular ritual like Shabbat that honors slowing down, seeking contemplation, and enacting alternative values. It can take the form of a daily habit, weekly practice, or even an annual holiday. An example of the latter is Take Back Your Time Day on October 24, which marks the date by which Americans have already logged more work hours than the average European does in a year. The Take Back Your Time (TYBT) movement promotes discussion about how overwork crowds out other elements of the meaningful life—health, parenthood, social relationships, community engagement—and how people can reassert control over their own daily rhythms.

In accord with Jewish mystical tradition, Rabbi Arthur Waskow, a TBYT leader, believes that people cannot *be* free if they don't have free time. "Imagine businesses setting aside seven minutes every morning and every afternoon in the midst of work as Quiet Time," he wrote in 2003, foreshadowing Intel's experiment. "No work, no telephone, no conversation. Time to sit quietly, to meditate, to drowse, to dream."[21] He urges religious communities to play a role in awakening their members to the wisdom of restfulness and in supporting public policies and workplace rituals devoted to spiritual search, family, and community.

Many approaches to media mindfulness create boundaries in time and space to delineate what kind of media to use *here* and what kind of media, if any, to use *there*. Some people engage in these practices independently while others join with their families, schools, or communities to explore non-digital or unmediated alternatives. Unplugging and other Slow Media rituals are helping to bring more people together in real time and physical space.

Post-Luddites Want Both

The Slow Medians described throughout this book are doing creative, cultural work that we have only begun to recognize. You might think that going Slow means being lazy, but in reality it requires a lot of effort. I can vouch for the fact that living the fast life and conforming to social expectations of media use is actually easier. Slow Media offers an attractive cultural narrative that underscores the rewards of making an effort to live more sustainably. Reframing these endeavors as an opportunity to pursue sustainability and create positive rituals of media use—rather than a struggle to break bad habits or resist technology—helps bring freedom, choice, and imagination to the fore.

Engaging in rituals of media non-use can help people build and maintain a satisfying cultural world. The venerable scholar James Carey described this ritual view of communication in essays that demythologize the digital revolution. He believed in the 1980s that people suffered already "from overloads of communication and overdoses of participation" and sympathized with the "new Ludditry" of his time.[22] Nonetheless, he criticized Neo-Luddites, too: not for protesting, but for failing to offer alternative ways of life.

Slow Medians defy this characterization. They *do* envision and enact a different relationship between society and its media. These post-Luddites want to enjoy the blessings of digital culture while preserving the gifts of analog culture, too. Making a place for Slow Media alongside fast ones enriches their lives. Reading expert Maryanne Wolf recommends such a balance in *Proust and the Squid*. Just as many children learn to switch between two or more oral languages, she says, they can learn to switch between books and screens, between Slow and fast—between different presentations of written language and different modes of analysis. Wolf hopes society can "preserve the capacities of two systems and appreciate why both are precious."[23] In other words, we do not have to make false choices. We have an opportunity, if we seize it, to enjoy both.

Eliminating the old binary, us-versus-them mentality could help move society forward, toward collective actions of the sort that I envision. A post-Luddite culture could accommodate diverse forms of media, multiple modes of interaction, and variable speeds of communication. Rather than forcing choices, we could preserve a wide range of options: fast *and* slow, digital *and* print, online *and* offline. People could be empowered to find more time away from digital devices and networks—and thus from work, business, and commerce—when they so choose. Accusations of "Luddism" just halt the conversation in its tracks. Admitting, finally, that we are all post-Luddites will mark a new beginning.

Slowness as Secular Oasis

The prospect of using media in Slower modes might feel intimidating to some people. You might perceive whatever you're "giving up" more acutely than whatever you're getting in return. The ingenious and industrious Benjamin Franklin cast a different light upon such acts of seeming self-deprivation. He referred to it as "philosophical self-denial": refusing to take an action you strongly desire because it would cost you more than it's worth.[24] Franklin was a great champion of rituals, which he used to fight his own worst tendencies and bring his overextended life under control, according to Powers. "What previously seemed a dreary, priggish way to live—denying oneself pleasure—suddenly becomes positive and even hedonistic," he wrote.[25] Instead of avoiding chatter and trivia, Franklin sought silence and tranquility, principles that bear no small resemblance to Slow Media ones.

Rituals are a sort of time-out, a way of setting aside rational, instrumental tasks for a brief period and immersing oneself in symbolic activities that hold spiritual, emotional, or communal meaning. Modern media rituals are often meaningful to people because their actions are voluntary and self-designed. Unlike religious Sabbaths, these activities are rarely compelled by authority and social duty. The fact that no creator is providing a structure for post-Luddites to follow serves as both a gift and a burden. (A day of rest would be easier for me to observe if I believed my god were commanding me to do so.)

Individuals confront a lot of systemic obstacles in pursuing alternative rituals of media usage and non-usage. Some schools and companies have led the way by promoting new ways of thinking about and using digital media. Other organizations have joined Intel and Boston Consulting Group in exploring the benefits of limiting media use. In Germany, Volkswagen no longer permits emailing certain employees after work hours, and Daimler employees are allowed to delete emails received while they're on vacation. The French IT company Atos switched from email to chat as a form of internal communication. Deutsche Telekom and Google have adopted measures to enforce scheduled breaks from the Internet.[26]

For better or worse, the presence or absence of a higher power influences one's ability to slow down. The case of Jack Lew is instructive. Anne-Marie Slaughter pointed to Lew as a role model for work-life balance in a much-discussed article for *The Atlantic*, "Why Women Still Can't Have It All."[27] Lew, a former White House chief of staff, was lauded by colleagues for carving out time to observe the Sabbath despite his demanding job. She contrasted the admiration people showed for Lew's commitment to faith with how she imagined people would react if a mother wanted to block out Friday afternoon, every week, to spend time with her children. "I suspect this would be seen as unprofessional, an imposition of unnecessary costs on co-workers," Slaughter wrote. "One of the great values of the Sabbath—whether Jewish or Christian—is precisely that it carves out a family oasis, with rituals and a mandatory setting-aside of work."

Slaughter's story ends on a hopeful note, pointing out that cultural assumptions about what can or cannot be done are subject to change. That's why we need to talk, as a society, about how to pursue sustainable values and practices in media use.

Slow Media Nation

Slow Media has helped launch a public conversation about what it means to be human, happy, wise, and free in a digital age. In its current state of development, Slow Media invites us to exercise our agency and creatively re-negotiate our relationships with media and with each other. Yet, Slow approaches transcend the private domain of choices and require institutional support. The individual power to choose Slow Media needs to be protected at a collective level, if it is to achieve its potential. A broad coalition of governments, schools, churches, businesses and other organizations could make incremental moves that empower people to incorporate some Slow Media principles into their lives.

Many institutions could join this discussion and make a greater commitment to sustainable media use and production. For starters, more schools could sensitize students to the influence of digital media on people and the planet, as many high-school and university educators have started to do. Academic administrators, educators, and their allies could pay more attention to mindfulness and promote it in schools, through programs that help kids self-regulate their behavior, improve their focus, and develop empathy.[28] More nonprofit organizations could participate in making Slow, green, mindful, and post-Luddite ideas accessible to diverse groups of people.

Businesses could take the environmental impact of their media use and production into greater account. They could foster dialogue about how to communicate more mindfully and enact policies that respect employees' private time, as Atos, Boston Consulting Group, Daimler, Deutsche Telekom, Google, Intel, Volkswagen, and others have done. More employers could try setting aside special times for creative thinking, special hours when email is restricted, or other approaches appropriate to their workplaces.

More elected officials could promote the benefits of sustainable media use, as Tim Ryan did in his book *Mindful Nation: How a Simple Practice Can Help Us Reduce Stress, Improve Performance and Recapture the American Spirit*. Government entities could recognize digital overtime as a compensable job duty and defend or shorten the 40-hour workweek—with possible perks such as bolstering job creation and civic participation while reducing carbon footprints.

And, more religious and spiritual communities could engage with issues such as protecting the environment and creating free time as ways of nourishing both divine creation and the sacred dimension of people's lives.

In addition to taking personal action, we could cultivate a greener political vision by supporting collective efforts that persuade media companies, employers, and lawmakers to improve working conditions and adopt eco-friendly policies. If demand-side reductions in media use and consumption are to take place on the scale required, "They cannot be left to the lifestyle decisions of earnest urbanites who like going to farmers' markets on Saturday afternoons and wearing up-cycled clothing," as Naomi Klein argues in *This Changes Everything*.[29] Low-carbon choices need to be made easier and more convenient for everyone, through policies and programs that require manufacturers to be responsible for the electronic waste they produce and to reduce built-in redundancies and obsolescences.

Some governmental bodies have started pursuing such policies. The European Parliament passed a law requiring all manufacturers to offer a common (standardized) battery charger—which might relegate Annie Leonard's struggle with tangled cords to the past. In the US, some states are working to recognize the right to a clean and sustainable environment in their constitutions. Two dozen states have passed e-waste recycling laws, covering more than half of all Americans. In Canada, labor leaders have pushed to make employers pay for the hours workers spend on devices when out of the office. In the US, some people have initiated lawsuits to recoup overtime pay for time spent on devices.

Governments could go further and work with employers and communities to establish a healthier balance between work and leisure. They could provide a regulatory framework that defines full-time work and guarantees fair compensation without excessive hours. They could show a commitment to environmental protection by ensuring that economic decisions are made to promote sustainability rather than exploit the planet.[30] Political representatives are unlikely to pursue such actions unless citizens demand action.

Another important step toward sustainability is improving our news environment (pardon the anthropocentric eco-metaphor). The 2016 presidential campaign in the US marked a watershed moment for public concern about the crisis in journalism and, especially, "fake news." Some say the reliability of political information, especially online, reached an all-time low. In an era when the status quo of commercial, corporate media is failing its democratic purpose of informing the electorate, the Slow Journalism movement has taken steps to boost news quality by adopting alternative economic models.

Media reform advocates, led by Robert McChesney and John Nichols, propose that the US government could make a difference by subsidizing journalism. In *People Get Ready: The Fight against a Jobless Economy and a Citizenless Democracy*, they suggest giving every American a $200 voucher to allocate to the nonprofit news organization of their choice. The idea is not as unprecedented or radical as it might seem at first glance. Historically, the federal government encouraged magazine publishing through generous postal subsidies. Some US states offer tax credits for citizens to donate to qualifying political campaigns of their choice. And the federal government currently subsidizes countless industries and companies, including immensely profitable ones that do not need support or serve the public interest. McChesney and Nichols imagine that the US could foster small, local producers who use less energy, pollute less, and exploit workers less by simply shifting a small portion of its vast farm subsidies away from corporate farming.[31]

Given the public's growing reluctance to pay for journalism, news as a commodity seems to be failing. What if subsidies helped tilt the playing field toward people who produce quality news with high democratic value? What if ethical production of journalism were encouraged by government regulation, rather than relegated to consumer choice? What if news organizations seeking support through citizen vouchers were asked to give information about how fair and clean their practices were? The voluntarily labeling or independent rating alternatives that I've proposed for Slow Journalism could give people information useful in determining which news producers are transparent, accountable, and sustainable enough to merit public funds.

Now Is the Time

You might have a hard time envisioning a large-scale movement, like those of the 1960s, happening today. In some ways, digital media have contributed to making us more isolated—"with our eyes glued to smart phones, attention scattered by click bait, loyalties split by the burdens of debt and insecurities of contract work," as Klein puts it. At the same time, many of us are significantly less isolated, thanks to social media, worker co-ops, farmers' markets, and other new cultural structures that help build community amid fragmented modern life. Like Slow Food before it, Slow Media could help bring people together to pursue common goals.

Pop quiz: What does a used book and record store have in common with an artisanal baker, a piano tuner, a letter-press artist, and a custom picture framer? In Viroqua, Wisconsin, these disparate cultural elements are joined philosophically and physically under the banner of the Driftless Centre for Slow Media, based in the evocatively named Forgotten Works Warehouse. The center supports and celebrates "intentional, thoughtfully crafted and homespun media," according to its founders. This community space has hosted zine exhibits, book and poetry readings, music performances, and the occasional record party or vaudeville show. (And, yes, the Driftless Centre promotes itself on the Internet and social media, as do most other Slow ventures. No "Luddism" here.) This joint enterprise shows how the concept of Slow Media can be used to consolidate and invigorate a wide range of popular practices whose shared ideals might otherwise be missed.

This Wisconsin warehouse suggests the potential of Slow values to unite people across political divides. After spending a couple of years in Viroqua (before the Driftless Centre existed), sociologist Lyn McGregor noted that area farmers had strong connections to the Slow Food Movement, selling organic and seasonal products to local consumers through community-supported agriculture programs as well as at farmers' markets and food coops. She also deduced that the town's "regular" residents who enjoy riding ATVs, frequenting the local VFW, and buying Walmart groceries and its "alternative" residents who favor Subaru Outbacks, Waldorf schools, and organic produce shared a commitment to frugality and a skepticism toward consumerism.[32] Social groups in this small town had enough in common to talk across their differences and work together to build their community.

The Driftless Centre was founded in a century-old tobacco warehouse in 2009. As we've seen, most of the cultural movement toward Slow Media occurred in the span between 2008 and 2016, a time when change *for the better* seemed possible. In fact, I wrote most of this book during an electoral season when progressive optimism was running high. In the current political context, the road to Slow Media appears rather longer and rougher. Indeed, you might be thinking that my vision seems utopian. That's not a bug; it's a feature.

With a little imagination and courage, we can find countless ways to put a little grit into the media system. Don't get me wrong—I am not an optimist. But a little idealism can give people motivation when we need it. Let's dream big, instead of limiting our hopes for the future by what seems possible today. The transition to a more sustainable way of living will not be fast, cheap, or easy. While there are justifiable grounds for pessimism, a sense of despair can become paralyzing and self-fulfilling. A Slow Media movement is unlikely to topple the political and economic status quo, but it can help people to reclaim some control over their own life worlds. One slow step at a time.

Actions like listening to vinyl records, taking an Internet sabbath, buying a Fairphone, and all the rest might sound like insignificant lifestyle choices. But the ensemble of Slow Media practices described in this book could, in aggregate, yield considerable social and environmental benefits.

People free to spend time away from digital media—and thus from work, business, commerce—could enjoy improved mental and physical health. They could become more active participants in local communities and better stewards of natural environments.[33] Journalists could produce more meaningful work, represent a greater range of public voices, and sustain longer careers (rather than decamping to PR or other fields). Interns at media organizations could get fairer compensation for their work, which could expand career options and improve diversity in the newsroom. Fewer workers could be sickened or injured at unhealthy media manufacturing facilities. Environmental decline could be slowed if digital products lasted longer, used fewer precious resources, and ended their life cycles more benignly.

Many activists believe that we are now living in "the age of the possible,"[34] at a critical juncture when entrenched interests are losing their power and the status quo cannot remain. This offers a great opening for reform or even radical change. McChesney and Nichols call it "a perfect storm moment." In historical instances like ours, the range of alternatives grows dramatically broader and "policies that were unthinkable suddenly move into play," they say. At a crossroads like this, when it is clear that neither society nor the economy are functioning well, people are more open to structural changes. Because of climate change, everything is going to change, one way or another. The environmental crisis neither trumps nor distracts from other pressing issues; as Klein said, "It supercharges each one of them with existential urgency."[35] The choice seems stark: sustainability or collapse.

The ideals and practices of Slow Media—wedded to movements for alternative media, mindfulness, green living, and more—strengthen this amalgam. Slow Media could help advance social and environmental well-being if all these like-minded groups and individuals join hands. Cultural creatives such as Slow

Journalists, green consumers, mindful media users, unpluggers, and post-Luddites are furnishing the imagination. The seeds of a better global media system are available to us, if we choose to nurture them. Facing the urgent problem of climate crisis, we need new tools for thinking, new ways of being, and new rousing ideals—now more than ever.

Acknowledgments

To the countless teachers and mentors who have given me advice and encouragement throughout the years. Jack Lule and Christine Ogan deserve special mention, as does Dave Nord—who indulged my Slow Media obsession by sending many postcards and letters, some of them manually typed on old library catalog cards and with newspaper cartoons glued on. (Ever the historian.)

To everyone who gave thoughtful feedback on previous versions on this manuscript and the proposals, pitches, and essays from which it derived, including Lisa Gettings, Alex Gilvarry, Corby Kummer, David Levy, William Swarts, and James Trimarco.

To all the journal and book editors who helped me develop ideas about alternative media, ritual communication, and Slow Media in earlier articles and chapters: Chris Atton, Grayson Cooke, John Downing, Paul Grosswiler, Julian Matthews, and Radhika Parameswaran among them.

To fellow panelists and organizers of conferences where I rehearsed many of these ideas about Slow Media, ecomedia literacy, and unplugging: Jack Bratich, Gabi Hadl, Antonio Lopez, Josh Meyrowitz, David Mindich, Mary Rothschild, Sarah Sharma, and many more.

To my talented editor, Hallie Stebbins, who helped me trust my voice, and everyone else at Oxford University Press who helped to make this book a reality.

To my colleagues at Long Island University Brooklyn, including Donald Bird, Ralph Engelman, and Curtis Stephen in Journalism, who supported me in every dimension of my career, as well as James Clarke in Honors, who gave me opportunities to teach classes exploring fun stuff like The Daily Show and YouTube.

To other colleagues inside and outside the academy who have given me inspiration, encouragement, and insight—not least of which Cory Armstrong, Janis Cakars, James Hamilton, Linda Jean Kenix, and Susan Maushart.

To Long Island University, for granting me leaves of absence that made the year-long Slow Media project and this book possible.

To the amazing students in my "Digital Disenchantment, Analog Alternatives" course (a.k.a. the Slow Media class) who kept Moleskine journals and spent a week without digital media, and to the journalism majors in my "Media and Culture" course who dared to tell me what they *really* thought about Neil Postman.

To my graduate assistants Ana Fernandez and Lionel Wininger, whose diligence helped bring research projects to fruition.

To Sabria David, for sharing her enthusiasm and research from the Slow Media Institute.

To Sally Herships, for helping to nudge Slow Media onto NPR and thus the public agenda.

To Megan Le Masurier, for editing superb special issues of *Journalism Practice* and *Digital Journalism* devoted to Slow Media.

To Tanya Schevitz and others at Reboot, whose Sabbath Manifesto inspires me to participate in the National Day of Unplugging each April.

To the Slow enablers who sent me postcards, faxes, and letters during my offline experiment: Sara Berret, Erika Bettencourt, Jared Burton, Rich Fravel, Alice Freda, Erdem Guven, J. Guy, Mike Kappa at Heavy Duty Press, Michele McClure, Christian McEwen, Jennifer McGill at AEJMC, Beverly Ogrodnick, Liz Perez, Paula Rempp, Amy Thompson, S. T. Van Airedale, and Sophia Wong. (If I've overlooked you, feel free to send a note and let me know.)

To my parents, who would have been thrilled to hold this book in their hands.

To my brother, Brad, who will buy a copy whether he reads it or not.

And to my partner in life and love, Michael Fanuzzi, who makes me wish every minute could last an hour.

Notes

Preface: The Bearable Lightness of Slowing

1. André Gregory and Wallace Shawn, *My Dinner with André*, directed by Louis Malle, 1981 (The Criterion Collection, 2015), DVD.
2. Nicholas Carr, "Exodus," *Rough Type*, April 8, 2010, http://www.roughtype.com/?p=1359.
3. Gary Shteyngart, *Super Sad True Love Story* (New York: Random House, 2011).
4. See my *Slow Media* blog at http://www.slow-media.org, as well as Jennifer Rauch, "The Origin of Slow Media: Early Diffusion of a Cultural Innovation through Press and Public Discourse," *Transformations* 20 (2011), http://www.transformationsjournal.org/wp-content/uploads/2016/12/Rauch_Trans20.pdf.
5. Sally Herships, "A Slow Media Movement," *Marketplace*, American Public Radio, November 17, 2009.
6. Stephen King, "Stephen King's Screen Addiction," *Entertainment Weekly*, July 24, 2009.
7. Malcolm Gladwell, interviewed by Patrick Brethour, "Malcolm Gladwell: The Quiet Canadian," *Globe and Mail*, April 4, 2010.
8. See "Oprah's What You Can Live Without" survival guide, http://media.oprah.com/tows/what-can-you-live-without-survival-guide.pdf.
9. See The Sabbath Manifesto, http://sabbathmanifesto.org.
10. Mark Bittman, "I Need a Virtual Break. No, Really," *New York Times*, March 2, 2008.
11. South By Southwest, "Tech Detox: Can You Survive a Day Without Technology?" http://schedule.sxsw.com/2012/events/event_IAP11664.
12. Michel Foucault, "Ethics of the Concern for Self as a Practice of Freedom," in *Ethics: Subjectivity and Truth*, ed. Paul Rabinow, 281–301 (New York: The New Press, 1997).
13. Benjamin Franklin and William Temple Franklin, *Memoirs of the Life and Writings of Benjamin Franklin* (London: Henry Coburn, 1818), 224.
14. In *The Paradox of Choice: Why Less Is More* (New York: Harper Perennial, 2005), Barry Schwartz espoused self-denial as a way to continue feeling satisfied—instead of running after ever-new pleasures.
15. Maggie Berg and Barbara Seeber offer a full discussion of the academic time crunch in *The Slow Professor: Challenging the Culture of Speed in the Academy* (Toronto: University of Toronto Press, 2016).
16. I describe my offline experience in "Living Offline: Artifacts of Life Before the Smartphone," *Medium*, March 5, 2015, https://medium.com/unplug-yourself/quick-3d59bbf2b92b.
17. André: "Yes, we are bored. We're all bored now. But has it ever occurred to you, Wally, that the process that creates this boredom that we see in the world now may very well be a self-perpetuating, unconscious form of brainwashing, created by a world totalitarian government based on money, and that all of this is much more dangerous than one thinks? And it's not just a question of individual survival, Wally, but that somebody who's bored is asleep, and somebody who's asleep will not say 'no'?" (Gregory and Shawn, *My Dinner with André*).

18. The comedian Stephen Fry, a British natural treasure perhaps best known from the ITV series *Jeeves and Wooster*, voiced my sentiments about digital-age conformity when he quit Facebook: "Who most wants you to stay on the grid? The advertisers. Your boss. Human Resources. The advertisers. Your parents (irony of ironies—once they distrusted it, now they need to tag you electronically, share your Facebook photos and message you to death). The advertisers. The government. Your local authority. Your school. Advertisers. Well, if you're young and have an ounce of pride, doesn't that list say it all?" Stephen Fry, "Off the Grid," *The Old Friary* (blog), April 20, 2016, http://www.stephenfry.com/2016/04/off-the-grid.

19. Sally Herships, "Woman Swears Off Internet for Six Months," *Marketplace*, American Public Radio, February 18, 2011.

20. For more on 21st-century Sabbath practices, see Jeremy Rifkin, *Time Wars: The Primary Conflict in Human History* (New York: Touchstone, 1987); Douglas Rushkoff, "Remember the Sabbath? Douglas Rushkoff Pleads for a Respite from E-Commerce," *Guardian*, March 8, 2000; and Judith Schulevitz, *The Sabbath World: Glimpses of a Different Order of Time* (New York: Random House, 2010).

21. Diane Zimmerman Umble, *Holding the Line: The Telephone in Old Order Mennonite and Amish Life* (Baltimore, MD: Johns Hopkins University, 1996).

22. Bill McKibben, *Enough: Staying Human in an Engineered Age* (New York: Henry Holt, 2003). He notes that, while Amish life is not perfect, their numbers are growing as most children opt to stay in Old Order societies, and their farms are more profitable by far than "English" farms. Amish societies also have a lower incidence of depression.

23. Jennifer Rauch, "Constructive Rituals of Demediatization: Spiritual, Corporeal and Mixed Metaphors in Popular Discourse about Unplugging." *Explorations in Media Ecology* 13, nos. 3–4 (2014): 231–246.

24. I talked more about students' reactions to the Slow Media assignment in an interview with the Australian Broadcasting Corporation. Antony Funnell, "The Slow Movement," *Future Tense*, Radio National, September 2, 2010.

25. For more on Slow Media as alternative media and the resistant power of using print and analog objects, see my chapter in The *Routledge Companion to Alternative and Community Media*, ed. Chris Atton (Oxford and New York; Routledge, 2015), 571–581.

26. See Jennifer Rauch, "Three Reasons I Don't Own a Smartphone," *HuffPost*, March 18, 2014, www.huffingtonpost.com/jennifer-rauch-.

27. Carr, "Exodus."

28. "Connecting and Communicating Online State of Media Report," MyLife.com, July 9, 2013. https://www.prnewswire.com/news-releases/national-mylifecom-survey-reveals-more-social-networks-and-message-services-more-problems-users-are-increasingly-overwhelmed-overloaded-214741101.html.

29. "The Communications Market Report: UK," *Ofcom*, August 4, 2016. People who reported trying a digital detox were around twice as likely to have a positive experience than a negative one. They felt more productive, liberated, and less distracted rather than lost, cut-off, or afraid of missing out.

30. Laurel J. Felt and Michael B. Robb, *Technology Addiction: Concern, Controversy, and Finding Balance* (San Francisco: Common Sense Media, 2016).

31. American Psychological Association, "Stress in America: Coping with Change," Stress in America Survey, 2017.

32. These anti-commercial events devised by Adbusters have been around since the early 1990s. They take place in the third week of April and on the Friday after Thanksgiving, respectively. You might consider the latter an appealing alternative to 6 a.m. mayhem at the local box store on Black Friday this year.

Chapter 1

1. Andres R. Edwards, *The Sustainability Revolution: Portrait of a Paradigm Shift* (Gabriola, BC: New Society Publishers, 2005).

2. Bill Tomlinson, *Greening through IT: Information Technology for Environmental Sustainability* (Cambridge, MA: MIT Press, 2010), 71.

3. Edwards, *Sustainability Revolution*.

4. Edwards, *Sustainability Revolution*.

5. Andrew Kirk gives a full account of Stewart Brand and the Bay Area countercultural movement in *Counterculture Green: Whole Earth Catalog and American Environmentalism* (Lawrence, KS: The University Press of Kansas), 2007.

6. According to NASA and the NOAA, 2016 was the hottest year in 137 years of record keeping—and the third year in a row to take the number one slot. See NASA, "NASA, NOAA Data Show 2016 Warmest Year on Record Globally," Report, January 2017. https://www.nasa.gov/press-release/nasa-noaa-data-show-2016-warmest-year-on-record-globally.

7. For more on McLuhan's pessimism about electronic media, see Paul Grosswiler, *Old New Media: From Oral to Virtual Environments* (New York: Peter Lang, 2013); Bob Hanke, "McLuhan, Viriolio, and Speed," in *Transforming McLuhan: Cultural, Critical, and Postmodern Perspectives*, ed. Paul Grosswiler (New York: Peter Lang, 2010), 203–226; Gerald Stearn, ed., *McLuhan: Hot and Cool* (New York: The Dial Press, 1967); and Peter Zhang, "Deluge's Relay and Extension of McLuhan: An Ethical Exploration," *Explorations in Media Ecology* 10, vols. 3 and 4 (2011): 207–224.

8. Malcolm Gladwell, Evgeny Morozov, and Micah White epitomize this line of thought. Gladwell argues that digital activism is a pale substitute for the face-to-face relationships that sustained the civil-rights movement. Morozov points out that mediated entertainment can distract people from social action, noting that East Germans living in areas without television reception participated in activism far more than those who had TV. White says that digital activists undermine social change by putting their faith in marketing metrics instead of in the power of words and deeds. See Gladwell, "Small Change: Why the Revolution Will Not Be Tweeted," *New Yorker*, October 4, 2010; Morozov, *The Net Delusion: The Dark Side of Internet Freedom* (New York: Public Affairs, 2011); and White, "Clicktivism Is Ruining Leftist Activism," *Guardian*, August 12, 2010, https://www.theguardian.com/commentisfree/2010/aug/12/clicktivism-ruining-leftist-activism.

9. Nicholas Carr, "Avatars Consume as Much Electricity as Brazilians," *Rough Type* (blog), December 5, 2006, http://roughtype.com/?p=611.

10. Justin Lewis, *Beyond Consumer Capitalism: Media and the Limits to Imagination* (Cambridge, UK and Malden, MA: Polity, 2013). By weight, a desktop computer is around 25% silica, 23% plastics, 20% iron, 14% aluminum, and 6% each of lead and copper—with smaller amounts of silver, gold, nickel, tin, zinc, beryllium, titanium, cobalt, manganese, tantalum, mercury, and arsenic.

11. Jennifer Gabrys, *Digital Rubbish: A Natural History of Electronics* (Ann Arbor, MI: University of Michigan Press, 2011).

12. Tomlinson, *Greening through IT*, 3.

13. See Nicole Starosielski and Janet Walker, *Sustainable Media: Critical Approaches to Media and Environment* (New York, Routledge 2016).

14. Tomlinson, *Greening through IT*, 4.

15. Some have expressed surprise and joy at the idea of being identified with this group. "Just knowing who we are, having a name as it were, gives Cultural Creatives more power to affect the world," said best-selling author Marianne Williamson (in Paul Ray and Sherry Ruth Anderson, *Cultural Creatives: How 50 Million People are Changing the World*, New York: Harmony Books, 2010). And California state senator John Vasconcellos: "Hallelujah! *The Cultural Creatives* brings us spectacular, inspiring good news: our long-desired sea change has occurred, each of us 'cultural creatives' is not alone, together we now amount to a critical mass sufficient to transform America!" (Ray and Anderson, *Cultural Creatives*).

16. See Edwards, *Sustainability Revolution*; Jeremy Rifkin, *Time Wars: The Primary Conflict in Human History* (New York: Touchstone, 1987).

17. Peter Senge, *The Necessary Revolution: How Individuals and Organizations are Working Together to Create a Sustainable World* (New York: Crown Business, 2010).

18. Paul Hawken, *Blessed Unrest: How the Largest Movement in the World Came into Being and No One Saw It Coming* (New York: Viking Books, 2007).

19. Rifkin, *Time Wars*, 229.

20. Starosielski and Walker, *Sustainable Media*.

21. Chris Atton, *Alternative Media* (Thousand Oaks, CA: Sage Publications, 2002).

22. For example, see Jennifer Rauch, "Activists as Interpretive Communities: Rituals of Consumption and Interaction in an Alternative Media Audience," *Media, Culture, and Society* 29, no. 6 (2007): 994–1013; and Jennifer Rauch, "Superiority and Susceptibility: How Activist Audiences Imagine the Influence of Mainstream News Messages on Self and Others," *Discourse and Communication* 4, no. 3 (2010): 263–277.

23. Jennifer Rauch, "Exploring the Alternative-Mainstream Dialectic: What 'Alternative Media' Means to a Hybrid Audience." *Communication, Culture and Critique* 8, no. 1 (2015): 124–143.

24. Rauch, "Activists as Interpretive Communities," 1002.

25. Rauch, "Activists as Interpretive Communities," 1001.

26. Rauch, "Exploring the Alternative Mainstream Dialectic."

27. Jenny Pickerill, *Cyberprotest: Environmental Activism Online* (Manchester, UK: Manchester University Press, 2003), 139. See also Chris Atton, "Are There Alternative Media After Computer-Mediated Communication?" *M/C Reviews* (April 12, 2000) and Linda Jean Kenix, *Alternative and Mainstream Media: The Converging Spectrum* (London: Bloomsbury Academic, 2012).

28. Carlo Petrini, *Slow Food: Collected Thoughts on Taste, Tradition, and the Honest Pleasures of Food*, (White River Junction, VT: Chelsea Green, 2001), 181.

Chapter 2

1. Grayson Cooke, "Editorial (Slow Media)," *Transformations: Journal of Media, Culture & Technology* 20 (2011), http://www.transformationsjournal.org/issue-20.

2. Carl Honoré, *In Praise of Slowness: Challenging the Cult of Speed* (New York: Harper Books, 2005).

3. Wendy Parkins and Geoffrey Craig, *Slow Living* (Oxford and New York: Berg, 2006), 123.

4. Folio Portinari, "The Slow Food Manifesto," *Slow Food*, December 10, 1989. Accessed November 2, 2017 at http://www.slowfoodusa.org/manifesto.

5. Corby Kummer, *The Pleasures of Slow Food: Celebrating Authentic Traditions, Flavors, and Recipes* (San Francisco, CA: Chronicle Books, 2002).

6. Alice Waters, "Fast Food and Slow Food Values," in *Ecological Literacy: Educating Our Children for a Sustainable World*, ed. Michael K. Stone and Zenobia Barlow (San Francisco, CA: Sierra Club Books, 2005).

7. Carlo Petrini, *Slow Food: Collected Thoughts on Taste, Tradition, and the Honest measures of Food* (White River Junction, VT: Chelsea Green, 2001), 8. Elsewhere, Petrini has talked about a principle that he calls "virtuous globalization" (interviewed by Parkins and Craig, *Slow Living*, 52).

8. Carlo Petrini, "Three Ideas, One Project," *Slow* 1 (2005).

9. Eric L. Hsu, "The Slow Food Movement and Time Shortage: Beyond the Dichotomy of Fast or Slow," *Journal of Sociology* 51, no. 3 (September 2015): 628–642.

10. Simon Gottschalk, "Speed Culture: Fast Strategies in Televised Commercial Ads," *Qualitative Sociology* 22, no. 4 (1999): 311–329.

11. Parkins and Craig, *Slow Living*.

12. Portinari, "Slow Food Manifesto."

13. Helen De Michiel, "Towards a Slow Media Practice," *Grantmakers in the Arts Reader* 13, no. 3 (Fall 2002), http://giarts.org/article/towards-slow-media-practice.

14. De Michiel, "Towards a Slow Media."

15. Jonathan Romney, "In Search of Lost Time," *Sight and Sound*, February 2010, 43.

16. Scott MacDonald, "Toward an Eco Cinema," *Interdisciplinary Studies in Literature and Environment* 11, no. 2 (Summer 2004), 109.

17. MacDonald, "Toward an Eco Cinema," 131.
18. Lisa Marr and Paolo Davanzo, "The Sound We See: Growing a Global Slow Film Movement," *Echo Park Film Center*, 2015. Another approach to eco-cinema considers the effects of the sprawling entertainment-industrial complex upon the environment. Research suggests the Hollywood film industry is the second biggest polluter in Los Angeles, after the oil industry. Filmmaking involves an enormous amount of energy consumption, waste generation, air pollution, greenhouse gas emissions, and physical disruptions on location. See Charles Corbett and Richard Turco, "Film and Television," in *South California Environmental Report Card 2006*, Institute of the Environment and Sustainability, University of California, Los Angeles, 4–11, https://www.ioes.ucla.edu/wp-content/uploads/RC06.pdf. See also the documentary film *Greenlit*, directed by Miranda Bailey (Los Angeles: Ambush Entertainment, 2010).
19. Simon Reynolds, *Retromania: Pop Culture's Addiction to its Own Past* (New York: Farrar, Straus and Giroux, 2011), 364.
20. Reynolds, *Retromania*, 427.
21. No Music Day was a series of events held on November 21 in 2005 through 2009. It was launched, paradoxically, by Scottish musician Bill Drummond, known for the novelty song "Doctorin' the Tardis," which remains a staple of American sports arenas. BBC Radio Scotland and other stations honored the day by playing no music during their broadcasts.
22. Reynolds, *Retromania*, 124.
23. Some examples include Elissa Altman, "Move Over Slow Food: Introducing Slow Media," *HuffPost*, November 29, 2009; Trevor Butterworth, "Time for a Slow-Word Movement," *Forbes*, December 29, 2009; De Michiel, "Toward a Slow Media"; Jennifer Rauch, "Is There a Slow Media Movement, or Is It Just Me?" *Slow Media* (blog), September 8, 2009; and Christopher Shea, "Slow-Media Movement," *Boston Globe*, January 25, 2010.
24. I discuss Slow Media philosophy and practices in Jennifer Rauch, "The Origin of Slow Media: Early Diffusion of a Cultural Innovation through Press and Public Discourse," *Transformations* 20 (2011), http://www.transformationsjournal.org/wp-content/uploads/2016/12/Rauch_Trans20.pdf, and Jennifer Rauch, "Slow Media as Alternative Media: On the Cultural Persistence of Print and Analog Forms," in *The Routledge Companion to Alternative and Community Media*, ed. Chris Atton (Oxford and New York: Routledge, 2015), 571–581.
25. Sally Herships, "A Slow Media Movement," *Marketplace*, American Public Media, November 17, 2009.
26. Nick Jones in Herships, "Slow Media Movement."
27. In my analysis, most of the stories that featured original reporting—interviews with people who practiced or promoted Slow Media—were linked to public broadcasters such as National Public Radio, German public radio, and the Australian Broadcasting Corporation. I speculated that the subject might not resonate with corporate-commercial journalists who have professional incentives to uncritically embrace digital technology. See Rauch, "Origins of Slow Media."
28. John Freeman, "Not So Fast," *Wall Street Journal*, August 22, 2009.
29. Maura Kelly, "A Slow Books Manifesto," *Atlantic*, March 26, 2012.
30. John Miedema in Malcolm Jones, "Slow Reading: An Antidote for a Fast World?" *Newsweek*, June 22, 2010, http://www.newsweek.com/slow-reading-antidote-fast-world-73395.
31. Henry David Thoreau, *Walden; or, Life in the Woods*, New York: Viking/Penguin, 1854/1983.
32. Parkins and Craig, *Slow Living*, 138.
33. Sabria David, Jorg Blumtritt, and Benedikt Kohler, "Slow Media Manifesto," *Slow-Media* (blog), January 2, 2010, http://en.slow-media.net/manifesto.
34. One notable difference between Petrini and these theorists is their support for industrial production of Slow Media, which they believed could still have "a special aura" and be "suggestive of being unique." See David, Blumtritt, and Kohler, "Slow Media Manifesto."
35. David, Blumtritt, and Kohler, "Slow Media Manifesto."
36. David, Blumtritt, and Kohler, "Slow Media Manifesto."

37. David, Blumtritt, and Kohler, "Slow Media Manifesto."

38. I have argued elsewhere for the progressive potential of not only Slow Media but also nostalgia. See Rauch, "Slow Media as Alternative Media."

39. David, Blumtritt, and Kohler, "Slow Media Manifesto."

40. Sabria David, "How 'Slow' Are the Germans?" *DCore/Slow Media Institut*, October 12, 2015. http://www.dcore.de/index.php/wie-slow-sind-die-deutschen-neue-slowtypes-studie-ermoeglicht-spannende-einblicke-in-die-lebenswelt-der-digitalen-mediengesellschaft.

41. David Shapiro, interviewed by Jenna Wortham, "Raised on the Web, But Liking a Little Ink," *New York Times*, October 22, 2011.

42. Jennifer Rauch, "Hands-on Communication: Zine Circulation Rituals and the Interactive Limitations of Web Self-Publishing," *Popular Communication* 2, no. 3 (2004): 153–169.

43. Negativland, "Shiny, Aluminum, Plastic, and Digital," *The Baffler* 8 (1996), 29–31.

44. Justin Lewis, *Beyond Consumer Capitalism: Media and the Limits to Imagination* (Cambridge, UK and Malden, MA: Polity, 2013), 139.

45. See Nielsen, "U.S. Music Industry Year-End Review 2013," *The Nielsen Company*, January 27, 2014, and Neil Shah, "The Biggest Music Comeback of 2014: Vinyl Records," *Wall Street Journal*, December 11, 2014.

46. Nielsen, "2017 U.S. Music Year-End Report," *The Nielsen Company*, January 3, 2018.

47. A forward-thinking technologist of my acquaintance (who shall remain nameless, to protect his reputation) hid the fact that he did not have a smartphone from his colleagues for *years*. The expectation in his office, like many tech workplaces, was that people have the latest devices. Without a fairly recent smartphone, he could not even lock or unlock the office door—which required an app.

48. David Sax, *The Revenge of Analog: Real Things and Why They Matter* (New York: Public Affairs, 2016).

49. Michiko Kakutani, "See It, Feel It, Touch It. Don't Click," *New York Times*, December 6, 2016.

50. Sax, *Revenge of Analog*, xvi.

51. Sax, *Revenge of Analog*, xvii.

52. For more on this, see Atton, *Alternative Media*; John D. H. Downing, *Radical Media: Rebellious Communication and Social Movements*, (Thousand Oaks, CA: Sage Publications, 2001); James F. Hamilton, *Democratic Communications: Formations, Projects, Possibilities*, (Washington: Lexington Books, 2008); Rauch, "Are There Still Alternatives? The Relationship Between Alternative and Mainstream Media in a Converged Environment," *Sociology Compass* 10, no. 9 (2016): 756–767.

53. Robert McChesney, *Digital Disconnect: How Capitalism Is Turning the Internet Against Democracy* (Boston: New Press, 2013).

54. Sean O'Hagan, "Analogue Artists Defying the Digital Age," *Observer*, April 23, 2011.

55. O'Hagan, "Analogue Artists," 13.

56. Radio Bra Red Waves, which Petrini founded in 1975 at age 26, was only the second radio station to break the state monopoly. For more on Petrini's background, see Kummer, *Pleasures of Slow Food*.

57. Kummer, *Pleasures of Slow Food*.

58. Kummer, *Pleasures of Slow Food*.

59. Kummer, *Pleasures of Slow Food*.

60. Sarah Sharma, *In the Meantime: Temporality and Cultural Politics* (Durham, NC: Duke University Press 2014), 110.

61. John Tomlinson, *The Culture of Speed: The Coming of Immediacy* (Thousand Oaks, CA: Sage Publications, 2007) 150.

62. A vivid example of the power of positive narratives comes from my classroom, where I ask students to experiment with device-free lifestyles. In one version, they are forbidden to use Fast Media for 24 hours. Normally, boredom ensues. The negative goal creates a void that's hard to fill, while prohibition incites rebels to resist authority. In another version, they are

instructed to spend a day using any Slow Media of their choice. Now, enthusiastic essays describe happy hours spent playing musical instruments, writing in journals, listening to old records, watching old videotapes, making art. They find it a lot easier, and more fun, to imagine living that way.

63. Sharma, *In the Meantime*, 128.

64. Sharma, *In the Meantime*, 128.

65. Hartmut Rosa, *Social Acceleration: A New Theory of Modernity* (New York: Columbia Unversity Press, 2013).

66. Parkins and Craig, *Slow Living*, 134.

Chapter 3

1. Delayed Gratification, "What We Do," accessed on November 2, 2017, https://www.slow-journalism.com/what-we-do.

2. Peter Laufer, *Slow News: A Manifesto for the Critical News Consumer* (Corvallis, OR: Oregon State University Press, 2011).

3. Michael Blanding, "The Value of Slow Journalism in the Age of Instant Information," *Nieman Reports*, Summer 2015.

4. David Dowling, "The Business of Slow Journalism," *Digital Journalism* 4, no. 4 (2015): 6.

5. Erik Neveu, "On Not Going Too Fast with Slow Journalism," *Journalism Practice* 10, no. 4 (2016): 448–460.

6. De Correspondent, "Our Principles." *De Correspondent*, accessed November 2, 2017, https://thecorrespondent.com/principles.

7. Alejandro Barranquero Carretero and Garbine Jaurrieta Bariain, "Slow Journalism in Spain: New Magazine Startups and the Paradigmatic Case of *Jot Down*," *Journalism Practice* 10, no. 4 (2016): 521–538.

8. Narratively, "About," *Narratively*, February 24, 2013, https://web.archive.org/web/20130224053212/http://narrative.ly/about.

9. Laurent Beccaria and Patrick de Saint-Exupery, "Content and Its Discontents," *Harper's Magazine*, October 2013.

10. Evan Osnos, "On Slow Journalism," *New Yorker*, January 21, 2013.

11. Sasha Anawalt, "The Slow Journalism Movement: Heard of It?" *ARTicles* (blog), National Arts Journalism Program, Sept. 7, 2008, http://www.najp.org/articles/sasha_anawalt/2008/09.

12. Genevieve Fussell, "The Sochi Project," *New Yorker*, November 24, 2013.

13. The word, a portmanteau of *churn* and *journalism*, was popularized by journalist Nick Davies in the book *Flat Earth News*. Obviously, press releases can make a positive contribution to journalism, when used wisely. Note also that the number of PR professionals exceeds the number of journalists by 2 to 1 (Martin Moore, "Churnalism Exposed," *Columbia Journalism Review*, March 3, 2011).

14. David Weaver and Lars Willnat, *The Global Journalist in the 21st Century* (New York: Routledge, 2012).

15. Bill Kovach and Tom Rosenstiel, *Warp Speed: America in the Age of Mixed Media* (New York: Century Foundation Press, 1999).

16. In the digital era, web metrics often drive journalism toward a race to the bottom. One AOL strategy aimed to increase page views by almost 500% while reducing the average cost per unit of content by around 15%. Compensation for many writers is determined by how many new viewers their work attracts. See James Fallows, "Learning to Love the New Media," *Atlantic*, April 2011.

17. Howard Rosenberg and Charles S. Feldman, *No Time to Think: The Menace of Media Speed and the 24-Hour News Cycle* (New York: Continuum International Publishing Group, 2008), 16.

18. Respected publications such as the *Chicago Tribune, Houston Chronicle*, and *San Francisco Chronicle* have subscribed to the Journatic service.

19. Leon Watson, "Humans Have Attention Spans Shorter Than Goldfish, Thanks to Smartphones," *Telegraph*, May 15, 2015.

20. I take a comprehensive look at the emergence of Slow Media and Slow Journalism in "The Origin of Slow Media: Early Diffusion of a Cultural Innovation through Press and Public Discourse," *Transformations* 20 (2011), http://www.transformationsjournal.org/issues/20/article-01.shtml.

21. Susan Greenberg, "Slow Journalism in the Digital Fast Lane," in *Global Literary Journalism: Exploring the Journalistic Imagination*, ed. Richard Keeble and John Tulloch (New York: Peter Lang, 2013), 381–382.

22. Greenberg, "Slow Journalism in the Digital Fast Lane," 2.

23. Megan Le Masurier, "What Is Slow Journalism?" *Journalism Practice* 9, no. 2 (2015): 138–152.

24. Megan Le Masurier, "Slow Journalism: An Introduction to a New Research Paradigm," *Journalism Practice* 10, no. 4 (2016): 405–413.

25. Neveu, "Not Going Too Fast."

26. Neveu, "Not Going Too Fast."

27. Neveu, "Not Going Too Fast," 6.

28. Mark Berkey-Gerard, "Tracking the 'Slow Journalism' Movement," *Campfire Journalism* (blog), July 29, 2009.

29. Carlo Petrini, *Slow Food Nation: Why Our Food Should Be Good, Clean, Fair* (New York: Rizzoli, 2007).

30. Petrini, *Slow Food Nation*, 98–99.

31. Petrini, *Slow Food Nation*, 122.

32. Petrini, *Slow Food Nation*, 128.

33. Petrini, *Slow Food Nation*, 135.

34. Petrini, *Slow Food Nation*, 136.

35. Harold Gess, "Climate Change and the Possibility of Slow Journalism," *Equid Novi: African Journalism Studies* 33, no. 1 (2012): 54–65.

36. Society of Professional Journalists, "SPJ Code of Ethics," September 6, 2016.

37. In Laura Oliver, "Delayed Gratification: New Magazine Launches Dedicated to 'Slow Journalism'," Journalism.co.uk, December 13, 2010.

38. McSweeney's. "A Look at the San Francisco Panorama," January 2, 2010, https://www.mcsweeneys.net/articles/a-look-at-the-san-francisco-panorama.

39. Trevor Butterworth, "Time for a Slow-Word Movement," *Forbes*, December 29, 2009.

40. Butterworth, "Time for a Slow."

41. Butterworth, "Time for a Slow."

42. Susan Greenberg, "Slow Journalism," *Prospect*, February 2007.

43. Greenberg, "Slow Journalism in the Digital Fast Lane."

44. David Leigh, "Are Reporters Doomed?" *Guardian*, November 12, 2007.

45. Blanding, "Value of Slow."

46. Per Le Masurier, "What Is Slow Journalism?"

47. In 2011, HuffPost had around 9,000 unpaid writers. Some interns have not only worked there for free but also paid up to $13,000 for the opportunity (with proceeds going to charity).

48. Sean Roach, "The Constant Gardener: My Two Years Tending AOL's Hyperlocal Experiment," *Columbia Journalism Review,* March/April 2012.

49. In Robert McChesney and John Nichols, *The Death and Life of American Journalism: The Media Revolution That Will Begin the World Again* (New York: Nation Books, 2010), 86.

50. Tim Rutten, "AOL? HuffPo? The Loser? Journalism," *Los Angeles Times*, February 9, 2011.

51. Robert McChesney, *Digital Disconnect: How Capitalism Is Turning the Internet Against Democracy* (Boston: New Press, 2013), 187.

52. Journalists often move into public relations. By some accounts, there are now twice as many PR professionals as there are working journalists; numbers of the former went up 22% in

the past decade while the latter went down 17%. See Maria Marron, "Content Creation Spans All Aspects of J-Programs," *Journalism and Mass Communication Editor* 69, no. 4 (2014): 347–348.

53. This turn reflects broader changes in the US workforce, of which freelancers now comprise a third—a 60% increase since 2001, totaling around 53 million US workers in 2014. See Guy Standing, *The Precariat: A Dangerous New Underclass* (London and New York: Bloomsbury Academic, 2014).

54. According to Thrive Global, http://www.thriveglobal.com/about.

55. Arianna Huffington, "Announcing My First Pick for the HuffPost Book Club: In Praise of Slowness," *HuffPost,* March 19, 2010.

56. McChesney and Nichols, "Death and Life."

57. The trend toward long-form narrative in online publishing also coincides with a shift from "page views" to "time on page" in the online attention metrics on which advertising and author payments are based—which puts a higher premium on "engaged time" and, thus, on engaging content.

58. De Correspondent, "Our Principles."

59. Ernst-Jan Pfauth, "How We Turned a World Record in Journalism Crowd-Funding into an Actual Publication," *Medium*, November 27, 2013.

60. Dowling, "Business of Slow," 10.

61. Barranquero and Juarrieta, "Slow Journalism in Spain."

62. Barranquero and Juarrieta, "Slow Journalism in Spain." See also James Breiner, "Cultural Publication Flirts with the 'Dark Side' in Spain," *News Entrepreneurs*, July 28, 2015.

63. While some publications identified here as Slow are still commercially financed, none are corporate-owned.

64. Dowling, "Business of Slow," 12.

65. Laufer, *Slow News*, 68.

66. Arianna Huffington, "The Slow News Movement," *HuffPost*, June 20, 2012.

67. Walter Shapiro, "After Breitbart and Shirley Sherrod, We Need a Slow-News Movement," *Politics Daily*, July 27, 2010, https://web.archive.org/web/20100728230512/http://www.politicsdaily.com/2010/07/27/after-breitbart-and-shirley-sherrod-we-need-a-slow-news-movemen.

68. Ruth Marcus, "After Shirley Sherrod, Time for the Slow Blogging Movement," *Washington Post*, July 23, 2010, http://voices.washingtonpost.com/postpartisan/2010/07/after_shirley_sherrod_time_for.html.

69. Gess, "Climate Change."

70. Megan Le Masurier, "Slow Journalism: An Introduction to a New Research Paradigm," *Journalism Practice* 10, no. 4 (2016).

71. Le Masurier, "Slow Journalism: An Introduction," 7.

72. Dowling, "Business of Slow," 12.

73. Le Masurier, "Slow Journalism: An Introduction," 5.

74. Nico Drok and Liesbeth Hermans, "Is There a Future for Slow Journalism?" *Journalism Practice* 10, no. 4 (2016): 539–554.

75. See John D. H. Downing, "Audiences and Readers of Alternative Media: The Absent Lure of the Virtually Unknown," *Media, Culture, and Society* 25, no. 5 (2003): 625–645; and Jennifer Rauch, "Activists as Interpretive Communities: Rituals of Consumption and Interaction in an Alternative Media Audience," *Media, Culture and Society* 29, no. 6 (2007): 994–1013.

76. Douglas Rushkoff, *Throwing Rocks at the Google Bus: How Growth Became the Enemy of Prosperity* (New York: Portfolio, 2016).

77. Le Masurier, "What Is Slow Journalism?" 6.

78. Petrini, *Slow Food Nation*, 125.

79. Justin Lewis, *Beyond Consumer Capitalism: Media and the Limits to Imagination* (Cambridge, UK and Malden, MA: Polity, 2013).

Chapter 4

1. Greenpeace International, "How Clean Is Your Cloud?" April 17, 2012, 6, https://www.greenpeace.org/international/publication/6986/how-clean-is-your-cloud/.
2. Greenpeace USA, "Clicking Clean: Who Is Winning the Race to Build a Greener Internet?" January 2017, https://www.greenpeace.org/usa/ending-the-climate-crisis/click-clean/#report.
3. Klint Finley, "Your Netflix Addiction Is Screwing the Climate." *Wired*, May 15, 2015.
4. Greenpeace USA, "Clicking Clean."
5. Ingrid Burrington, "The Environmental Toll of a Netflix Binge." *Atlantic*, December 16, 2015.
6. Greenpeace International, "How Clean?"
7. Adam Clark Estes, "What Is the Cloud, and Where Is It?" *Gizmodo*, January 29, 2015, http://gizmodo.com/what-is-the-cloud-and-where-is-it-1682276210.
8. Estes, "What Is the Cloud?"
9. Natural Resources Defense Council, "America's Data Centers Are Wasting Huge Amounts of Energy," Issue Brief, August 2014. In this paper, the NRDC points out an even bigger problem than large data centers run by large cloud providers (which can be ultra-efficient): thousands of mainstream business and government data centers and small, corporate, or multi-tenant operations, which account for around 95% of all data center energy use. See also Greenpeace USA, "Clicking Clean."
10. Greenpeace USA, "Clicking Clean."
11. Giulio Boccaletti, Marcus Loftier, and Jeremy M. Oppenheim, "How IT Can Cut Carbon Emissions," *The McKinsey Quarterly*, October 2008.
12. Greenpeace International, "Make IT Green: Cloud Computing and Its Contribution to Climate Change," March 30, 2010.
13. Richard Maxwell and Toby Miller, "Greening the Media," *HuffPost*, March 16, 2012.
14. Jennifer Gabrys, *Digital Rubbish: A Natural History of Electronics* (Ann Arbor, MI: The University of Michigan Press, 2011), 1.
15. See Nicole Starosielski, *The Undersea Network: Sign, Storage, Transmission* (Durham, NC: Duke University Press, 2015); and Lisa Parks and Nicole Starosielski, *Signal Traffic: Critical Studies of Media Infrastructures* (Champaign, IL: University of Illinois Press, 2015).
16. Nicole Starosielski and Janet Walker, *Sustainable Media: Critical Approaches to Media and Environment* (New York: Routledge, 2016), x.
17. Jussi Parikka, "The Geology of Media." *Atlantic*, October 11, 2013.
18. Sean Cubitt, "I Took Off My Pants and Felt Free: Environmentalism in Countercultural Radio," in *Ecomedia: Key Issues*, ed. Stephen Rust, Salma Monani, and Sean Cubitt (Abingdon, UK and New York: Routledge, 2015), 1.
19. Gabrys, *Digital Rubbish*, 151.
20. Bill Tomlinson, *Greening through IT: Information Technology for Environmental Sustainability* (Cambridge, MA: MIT Press), 2010.
21. Jennifer Gabrys, "Powering the Digital: From Energy Ecologies to Electronic Environmentalism," in *Media and the Ecological Crisis*, ed. Richard Maxwell, Jon Raundalen, and Nina Lager Vestberg, (New York and London: Routledge, 2015), 5.
22. Richard Maxwell and Toby Miller, *Greening the Media* (New York: Oxford University Press, 2012), 159.
23. Maxwell and Miller, *Greening the Media*, 16.
24. For instance, stockholders in Chevron and Exxon voted in May 2016 on proposals that would have required the giant oil companies to release climate impact reports, increase transparency of climate change lobbying efforts, and adopt greenhouse gas emission reduction targets. Executives urged shareholders to reject the proposals as bad for business, and they did.
25. Maxwell and Miller are not alone in vilifying Earth Day. I. F. Stone called the celebration a "snow job" that uses "rock and roll, idealism and noninflammatory social issues" to distract

people from more urgent concerns that might threaten the power structure (I. F. Stone, "Con Games," speech delivered at Sylvan Theater, Washington, DC, April 22, 1970). Naomi Klein called Earth Day "an annual ritual of mass corporate greenwashing," noting that companies spend more time, money, and energy promoting the event than they do improving their environmental practices or cleaning up their pollution. See *This Changes Everything: Capitalism vs. the Climate.* New York: Simon and Schuster, 2014.

26. Peter Senge, *The Necessary Revolution: How Individuals and Organizations are Working Together to Create a Sustainable World* (New York: Crown Business, 2010).

27. See Daniel Czitrom, *Media and the American Mind: From Morse to McLuhan* (Chapel Hill, NC: University of North Carolina Press, 1983); Maxwell, Raundalen, and Vestberg, "Media Ecology Recycled," in *Media and the Ecological Crisis*, xi.

28. "The Playboy Interview: Marshall McLuhan," *Playboy*, March 1969.

29. Marshall McLuhan, *Understanding Media: The Extensions of Man* (New York: McGraw-Hill, 1964). He also argued that nature was obsolete, thanks to media technology; see Richard Maxwell and Toby Miller, "The Fantasies of Marshall McLuhan," *Psychology Today*, November 3, 2014.

30. Neil Postman, "The Reformed English Curriculum," in *High School 1980: The Shape of the Future in American Secondary Education*, ed. A. C. Zurich (New York: Pittman, 1970).

31. Neil Postman, *Technopoly: The Surrender of Culture to Technology* (New York: Vintage, 1993), 18.

32. Postman, "Reformed English Curriculum."

33. Jennifer Daryl Slack, "Environment/Ecology," in *New Keywords: A Revised Vocabulary of Culture and Society*, ed. Tony Bennett, Lawrence Grossberg, and Meaghan Morris, 106–108 (Oxford, England: Blackwell, 2005).

34. Maxwell, Raundalen, and Vestberg, "Media Ecology Recycled," xii.

35. Cory Doctorow, "Writing in the Age of Distraction," *Locus*, January 2009, http://www.locusmag.com/Features/2009/01/cory-doctorow-writing-in-age-of.html.

36. Jason Bloomberg, "Amazon Cloud Ecosystem: Where the Cloud Action Is," *Forbes*, July 13, 2015. http://www.forbes.com/sites/jasonbloomberg/2015/07/13/amazon-cloud-ecosystem-where-the-cloud-action-is.

37. For example, see Antonio Lopez, *The Media Ecosystem* (Berkeley, CA: Revolver, 2012) and Maxwell and Miller, *Greening the Media.*

38. Maxwell, Raundalen, and Vestberg, "Media Ecology Recycled," xi.

39. Lopez, *Media Ecosystem*, 19.

40. Maxwell and Miller, *Greening the Media.*

41. Antonio Lopez, "Putting the Eco Back in Ecosystems," in Maxwell, Raundalen, and Vestberg, *Media and the Ecological Crisis*, 152. See also Maxwell, Raundalen, and Vestberg, "Media Ecology Recycled," xi.

42. Lopez, *Media Ecosystem.*

43. Maxwell, Raundalen, and Westberg, "Media Ecology Recycled," 9.

44. There are two stances on sustainability: a "soft" one that seeks to accommodate growth and a "tougher" one that "thoroughly discredits the growth model that subtends capitalism itself" (Maxwell and Miller, *Greening the Media*, 26). The latter version views the Earth as a closed system that cannot keep giving more and more resources or absorbing more and more waste without eventually hitting a material limit. The idea of sustainable growth is, they write, "a bad oxymoron—self-contradictory as prose and unevocative as poetry."

45. See James Gustave Speth, *The Bridge at the Edge of the World: Capitalism, the Environment, and Crossing from Crisis to Sustainability* (New Haven, CT: Yale University, 2008), 155.

46. Lopez, *Media Ecosystem*; and Antonio Lopez, *Greening Media Education: Bridging Media Literacy with Green Cultural Citizenship* (New York: Peter Lang, 2014).

47. Jim Nail, "If It's Not 'Green,' What Is 'Sustainability Communications'?" *Speaking Sustainability* (blog), Nov. 20, 2010, https://web.archive.org/web/20120227032853/http://speakingsustainability.com:80/2010/11/30/if-its-not-green-what-is-sustainability-communications/.

48. David Kiron et al., "Sustainability's Next Frontier: Walking the Talk on Issues that Matter Most," *MIT Sloan Management Review*, December 2016.

49. Gregory Unruh et al., "Investing for a Sustainable Future," *MIT Sloan Management Review*, May 2016.

50. Claudia Rademaker, *Green Media: Exploring Green Media Selection and its Impact on Communication Effectiveness* (Dusseldorf: Lambert Academic Publishing, 2013).

51. John Parnham, *Green Media and Popular Culture: An Introduction* (London: Palgrave, 2015).

52. Charles W. Schmidt, "E-Junk Explosion," *Environmental Health Perspectives* 110, no. 4 (April 2002): 190.

53. Maxwell and Miller, "Greening the Media."

54. Annie Leonard, "Annotated Script," *The Story of Electronics*, 2011.

55. Greenpeace was the first group to "explore fully and trust in the progressive potential of television, reflecting their Canadian lineage and the influence of Marshall McLuhan on key original members," said Kevin Michael DeLuca, in *Image Politics: The New Rhetoric of Environmental Activism* (New York, Routledge, 1999), 4. Founding members, one of whom called McLuhan their "greatest prophet" in 1971, "took to heart McLuhan's aphorism 'the medium is the message' and accepted McLuhan's challenge not to cower in their ivory towers bemoaning change but to plunge into the vortex of electronic technology in order to understand it and dictate the new environment, to 'turn ivory tower into control tower.'"

56. On the human front, Amazon has been condemned for the working conditions of its third-party logistics contractor, Amalgamated Product Giant Shipping Worldwide (APGSW). One undercover journalist reported from a warehouse where employees experienced physical danger, injuries, and electrical shocks. According to *Mother Jones*, an APGSW employee might earn $60 per day after taxes for a 10.5-hour workday. In some places, such a job was the only game in town (Mac McLelland, "Shelf Lives," *Mother Jones*, March/April 2012).

57. Barbara Grady, "Amazon Moves on Renewables after Push from Greenpeace," *GreenBiz*, June 12, 2015.

58. Maxwell and Miller, *Greening the Media*, 25.

59. One commentator, considering the virtues of a Fairphone, described the pleasure of replacing a cracked e-reader screen himself: "I managed to source a £60 replacement screen from an internet trader in Hong Kong, and spent an hour, working painstakingly with a trembling screwdriver and repeated re-plays of the instructions someone had kindly posted on YouTube, before I lit up (like my new screen) with, well, sheer joy. There's no better word for that sense of empowerment and accomplishment" (Nick Thorpe, "The Love of Stuff: Why We Should Love Material Things More, Not Less," *Aeon*, March 3, 2014). He bemoaned that screens were glued rather than screwed into later models—designed for the dump, in other words. Thorpe wondered whether Fairphone's business model is as sustainable as its product: "Will it make enough money for any long-term market presence, if nobody needs to replace it?"

60. Some overseas subcontractors in the electronics industry have been caught illegally dumping toxic and radioactive waste that can cause miscarriages, childhood leukemia, and mental disabilities among local people.

61. Chris Sweeney, "Is Your Phone Smart Enough Not to Poison the People Making It? This One Is," *Yes! Magazine*, October 2013, http://www.yesmagazine.org/issues/the-human-cost-of-stuff/smart-phone-why-its-time-for-a-kind-phone.

62. "GoodElectronics Vision, Mission, Common Demands on the Electronics Industry," International Network on Human Rights and Sustainability in Electronics, January 20, 2012, https://goodelectronics.org/goodelectronics-vision-mission-common-demands-on-the-electronics-industry.

63. Lynn Stuart Parramore, "Six Reasons Your Apple Product Has Become Very Uncool," *AlterNet*, June 3, 2013, http://www.alternet.org/economy/apple-not-cool. She notes that Apple has been accused of tax dodging, fixing prices on eBooks, and buying back stocks to manipulate its share prices and reward its executives.

64. Charlie Sorrel, "10 Things Missing from the iPad," *Wired*, January 28, 2010, https://www.wired.com/2010/01/ten-things-missing-from-the-ipad.

65. Pete Pachal, "Why the iPad 2 Is Far More Likely to Break than the Original," *Mashable*, March 3, 2012.

66. Workers usually live in on-site dormitories, where they are sometimes awoken in the middle of the night when managers urgently need them to do something. Factories can scale up and down quickly, sometimes aided by subsidies from the Chinese government. Charles Duhigg and Keith Bradsher, "How the U.S. Lost Out on iPhone Work," *New York Times*, January 21, 2012.

67. To give some perspective: The number of FoxConn's 1.2 million workers who committed suicide is lower than China's national rate. It's also lower than the suicide rate among US college students.

68. Joel Johnson, "1 Million Workers. 90 Million iPhones. 17 Suicides. Who's to Blame?" *Wired*, February 28, 2011.

69. Kiera Butler, "Killer App," *Mother Jones*, November/December 2012.

70. Quoted in Maxwell and Miller, *Greening the Media*.

71. David Segal, "Apple's Retail Army: Long on Loyalty but Short on Pay," *New York Times*, June 23, 2012. See also Parramore, "Six Reasons."

72. In 1955, General Motors employed around 576,000 people and General Electric around 210,000. In 2013, GM's workforce was still around 202,000 and GE's had grown to around 304,000.

73. Douglas Rushkoff, *Throwing Rocks at the Google Bus: How Growth Became the Enemy of Prosperity* (New York: Portfolio, 2016), 51–54.

74. There are at least 27 million slaves worldwide, according to Slavery Footprint. You can find out how many slaves toil to support your consumption lifestyle at SlaveryFootprint.org.

75. John Davis, "Going Analogue: Vinylphiles and the Consumption of the 'Obsolete' Vinyl Record," in *Residual Media*, ed. Charles Acland (Minneapolis: University of Minnesota Press, 2007).

76. Rob Walker, "Replacement Therapy: Why Our Gadgets Can't Wear Out Fast Enough." *Atlantic*, September 2011.

77. Rauch, "Slow Media as Alternative Media: On the Cultural Persistence of Print and Analog Forms," in *The Routledge Companion to Alternative and Community Media*, ed. Chris Atton (Oxford and New York: Routledge, 2015), 571–581.

78. Rauch, "Slow Media as Alternative Media."

79. Ashlea Halpern, "The Analog Underground," *New York*, July 11, 2011, 59.

80. Halpern, "Analog Underground."

81. Some critics contend that the question of whether cloud computing is less or more damaging to the environment than analog predecessors is a red herring. The real question is "whether networked computing is sustainable in the technical and corporate model currently being deployed," and the answer is "no." See Sean Cubitt, Robert Hassan, and Ingrid Volkmer, "Does Cloud Computing Have a Silver Lining?" *Media, Culture and Society* 33, no. 1 (2011).

82. Nicholas Carr, "The iPad Luddites," *Rough Type* (blog), April 7, 2010, http://roughtype.com/?p=1357.

83. Some have noted the irony of the music industry having championed the CD format, which ultimately undermined sales by arming fans with digital files that could so easily be copied and shared.

84. David Sax, *The Revenge of Analog: Real Things and Why They Matter* (New York: Public Affairs, 2016).

85. Raymond Williams, *Marxism and Literature* (New York: Oxford University Press, 1977); Jakob Nielsen, "The End of Legacy Media," *Nielsen Norman Group*, August 23, 1998.

86. Garnet Hertz, "Dead Media," *Dead Media Research Lab*, 2009; Garnet Hertz and Jussi Parikka, "Zombie Media: Circuit Bending Media Archaeology into an Art Method," *Leonardo* 45, no. 5 (2012).

87. Esther Dyson, George Gilder, George Keyworth, and Alvin Toffler, "Cyberspace and the American Dream: A Magna Carta for the Knowledge Age," The Progress and Freedom Foundation, August 1994, http://www.pff.org/issues-pubs/futureinsights/fi1.2magnacarta. html.

88. Dyson's thinking might have evolved, as a board member of the Long Now Foundation, along with Stewart Brand, Kevin Kelly, Brian Eno, and others. The group "hopes to provide a counterpoint to today's accelerating culture and help make long-term thinking more common," according to its website, http:///longnow.org/about. "We hope to foster responsibility in the framework of the next 10,000 years."

89. Stephen Rust, Salma Monani, and Sean Cubitt, *Ecomedia: Key Issues* (Abingdon, UK and New York: Routledge, 2015).

90. Elizabeth Grossman, *High-Tech Trash: Digital Devices, Hidden Toxins, and Human Health* (Washington: Island Press, 2006).

91. Bill McKibben, *Deep Economy: The Wealth of Communities and the Durable Future* (New York: Times Books, 2007).

92. James Gustave Speth, *The Bridge at the End of the World: Capitalism, the Environment, and Crossing from Crisis to Sustainability* (New Haven, CT: Yale University Press, 2008).

93. Speth, *Bridge at the End*.

94. Lopez, *Media Ecosystem*; and Lopez, *Greening Media Education*.

Chapter 5

1. Maggie Jackson, *Distracted: The Erosion of Attention and the Coming Dark Age* (Amherst, NY: Prometheus Books, 2008), 9.

2. Some books that jump-started public discussions of over-mediated life include: *Irresistible: The Rise of Addictive Technology and the Business of Keeping Us Hooked* by marketing professor Adam Alter (New York: Penguin, 2017); *The Dumbest Generation: How the Internet Stupefies Young Americans and Jeopardizes Our Future* by English professor and former National Endowment for the Arts director Mark Bauerlein (New York: Tarcher, 2008); *The Shallows: What the Internet Is Doing to Our Brains* by tech writer Nicholas Carr (New York: Norton, 2010); *Distracted: The Erosion of Attention and the Coming Dark Age* by journalist Maggie Jackson (New York: Prometheus, 2008); and *The Distraction Addiction: Getting the Information You Need and the Communication You Want, without Enraging Your Family, Annoying Your Colleagues, and Destroying Your Soul* by tech consultant and scholar Alex Soojung-Kim Pang (New York: Little, Brown and Co., 2013).

3. According to Facebook marketing head Michelle Klein, quoted at https://socialmediaweek. org/newyork/2016/05/31/millennials-check-phones-157-times-per-day.

4. Bank of America, *Trends in Consumer Mobility Report 2016*, August 17, 2017, https://newsroom.bankofamerica.com/content/newsroom/press-releases/2017/08/keeping-digital-natives.html.

5. According to Clifford Nass, talking with Ira Flatow on "The Myth of Multitasking," *Talk of the Nation*, National Public Radio, May 10, 2013. Nass gives the example of Stanford students who listen to music, text friends, and use Facebook or Twitter while writing a paper.

6. In addition, 60% of respondents claimed they were frequently too tired for leisure activities and 42% attributed ill health to stress. Kaiser Family Foundation, "Daily Media Use Among Children and Teens Up Dramatically from Five Years Ago," January 20, 2010, http://kff.org/disparities-policy/press-release/daily-media-use-among-children-and-teens-up-dramatically-from-five-years-ago.

7. Soren Gordhamer, *Wisdom 2.0: Ancient Secrets for the Creative and Constantly Connected* (New York: Harper Collins, 2009).

8. Gloria J. Mark, Stephen Voida, and Armand V. Cardello, "A Pace Not Dictated by Electrons: An Empirical Study of Work Without Email," *Proceedings of the SIG CHI Conference on Human Factors in Computer Systems* (2012): 555–564.

9. See Sara Konrath, Edward H. O'Brien, and Courtney Hsing, "Changes in Dispositional Empathy in American College Students over Time: A Meta-Analysis," *Personality and Social Psychology Review* 15, no. 2 (May 2011): 180–198; Andrew Przybyliski and Netta Weinstein, "Can You Connect with Me Now? How the Presence of Movie Communication Technology Influences Face-to-Face Conversation Quality," *Journal of Social and Personal Relationships* (2012): 1–10; and Stalin Misra et al., "The iPhone Effect: The Quality of In-Person Social Interactions in the Presence of Mobile Devices," *Environment and Behavior* (2014): 124.

10. Stephen Marche reviews many studies correlating media use with loneliness in an article that sparked much discussion, "Is Facebook Making Us Lonely?" *Atlantic*, May 2012.

11. Alter, *Irresistible*.

12. There's substantial disagreement, ambiguity, and controversy among psychologists about what "Internet addiction" is, given the many things you can do on the Internet. It is not currently included in the *Diagnostic and Statistical Manual of Mental Disorders* (the *DSM-V*), the medical resource that classifies psychiatric disorders. Internet gaming disorder (IGD), which refers to unhealthy patterns of engagement with games, mostly by male adolescents and young adults, is being considered for inclusion in the next *DSM*. There is evidence that the brains of IGD patients resemble the brains of substance users and pathological gamblers. "Problematic media use" is a term used to describe dysfunctional ways of engaging with media and encompasses Internet addiction, technology addiction, Internet gaming disorder, and others. Many psychologists characterize problematic relationships with media and devices, such as smartphones, as *compulsive, obsessive,* or *unhealthy*. See Laurel J. Felt and Michael B. Robb, *Technology Addiction: Concern, Controversy, and Finding Balance.* San Francisco, CA: Common Sense Media, 2016.

13. Alter, *Irresistible*, 4.

14. In Julian Morgans, "Your Addiction to Social Media Is No Accident," *Vice*, May 19, 2017, https://www.vice.com/en_us/article/the-secret-ways-social-media-is-built-for-addiction.

15. Morgans, "Your Addiction."

16. Alexis Madrigal compares social networks to Vegas slot machines in "The Machine Zone: This Is Where You Go When You Just Can't Stop Looking at Pictures on Facebook." *Atlantic*, July 21, 2013; see also Natasha Dow Schull, *Addiction by Design* (Princeton, 2012). The machine zone represents the dark side of "flow"—a trancelike state of deep, joyful absorption in which people lose their sense of a separate self and merge their identity with the environment. People talk of artists, athletes, and musicians who experience flow when intensely engaged in creative activities—but playing jazz is not the equivalent to playing slot machines or Candy Crush. Losing your sense of time awareness severs bonds with the larger environment and the rhythms of nature. It also makes people manipulable; totalitarian regimes and brainwashing techniques often work by removing victims' control over their own time orientation. For more on this, see Jeremy Rifkin, *Time Wars: The Primary Conflict in Human History* (New York: Touchstone, 1987).

17. Other digerati who constrain their kids' media use include people from Microsoft, Oracle, Intel, PlayStation, 23andMe, Twitter, and Vine. Amy Fleming offers some profiles in "Screen Time vs. Play Time: What Tech Leaders Won't Let Their Own Kids Do." *Guardian*, May 23, 2015.

18. Alter, *Irresistible*.

19. The number of published scientific papers with the word "mindfulness" in the title and of proposals to the National Institutes for Health that seek funding for mindfulness work has "gone exponential," Jon Kabat-Zinn told Krista Tippett. Kabat-Zinn, "Opening to Our Lives," *On Being with Krista Tippett*, December 27, 2012.

20. Kirk Warren Brown and Richard M. Ryan, "The Benefits of Being Present: Mindfulness and Its Role in Psychological Well-Being," *Journal of Personality and Social Psychology* 84, no. 4 (2003): 822–848.

21. Brown and Ryan, "Benefits of Being Present."

22. Winifred Gallagher, *Rapt: Attention and the Focused Life* (New York: Penguin Press, 2009), 9.

23. Gallagher, 11.

24. William James, *The Principles of Psychology* (New York: Dover, 1890), 5.
25. James, *Principles*.
26. Jon Kabat-Zinn, *Mindfulness for Beginners: Reclaiming the Present Moment—And Your Life* (Boulder, CO: Sounds True, 2012), 17.
27. For more on the spiritual origins of mindfulness, see Levy, *Mindful Tech*; David Shi, *In Search of the Simple Life* (Leyton, UT: Gibbs Smith, 1986); Daniel Siegel, *The Mindful Brain: Reflection and Attunement in the Cultivation of Well-Being* (New York: Norton, 2009); and Jeff Wilson, *Mindful America: The Mutual Transformation of Buddhist Meditation and American Culture* (New York: Oxford University Press, 2014).
28. Jon Kabat-Zinn, *Wherever You Go, There You Are* (New York: Hyperion Press, 1994), 174.
29. Judy Lief, "The Dharma of Distraction," *Shambhala Sun*, September 2014, 46.
30. Sharon Salzberg, "The Myth of Multitasking," *Shambhala Sun*, May 2014.
31. Sharon Salzberg, *Real Happiness: The Power of Meditation* (New York: Workman Publishing Group, 2010).
32. Craig Hassed and Richards Chambers, *Mindful Learning* (Boston: Shambhala Publications, 2015).
33. Hassed and Chambers, *Mindful Learning*.
34. Nicholas Carr, *The Shallows: What the Internet Is Doing to Our Brains* (New York: Norton, 2010), 34.
35. Richard Davidson et al. "Alterations in Brain and Immune Function Produced by Mindfulness Meditation," *Psychosomatic Medicine* 65 (2003): 564–570.
36. For example, see Mattieu Ricard, Antoine Lutz, and Richard Davidson, "The Mind of the Meditator," *Scientific American* 311, no 5. (Nov. 2014): 38–45.
37. Hassed and Chambers, *Mindful Learning*.
38. Ellen Langer, *Mindfulness* (Cambridge, MA: De Capo Press, 1989), 49.
39. For example, see Eval Ophir, Clifford Nass, and Anthony D. Wagner, "Cognitive Control in Media Multitaskers," Proceedings of the National Academy of Sciences USA 106, no. 37 (September 15, 2009): 15583–15587.
40. For example, see Zheng Wang and John M. Tcherhov, "The 'Myth' of Media Multitasking: Reciprocal Dynamics of Media Multitasking, Personal Needs, and Gratifications," *Journal of Communication* 62 (2012): 493–513.
41. See David L. Strayer and Jason M. Watson, "Supertaskers and the Multitasking Brain," *Scientific American Mind*, (March/April 2012); and Maria Konnikova, "The Multitask Masters," *New Yorker*, May 7, 2014.
42. Ricard, Lutz, and Davidson, "Mind of the Meditator."
43. Wang and Tchernev, "'Myth.'"
44. Roy Pea et al. "Media Use, Face-to-Face Communication, Media Multitasking, and Social Well-Being Among 8- to 12-Year-Old Girls," *Developmental Psychology* 48, no. 2 (2012): 327–336.
45. Some research has found that people show greater attentiveness, stronger memory, and improved cognition after spending time in a quiet rural setting, close to nature. For example, an experimental group that went to a secluded woodland park showed significant improvement in these mental faculties by comparison to another group that went to busy downtown streets. Even just looking at pictures of nature scenes can have a positive effect on your brain. See Marc G. Berman, John Jonides, and Stephen Kaplan, "The Cognitive Benefits of Interacting with Nature," *Psychological Science* 19, no. 12 (December 2008): 1207–1212.
46. See Mark, Voida, and Cardello, "Pace Not Dictated."
47. Langer, *Mindfulness*, 137.
48. Langer, *Mindfulness*.
49. Langer, *Mindfulness*.
50. Jonathan B. Spira and Cody Burke, "Intel's War on Information Overload: A Case Study," Basex, August 2009, http://iorgforum.org/wp-content/uploads/2011/06/IntelWarIO.BasexReport1.pdf.
51. Spira and Burke, "Intel's War."
52. Mark, Voida, and Cardello, "Pace Not Dictated."

53. Ray Williams, "Why It's So Hard to Unplug from the Digital World," *Psychology Today*, May 6, 2012.

54. Williams, "Why It's So Hard."

55. Leslie Perlow, *Sleeping with Your Smartphone: How to Break the 24/7 Habit and Change the Way You Work* (Cambridge, MA: Harvard Business Review Press, 2012).

56. Perlow, *Sleeping with Your Smartphone*, 104.

57. Susan Moeller, "A Day Without Media," *International Center for Media and the Public Agenda and the University of Maryland*, 2010.

58. Research suggests that young people benefit from media time-outs, too. College students around the world who gave up their devices for a day reported feeling more peaceful, invigorated, happy, liberated, focused, and creative. Preteens who spent five days in the woods without devices got significantly better at reading people's nonverbal emotional cures than a control group did—and they still enjoyed camp. See Susan Moeller, "A Day Without Media," and Yalta T. Urls et al., "Five Days at Outdoor Education Camp Without Screens Improves Preteen Skills with Nonverbal Emotional Cues," *Computers in Human Behavior* 39 (2014): 387–392.

59. Personal communication, 2015.

60. David Levy, *Mindful Tech: How to Bring About Balance in Our Digital Lives* (New Haven, CT: Yale University Press, 2016), 82.

61. Levy, *Mindful Tech*.

62. Hassed and Chambers, *Mindful Learning*, 161.

63. Linda Stone, "Just Breathe: Building the Case for Email Apnea," *HuffPost*, February 8, 2008, https://www.huffpost.com/entry/just-breathe-building-the_b_85651.

64. Stone, "Just Breathe"; Linda Stone, "Conscious Computing," *HuffPost*, April 20, 2012, https://lindastone.net/2012/04/20/conscious-computing-36.

65. Linda Stone, "The Connected Life: From Email Apnea to Conscious Computing," *HuffPost*, May 7, 2012, https://www.huffpost.com/entry/email-apnea-screen-apnea-_b_1476554.

66. Margaret Chesney and David Anderson, quoted in Stone, "Just Breathe."

67. Quoted in Stone, "Just Breathe."

68. Linda Stone, "Continuous Partial Attention," *Linda Stone* (blog), https://lindastone.net/2009/11/30/beyond-simple-multi-tasking-continuous-partial-attention/.

69. Stone, "Just Breathe."

70. Alex Soojung-Kim Pang, *The Distraction Addiction: Getting the Information You Need and the Communication You Want, without Enraging Your Family Annoying Your Colleagues, and Destroying Your Soul* (New York: Little, Brown and Co., 2013).

71. One self-described contemplative-computing "devotee" is Evgeny Morozov, who bought a safe with a built-in timer and locked his smartphone in it for days at a time. Morozov compares today's struggle against mediated distraction to the anti-noise campaigns of the early 20th century. People did not promote individual acts like buying earplugs or moving to the countryside. They sought collective solutions to the problem of noise: by turning silence into a right. See Morozov, "Only Disconnect: Two Cheers for Boredom," *New Yorker*, October 28, 2013.

72. Stone, "Conscious Computing."

73. For more on how the fields of positive psychology and happiness studies influenced the positive computing movement, see Rafael Calvo and Dorian Peters, *Positive Computing: Technology for Well-Being and Human Potential* (Cambridge, MA: MIT Press, 2014).

74. Calvo and Peters, *Positive Computing*, 8.

75. For example, see Hsu, "Slow Media Movement"; Daisy Tam, "Slow Journeys: What Does It Mean to Go Slow?" *Food, Culture and Society* 11, no. 2 (2008): 208–218; Rudy Dunlap, "Recreating Culture: Slow Food as a Leisure Education Movement," *World Leisure Journal* 54, no. 1 (2012): 38–47; and Wendy Parkins, "Out of Time: Fast Subjects and Slow Living." *Time and Society* 16, nos. 2 and 3 (2004): 311–332.

76. Siegel, *Mindful Brain*, 105.

77. See Daniel Levitin, *The Organized Mind: Thinking Straight in the Age of Information Overload* (New York: Plume Books, 2014).

78. Pang, *Distraction Addiction*.

79. Patrick Kingsley, "The Art of Slow Reading." *Guardian*, July 15, 2010.

80. Carr, *The Shallows*.

81. Levy, *Mindful Tech*, xi.

82. Damasio, quoted in Carr, *The Shallows*, 220.

83. Nicholas Carr, "Is Google Making Us Stupid?" *Atlantic*, July/August 2008.

84. Alex Pang talks about the value of mind wandering in his book *Rest: Why You Get More Done When You Work Less*, (New York: Penguin, 2016), which describes how scores of artists, scientists, and scholars have prospered by balancing deliberate practice with deliberate rest.

85. Edgar Allen Poe, "A Descent into the Maelstrom" (1841).

86. Jeff Wilson, *Mindful America: The Mutual Transformation of Buddhist Meditation and American Culture* (New York: Oxford University Press, 2014), 119.

87. American Psychological Association, "Stress in America: Coping with Change," Stress in America Survey, 2017.

88. For more on the adult coloring-book trend, see Thu-Huang Ha, "America's Obsession with Adult Coloring Is a Cry for Help," *Quartz*, April 24, 2016, http://qz.com/650378/the-sad-reason-american-adults-are-so-obsessed-with-coloring-books.

89. For more on the marketing of Buddhist products, see Wilson, *Mindful America*.

90. Calvo and Peters, *Positive Computing*, 267.

91. Wilson, *Mindful America*, 5.

92. Ha, "America's Obsession."

Chapter 6

1. Neil Postman, *Technopoly: The Surrender of Culture to Technology* (New York: Vintage, 1993), 44.

2. Bill Joy, "Why the Future Doesn't Need Us," *Wired* 8, no. 4 (April 2000). Environmentalist Bill McKibben calls this article "one of the great Paul Revere moments of our time" (*Enough*, 86).

3. Even the IEEE, a group of engineers self-described as the world's largest technical professional organization dedicated to advancing technology for the benefit of humanity, was called Luddite when it disputed claims in 1998 that there was a shortage of US computer programmers—a business argument aimed at easing visa access for (cheaper) foreign workers.

4. Paulina Borsook, *Cyberselfish: A Critical Romp through the Terribly Libertarian Culture of High Tech* (New York: Public Affairs, 2000).

5. For more about Luddite history, see Kevin Binfield, ed., *Writings of the Luddites* (Baltimore, MD: John Hopkins University Press, 2004); Richard Conniff, "What the Luddites Really Fought Against," *Smithsonian*, March 2011; Steven E. Jones, *Against Technology: From the Luddites to Neo-Luddism* (New York: Routledge, 2006); E. P. Thompson, *The Making of the English Working Class* (New York: Vintage Books, 1963); and Jeffrey Wasserstrom, "'Civilization' and its Discontents: The Boxers and Luddites as Heroes and Villains," *Theory and Society* 16 (1987): 675–707.

6. Richard Byrne, "A Nod to Ned Ludd," *The Baffler* 23 (2013); and Kevin Robins and Frank Webster, *Times of the Technoculture: From the Information Society to the Virtual Life* (New York: Routledge, 1999).

7. Byrne, "Nod to Ned Ludd," and Kirkpatrick Sale, *Rebels against the Future: The Luddites and Their War on the Industrial Revolution: Lessons for the Computer Age* (Boston: Addison-Wesley, 1995).

8. Conniff, "What the Luddites Really Fought Against"; Thomas R. Pynchon, "Is It O.K. to Be a Luddite?" *New York Times Book Review*, October 28, 1984.

9. In Conniff, "What the Luddites."

10. In William Safire, "The Return of the Luddites," *New York Times Magazine*, December 6, 1998.

11. Jennifer Daryl Slack, *Communication Technologies and Society: Conceptions of Causality and the Politics of Technological Intervention* (Norwood, NJ: Ablex Publishing, 1984).

12. David Noble, *Progress without People: New Technology, Unemployment, and the Message of Resistance* (Toronto: Between the Lines, 1995), 7.

13. Noble, *Progress without People.*

14. Robins and Webster, *Times of the Technoculture.*

15. Byrne, "Nod to Ned Ludd."

16. Byrne, "Nod to Ned Ludd."

17. Byrne, "Nod to Ned Ludd."

18. See Noble, *Progress without People*; Robins and Webster, *Times of the Technoculture*; Robert McChesney and John Nichols, *People Get Ready: The Fight against a Jobless Economy and a Citizenless Democracy* (New York: Nation Books, 2016); and Langdon Winner, "Look Out for the Luddite Label," *MIT Technology Review,* November/December 1997.

19. Eric Hobsbawm, "The Machine Breakers," *Past and Present* 1, no. 1 (1952): 57–70.

20. Thompson, *Making of the English*, 553, quoted in Slack, *Communication Technologies and Society*, 42.

21. Chellis Glendinning, "Notes towards a Neo-Luddite Manifesto," *Utne Reader*, March/April 1990.

22. E. F. Schumacher, *Small Is Beautiful: Economics as if People Mattered* (New York: Harper Perennial, 2010).

23. Marshall McLuhan and Bruce Powers, *The Global Village: Transformations in World Life and Media in the 21st Century* (New York: Oxford University Press, 1992), 97.

24. Marshall McLuhan, quoted in Nicholas Carr, "The Luddite McLuhan," *Rough Type* (blog), March 1, 2009, http://www.roughtype.com/?p-123.

25. Glendinning, "Notes Toward a Neo-Luddite Manifesto."

26. Robins and Webster, *Times of the Technoculture.*

27. In defense of pre-industrial and pre-agricultural societies, let's note that hunter-gatherers spend around half as much time working as people in advanced nations do. Research in the 1960s found that the Bushmen of the Kalahari took only 17 hours a week to find food and another 19 hours to perform domestic activities. By comparison, the average American worked 40 hours at a job and 36 in domestic labor. (Subsistence societies might not accumulate material surpluses, but they don't accumulate any debt, either.)

28. John Katz, "Return of the Luddites," *Wired* 3, no. 6 (July 1995).

29. See Sherry Turkle, *Alone Together: Why We Expect More from Technology and Less from Each Other* (Cambridge, MA: Basic Books, 2011).

30. Katz, "Return of the Luddites."

31. Kelly, Kevin, "Interview with a Luddite," *Wired* 3, no. 6 (July 1995).

32. Kelly, "Interview with a Luddite."

33. The serial bomber, whose identity was still unknown at the time of publication, had promised to renounce terrorism and halt his attacks if the manuscript was printed. Publishers decided to agree with the request after consulting with law-enforcement authorities.

34. It might seem hard to believe now, but highway trash was a big problem at the time. It might be easier to believe that Iron Eyes Cody, who played the chief, was an actor of Sicilian descent who sustained a long career pretending to be Native American.

35. Wasserstrom, "'Civilization' and its Discontents," 705.

36. Sale, *Rebels against the Future*, 266.

37. Jerry Mander, "Six Grave Doubts about Computers," *Whole Earth Review* 44 (1985), 20.

38. Ronald Bailey, "Rage Against the Machines," *Reason* 33, no. 3 (July 2001): 26–35.

39. Noble, *Progress without People.*

40. Conniff, "What the Luddites."

41. Zachary Loeb, "Warding Off General Ludd: The Absurdity of the Luddite Awards," *Boundary 2*, January 7, 2015, http://www.boundary2.org/2015/01/warding-off-general-ludd-the-absurdity-of-the-luddite-awards-2.

42. Robert D. Atkinson, "The 2015 ITIF Luddite Award Nominees: The Worst of the Year's Worst Innovation Killers," *Information Technology and Innovation Foundation,* December 21, 2015.

43. Robins and Webster, *Times of the Technoculture,* 61.

44. Byrne, "Nod to Ned Ludd."

45. David Shenk, Andrew Shapiro, and Steven Johnson, *Technorealism,* 1998, http://technorealism.org.

46. Borsook, *Cyberselfish,* 258.

47. Lee Siegel, *Against the Machine: Being Human in the Age of the Electronic Mob* (New York: Spiegel and Grau, 2008).

48. Howard Rheingold, "Technology 101: What Do We Need to Know About the Future We're Creating?" *Howard Rheingold* (blog), May 5, 1998, http://www.rheingold.com/texts/techcrit/technophiles.html.

49. Howard Rheingold, *Net Smart: How to Thrive Online,* (Cambridge, MA: MIT Press, 2012).

50. Turkle, *Alone Together.*

51. Jaron Lanier, *You Are Not a Gadget: A Manifesto* (New York: Knopf, 2010).

52. Simon Reynolds, "Back to the Future," *Salon,* May 12, 2007.

53. Michiko Kakutani, "A Rebel in Cyberspace, Fighting Collectivism," *New York Times,* January 14, 2010; and John Tierney, "Jaron Lanier Is Rethinking the Open Culture of the Internet," *New York Times,* January 12, 2010.

54. Rheingold, *Net Smart.*

55. Malcolm Gladwell, *The Tipping Point: How Little Things Can Make a Big Difference* (Boston: Back Bay Books, 2002).

Chapter 7

1. Ben Agger, *Speeding Up Fast Capitalism* (Boulder, CO: Paradigm, 2004), 163.

2. Agger, *Speeding Up Fast Capitalism,* 165.

3. John Tomlinson, *The Culture of Speed: The Coming of Immediacy,* (Thousand Oaks, CA: Sage Publications, 2007), 150; and Wendy Parkins and Geoffrey Craig, *Slow Living* (Oxford and New York: Berg, 2006), 125.

4. Maggie Berg and Barbara Seeber, *The Slow Professor: Challenging the Culture of Speed in the Academy* (Toronto: University of Toronto, 2017), 57.

5. Maxwell and Miller, *Greening the Media,* 26.

6. Modern women spend as much time on housework as their colonial counterparts did. Whereas cleaning tasks were once performed with more assistance from men, children, and servants, these duties increasingly fell, and still fall, to the woman of the household—whose labor was, and remains, mostly unpaid.

7. Daniel Levitin, *The Organized Mind: Thinking Straight in the Age of Information Overload* (New York: Plume Books, 2014).

8. One of David Levy's experiments suggests that people who strongly favor technology are less tolerant of alternative viewpoints. He invited a cohort of students to vote on whether or not they would be allowed to use digital devices in the classroom. The majority preferred *not* to use technology but hesitated to force their preference on others; they respected the rights of other class members to choose for themselves. By contrast, the tech-inclined minority were aggressive about imposing their own choice, with little concern about other students' preferences. See Levy, *Mindful Tech: How to Bring Balance to Our Digital Lives* (New Haven, CT: Yale, 2015), 181.

9. Some politicians have pondered changing this exemption. Job creators, take note. (The decline of the standardized work week can also be framed as a labor-market issue: workers cannot effectively compare and evaluate job offers when they do not know how many hours of labor they are exchanging for whatever compensation they might receive.)

10. For more on the social and environmental impact of overwork, see Naomi Klein, *This Changes Everything: Capitalism vs. the Climate* (New York: Simon and Schuster, 2014); Bill McKibben, *Deep Economy: The Wealth of Communities and the Durable Future* (New York: Times Books,

2007); and Juliet B. Schor, *True Wealth: How and Why Millions of Americans are Creating a Time-Rich, Ecologically Light, Small-Scale, High-Satisfaction Economy* (New York: Penguin, 2011).

11. Juliet B. Schor, *The Overworked American: The Unexpected Decline of Leisure* (New York: Basic Books, 1992).

12. David Rosnick, "Shorter Work Hours as a Means of Slowing Climate Change," Center for Economic and Policy Research, February 2013.

13. David Rosnick and Mark Weisbrot, "Are Shorter Work Hours Good for the Environment? A Comparison of U.S. and European Energy Consumption," Center for Economic and Policy Research, December 2006.

14. Douglas Rushkoff, *Throwing Rocks*. See also Jenny Brundin, "Utah Finds Surprising Benefits in 4-Day Workweek," *Morning Edition*, National Public Radio, April 10, 2009; and John de Graaf, "Life Away from the Rat Race: Why One Group of Workers Decided to Cut Their Own Hours and Pay," AlterNet, July 2, 2012, https://www.alternet.org/story/156126/life_away_from_the_rat-race%3A_why_one_group_of_workers_decided_to_cut_their_own_hours_and_pay.

15. Anna Coote, "Shorten the Workweek to Thirty Hours," *New York Times*, January 13, 2015.

16. Alec MacGillis, "Revenge of the Forgotten Class," ProPublica, November 10, 2016. https://www.propublica.org/article/revenge-of-the-forgotten-class.

17. William Powers, *Hamlet's Blackberry: A Practical Philosophy for Building a Good Life in the Digital Age* (New York: Harper Books, 2010).

18. Barry Schwartz, *The Paradox of Choice: Why More Is Less* (New York: Harper Perennial, 2005).

19. Kalle Lasn, *Culture Jam: How to Reverse America's Suicidal Consumer Binge—and Why We Must* (New York: William Morrow and Co., 1999).

20. For example, see Jeremy Rifkin, *Time Wars: The Primary Conflict in Human History* (New York: Touchstone, 1987).

21. Rabbi Arthur Waskow, "Can America Learn from Shabbat?" in *Take Back Your Time: Fighting Time Poverty and Overwork in America*, ed. John de Graaf (San Francisco: Berrett-Koehler, 2003).

22. James Carey, *Communication as Culture: Essays on Media and Society* (New York: Routledge, 1989).

23. Maryanne Wolf, *Proust and the Squid: The Story and Science of the Reading Brain* (New York: Harper Perennial, 2008), 213–214, 228.

24. Benjamin Franklin and William Temple Franklin, *Memoirs of the Life and Writings of Benjamin Franklin* (London: Henry Coburn, 1818), 224.

25. Powers, *Hamlet's Blackberry*, 168.

26. Miriam Moser, "Slow Media: Using Digital Media Responsibly," *AlumniPortal Deutschland Career Magazine*, August 2014; and Ray Williams, "Why It's So Hard to Unplug from the Digital World," *Psychology Today*, May 6, 2012.

27. Anne-Marie Slaughter, "Why Women Still Can't Have It All." *Atlantic*, July/August 2012.

28. Two notable examples are the Mindful Schools Program, founded with help from Jon Kabat-Zinn and Soren Gordhamer, and the MindUp Program, developed by the Hawn Foundation in collaboration with neuroscientists, psychologists, and educators.

29. Klein, *This Changes Everything*.

30. Robert McChesney and John Nichols, *People Get Ready: The Fight against a Jobless Economy and a Citizenless Democracy* (New York: Nation Books, 2016).

31. McKibben, *Deep Economy*.

32. See Lyn Christine McGregor, *Habits of the Heartland: Modern Life in Small-Town America* (Ithaca, NY: Cornell University, 2010).

33. People are more engaged in civic life and commit more time to social issues when they work fewer days. For more on this, see Rushkoff, *Throwing Rocks*.

34. McChesney and Nichols, *People Get Ready*, 34.

35. Klein, *This Changes Everything*, 153.

References

Agger, Ben. *Speeding Up Fast Capitalism*. Boulder, CO: Paradigm, 2004.

Alter, Adam. *Irresistible: The Rise of Addictive Technology and the Business of Keeping Us Hooked*. New York: Penguin Press, 2017.

Altman, Elissa. "Move Over Slow Food: Introducing Slow Media." *HuffPost*, November 29, 2009. http://huffingtonpost.com/elissa-altman/move-over-slow-food-intro_b_367517.html.

American Psychological Association. *Stress in America: Coping with Change*. Stress in America Survey, 2017.

Anawalt, Sasha. "The Slow Journalism Movement: Heard of It?" *ARTicles* (blog). National Arts Journalism Program, September 7, 2008. http://www.najp.org/articles/sasha_anawalt/2008/09.

Atkinson, Robert D. "The 2015 ITIF Luddite Award Nominees: The Worst of the Year's Worst Innovation Killers." *Information Technology and Innovation Foundation*, December 21, 2015. https://itif.org/publications/2015/12/21/2015-itif-luddite-award-nominees-worst-year%E2%80%99s-worst-innovation-killers.

Atton, Chris. "Are There Alternative Media After Computer-Mediated Communication?" *M/C Reviews*, April 12, 2000.

Atton, Chris. *Alternative Media*. Thousand Oaks, CA: Sage Publications, 2002.

Bailey, Miranda. *Greenlit*. Movie. Produced by Miranda Bailey, Marc Lesser, and Lauren Selman. Los Angeles: Ambush Entertainment, 2010. DVD.

Bailey, Ronald. "Rage Against the Machines." *Reason* 33, no. 3 (July 2001): 26–35.

Bank of America. *Trends in Consumer Mobility Report 2016*. August 17, 2017. https://newsroom.bankofamerica.com/content/newsroom/press-releases/2017/08/keeping-digital-natives.html.

Barranquero Carretero, Alejandro, and Garbiñe Jaurrieta Bariain 2016. "Slow Journalism in Spain: New Magazine Startups and the Paradigmatic Case of *Jot Down*." *Journalism Practice* 10, no. 4 (2016): 521–538.

Bauerlein, Mark. *The Dumbest Generation: How the Internet Stupefies Young Americans and Jeopardizes Our Future (Or, Don't Trust Anyone Under 30)*. New York: Tarcher/Penguin, 2008.

Beccaria, Laurent, and Patrick de Saint-Exupéry. "Content and Its Discontents." *Harper's Magazine*, October 2013.

Berg, Maggie, and Barbara Seeber. *The Slow Professor: Challenging the Culture of Speed in the Academy*. Toronto: University of Toronto, 2016.

Berkey-Gerard, Mark. "Tracking the 'Slow Journalism' Movement." *Campfire Journalism* (blog), July 29, 2009. https://web.archive.org/web/20120911165001/markberkeygerard.com/2009/07/tracking-the-%E2%80%9Cslow-journalism%E2%80%9D-movement.

Berman, Marc G., John Jonides, and Stephen Kaplan. "The Cognitive Benefits of Interacting with Nature." *Psychological Science* 19, no. 12 (December 2008): 1207–1212.

Binfield, Kevin, ed. *Writings of the Luddites*. Baltimore, MD: Johns Hopkins University Press, 2004.

Bittman, Mark. "I Need a Virtual Break. No, Really." *New York Times*, March 2, 2008.

Blanding, Michael. "The Value of Slow Journalism in the Age of Instant Information." *Nieman Reports*, Summer 2015.

Bloomberg, Jason. "Amazon Cloud Ecosystem: Where the Cloud Action Is." *Forbes*, July 13, 2015. http://www.forbes.com/sites/jasonbloomberg/2015/07/13/amazon-cloud-ecosystem-where-the-cloud-action-is.

Boccaletti, Giulio, Marcus Löffler, and Jeremy M. Oppenheim. "How IT Can Cut Carbon Emissions." *The McKinsey Quarterly*, October 2008. http://www.kyotoclub.org/docs/mckinsey_it_ott08.pdf.

Borsook, Paulina. *Cyberselfish: A Critical Romp through the Terribly Libertarian Culture of High Tech*. New York: Public Affairs, 2000.

Breiner, James. "Cultural Publication Flirts with the 'Dark Side' in Spain." *News Entrepreneurs*, July 18, 2015. http://newsentrepreneurs.blogspot.com/2015/07/digital-publication-flirts-with-dark.html.

Brethour, Patrick. "Malcolm Gladwell: The Quiet Canadian," *Globe and Mail*, April 4, 2010.

Brown, Kirk Warren, and Richard M. Ryan. "The Benefits of Being Present: Mindfulness and Its Role in Psychological Well-Being." *Journal of Personality and Social Psychology* 84, no. 4 (2003): 822–848.

Brundin, Jenny. "Utah Finds Surprising Benefits in 4-Day Workweek." *Morning Edition*, National Public Radio, April 10, 2009.

Burrington, Ingrid. "The Environmental Toll of a Netflix Binge." *Atlantic*, December 16, 2015.

Butler, Kiera. "Killer App." *Mother Jones*, November/December 2012.

Butterworth, Trevor. "Time for a Slow-Word Movement." *Forbes*, December 30, 2009. http://forbes.com/2009/12/29/media-newspapers-internet-opinions-columnists-trevor-butterworth.html.

Byrne, Richard. "A Nod to Ned Ludd." *The Baffler* 23 (2013). http://thebaffler.com/articles/a-nod-to-ned-ludd.

Calvo, Rafael, and Peters, Dorian. *Positive Computing: Technology for Well-Being and Human Potential*. Cambridge, MA: MIT Press, 2014.

Carey, James. *Communication as Culture: Essays on Media and Society*. New York: Routledge, 1989.

Carr, Nicholas. "Avatars Consume as Much Electricity as Brazilians." *Rough Type* (blog), December 5, 2006. http://roughtype.com/?p=611.

Carr, Nicholas. "Exodus." *Rough Type* (blog), April 8, 2010. http://www.roughtype.com/?p=1359.

Carr, Nicholas. "The iPad Luddites." *Rough Type* (blog), April 7, 2010. http://roughtype.com/?p=1357.

Carr, Nicholas. "Is Google Making Us Stupid?" *Atlantic*, July/August 2008.

Carr, Nicholas. "The Luddite McLuhan." *Rough Type* (blog), March 1, 2009. http://www.roughtype.com/?p=1230.

Carr, Nicholas. *The Shallows: What the Internet is Doing to Our Brains*. New York: Norton, 2010.

Conniff, Richard. "What the Luddites Really Fought Against." *Smithsonian*, March 2011.

Cooke, Grayson. "Editorial (Slow Media)." *Transformations: Journal of Media, Culture & Technology* 20 (2011). http://www.transformationsjournal.org/issue-20.

Coote, Anna. "Shorten the Workweek to Thirty Hours." *New York Times*, January 13, 2015.

Corbett, Charles, and Richard Turco. "Film and Television," in *South California Environmental Report Card 2006*, 4–11. Institute of the Environment and Sustainability, University of California, Los Angeles. https://www.ioes.ucla.edu/wp-content/uploads/RC06.pdf.

Cubitt, Sean. "I Took Off My Pants and Felt Free: Environmentalism in Countercultural Radio." In *Ecomedia: Key Issues*, edited by Stephen Rust, Salma Monani, and Sean Cubitt. Abingdon, UK and New York: Routledge, 2015.

Cubitt, Sean, Robert Hassan, and Ingrid Volkmer. "Does Cloud Computing Have a Silver Lining?" *Media, Culture and Society* 33, no. 1 (2011): 149–158.

Czitrom, Daniel. *Media and the American Mind: From Morse to McLuhan*. Chapel Hill, NC: University of North Carolina Press, 1983.

David, Sabria. "How 'Slow' Are the Germans?" *DCore/Slow Media Institut,* October 12, 2015. http://www.dcore.de/index.php/wie-slow-sind-die-deutschen-neue-slowtypes-studie-ermoeglicht-spannende-einblicke-in-die-lebenswelt-der-digitalen-mediengesellschaft.

David, Sabria, Jorg Blumtritt, and Benedikt Kohler. "Slow Media Manifesto." *Slow-Media* (blog), January 2, 2010. http://en.slow-media.net/manifesto.

Davidson, Richard, Jon Kabat-Zinn, Jessica Schumacher, Melissa Rosenkranz, Daniel Muller, Saki F. Santorelli, Ferris Urbanowski, Anne Harrington, Katherine Bonus, and John F. Sheridan. "Alterations in Brain and Immune Function Produced by Mindfulness Meditation." *Psychosomatic Medicine* 65 (2003): 564–570

Davis, John. "Going Analog: Vinylphiles and the Consumption of the 'Obsolete' Vinyl Record." In *Residual Media*, edited by Charles Acland. Minneapolis, MN: University of Minnesota Press, 2007.

De Correspondent. "Our Principles." *The Correspondent.* Accessed on November 2, 2017. https://thecorrespondent.com/principles.

de Graff, John. "Life Away from the Rat Race: Why One Group of Workers Decided to Cut Their Own Hours and Pay." *Alternet,* July 2, 2012. https://www.alternet.org/story/156126/life_away_from_the_rat-race%3A_why_one_group_of_workers_decided_to_cut_their_own_hours_and_pay.

De Michiel, Helen. "Towards a Slow Media Practice." *Grantmakers in the Arts Reader* 13, no. 3 (Fall 2002). http://giarts.org/article/towards-slow-media-practice.

Delayed Gratification. "What We Do." Accessed on November 2, 2017. https://www.slow-journalism.com/what-we-do.

DeLuca, Kevin Michael. *Image Politics: The New Rhetoric of Environmental Activism.* New York: Routledge, 1999.

Doctorow, Cory. "Writing in the Age of Distraction." *Locus,* January 2009. http://www.locusmag.com/Features/2009/01/cory-doctorow-writing-in-age-of.html.

Dowling, David. "The Business of Slow Journalism." *Digital Journalism* 4, no. 4 (2015): 530–546.

Downing, John D. H. *Radical Media: Rebellious Communication and Social Movements.* Thousand Oaks, CA: Sage Publications, 2001.

Downing, John D. H. "Audiences and Readers of Alternative Media: The Absent Lure of the Virtually Unknown." *Media, Culture and Society* 25, no. 5 (2003): 625–645.

Drok, Nico, and Liesbeth Hermans. "Is There a Future for Slow Journalism?" *Journalism Practice* 10, no. 4 (2016): 539–554.

Duhigg, Charles, and Keith Bradsher. "How the U.S. Lost Out on iPhone Work." *New York Times,* January 21, 2012.

Dunlap, Rudy. "Recreating Culture: Slow Food as a Leisure Education Movement," *World Leisure Journal* 54, no. 1 (2012): 38–47.

Dyson, Esther, George Gilder, George Keyworth, and Alvin Toffler. "Cyberspace and the American Dream: A Magna Carta for the Knowledge Age." The Progress and Freedom Foundation, August 1994. http://www.pff.org/issues-pubs/futureinsights/fi1.2magnacarta.html.

Edwards, Andres R. *The Sustainability Revolution: Portrait of a Paradigm Shift.* Gabriola, BC: New Society Publishers, 2005.

Estes, Adam Clark. "What is the Cloud, and Where is It?" *Gizmodo,* January 29, 2015. http://gizmodo.com/what-is-the-cloud-and-where-is-it-1682276210.

Fallows, James. "Learning to Love the New Media." *Atlantic,* April 2011.

Felt, Laurel J., and Michael B. Robb. *Technology Addiction: Concern, Controversy, and Finding Balance.* San Francisco: Common Sense Media, 2016.

Finley, Klint. "Your Netflix Addiction is Screwing the Climate." *Wired,* May 14, 2015. http://www.wired.com/2015/05/binge-watching-making-planet-warmer.

Nass, Clifford, interview by Ira Flatow. "The Myth of Multitasking." *Talk of the Nation,* National Public Radio, May 10, 2013.

Fleming, Amy. "Screen Time vs. Play Time: What Tech Leaders Won't Let Their Own Kids Do," *Guardian,* May 23, 2015.

Foucault, Michel. "Ethics of the Concern for the Self as a Practice of Freedom." In *Ethics: Subjectivity and Truth*, edited by Paul Rabinow, 281–301. New York: New Press, 1997.

Franklin, Benjamin, and William Temple Franklin. *Memoirs of the Life and Writings of Benjamin Franklin*. London: Henry Colburn, 1818.

Freeman, John. "Not So Fast." *Wall Street Journal*, August 21, 2009. https://www.wsj.com/articles/SB10001424052970203550604574358643117407778.

Freeman, John. *The Tyranny of E-mail: The Four-Thousand-Year Journey to Your Inbox*. New York: Scribner, 2009.

Fry, Stephen. "Off the Grid." *The Old Friary* (blog). April 20, 2016. http://www.stephenfry.com/2016/04/off-the-grid.

Funnell, Antony. "The Slow Movement." *Radio National/Australian Broadcasting Corporation*. September 2, 2010.

Fussell, Genevieve. "The Sochi Project." *New Yorker*, November 24, 2013.

Gabrys, Jennifer. *Digital Rubbish: A Natural History of Electronics*. Ann Arbor, MI: University of Michigan Press, 2011.

Gabrys, Jennifer. "Powering the Digital: From Energy Ecologies to Electronic Environmentalism." In *Media and the Ecological Crisis*, edited by Richard Maxwell, Jon Raundalen, and Nina Lager Vestberg, 3–18. New York and London: Routledge, 2015.

Gallagher, Winifred. *Rapt: Attention and the Focused Life*. New York: Penguin Press, 2009.

Gane, Nicholas. "Speed Up or Slow Down? Social Theory in the Information Age," *Information, Communication and Society* 9, no. 1 (February 2006): 20–38.

Gess, Harold. "Climate Change and the Possibility of Slow Journalism." *Ecquid Novi: African Journalism Studies* 33, no. 1 (2012): 54–65.

Gladwell, Malcolm. "Small Change: Why the Revolution Will Not Be Tweeted." *New Yorker*, October 4, 2010.

Gladwell, Malcolm. *The Tipping Point: How Little Things Can Make a Big Difference*. Boston: Back Bay Books, 2002.

Glendinning, Chellis. "Notes towards a Neo-Luddite Manifesto." *Utne Reader*, March/April 1990.

"GoodElectronics Vision, Mission, Common Demands on the Electronics Industry." International Network on Human Rights and Sustainability in Electronics, January 20, 2012. https://goodelectronics.org/goodelectronics-vision-mission-common-demands-on-the-electronics-industry.

Gordhamer, Soren. *Wisdom 2.0: Ancient Secrets for the Creative and Constantly Connected*. New York: Harper Collins, 2009.

Gottschalk, Simon. "Speed Culture: Fast Strategies in Televised Commercial Ads." *Qualitative Sociology* 22, no. 4 (1999): 311–329.

Grady, Barbara. "Amazon Moves on Renewables After Push From Greenpeace." *GreenBiz*, June 12, 2015. https://www.greenbiz.com/article/amazon-moves-renewables-after-push-greenpeace.

Greenberg, Susan. "Slow Journalism." *Prospect*, February 2007.

Greenberg, Susan. "Slow Journalism in the Digital Fast Lane." In *Global Literary Journalism: Exploring the Journalistic Imagination*, edited by Richard Keeble and John Tulloch, 381–393. New York: Peter Lang, 2013.

Greenpeace International. "How Clean Is Your Cloud?" April 17, 2012. https://www.greenpeace.org/international/publication/6986/how-clean-is-your-cloud/.

Greenpeace International. "Make IT Green: Cloud Computing and Its Contribution to Climate Change." March 30, 2010. http://www.greenpeace.org/international/en/publications/reports/make-it-green-cloud-computing.

Greenpeace USA. "Clicking Clean: Who's Winning the Race to Build a Green Internet?" January 2017. https://www.greenpeace.org/usa/ending-the-climate-crisis/click-clean/#report.

Gregory, André, and Wallace Shawn. *My Dinner with André*. Movie. Directed by Louis Malle. 1981. New York: The Criterion Collection, 2015. DVD.

Grossman, Elizabeth. *High-Tech Trash: Digital Devices, Hidden Toxins, and Human Health.* Washington, DC: Island Press, 2006.

Grosswiler, Paul. *Old New Media: From Oral to Virtual Environments.* New York: Peter Lang, 2013.

Ha, Thu-Huang. "America's Obsession with Adult Coloring is a Cry for Help." *Quartz*, April 24, 2016. http://qz.com/650378/the-sad-reason-american-adults-are-so-obsessed-with-coloring-books.

Halpern, Ashlea. "The Analog Underground." *New York*, July 11, 2011.

Hamilton, James F. *Democratic Communications: Formations, Projects, Possibilities.* Washington, DC: Lexington Books, 2008.

Hanke, Bob. "McLuhan, Virilio, and Speed." In *Transforming McLuhan: Cultural, Critical, and Postmodern Perspectives*, edited by Paul Grosswiler, 203–226. New York: Peter Lang, 2010.

Hassed, Craig and Richards Chambers. *Mindful Learning.* Boston: Shambhala Publications, 2015.

Hawken, Paul. *Blessed Unrest: How the Largest Movement in the World Came into Being and No One Saw It Coming.* New York: Viking Books, 2007.

Herships, Sally. "A Slow Media Movement." *Marketplace*, American Public Media, November 17, 2009.

Herships, Sally. "Woman Swears Off Internet for Six Months." *Marketplace*, American Public Radio, February 18, 2011.

Hertz, Garnet. "The Problem: How to Creatively Repurpose and Reuse Electronic Waste." *Dead Media Research Lab*, September 2009. http://www.conceptlab.com/deadmedia.

Hertz, Garnet, and Jussi Parikka. "Zombie Media: Circuit Bending Media Archaeology into an Art Method." *Leonardo* 45, no. 5 (2012): 424–430.

Hobsbawm, Eric. "The Machine Breakers." *Past and Present* 1, no. 1 (1952): 57–70.

Honoré, Carl. *In Praise of Slowness: Challenging the Cult of Speed.* New York: Harper Books, 2005.

Hsu, Eric L. "The Slow Food Movement and Time Shortage: Beyond the Dichotomy of Fast or Slow." *Journal of Sociology* 51, no. 3 (September 2015): 628–642.

Huffington, Arianna. "Announcing My First Pick for the HuffPost Book Club: In Praise of Slowness." *Huffington Post*, March 19, 2010. http://www.huffingtonpost.com/arianna-huffington/announcing-my-first-pick-_b_310544.html.

Huffington, Arianna. "The Slow News Movement." *Huffington Post*, June 20, 2012. http://www.huffingtonpost.com/arianna-huffington/the-slow-news-movement_1_b_1613631.html.

Jackson, Maggie. *Distracted: The Erosion of Attention and the Coming Dark Age.* Amherst, NY: Prometheus Books, 2008.

James, William. *The Principles of Psychology.* New York: Dover, 1890.

Johnson, Joel. "1 Million Workers. 90 Million iPhones. 17 Suicides. Who's to Blame?" *Wired*, February 28, 2011. https://www.wired.com/2011/02/ff_joelinchina.

Jones, Malcolm. "Slow Reading: An Antidote for a Fast World?" *Newsweek*, June 22, 2010. http://www.newsweek.com/slow-reading-antidote-fast-world-73395

Jones, Steven E. *Against Technology: From the Luddites to Neo-Luddism.* New York: Routledge, 2006.

Joy, Bill. "Why the Future Doesn't Need Us." *Wired* 8, no. 4 (April 2000).

Kabat-Zinn, Jon. *Mindfulness for Beginners: Reclaiming the Present Moment—And Your Life.* Boulder, CO: Sounds True, 2012.

Kabat-Zinn, Jon. *Wherever You Go, There You Are.* New York: Hyperion Press, 1994.

Kaiser Family Foundation. "Daily Media Use Among Children and Teens Up Dramatically from Five Years Ago." January 20, 2010. http://kff.org/disparities-policy/press-release/daily-media-use-among-children-and-teens-up-dramatically-from-five-years-ago.

Kakutani, Michiko. "A Rebel in Cyberspace, Fighting Collectivism," *New York Times*, January 14, 2010.

Kakutani, Michiko. "See It, Feel It, Touch It. Don't Click," *New York Times*, December 6, 2016.

Katz, Jon. "Return of the Luddites." *Wired* 3, no. 6 (July 1995).

Kelly, Kevin. "Interview with a Luddite." *Wired* 3, no. 6, (July 1995).

Kelly, Maura. "A Slow Books Manifesto." *Atlantic*, March 26, 2012. http://www.theatlantic.com/entertainment/archive/2012/03/a-slow-books-manifesto/254884.

Kenix, Linda Jean. *Alternative and Mainstream Media: The Converging Spectrum.* London: Bloomsbury Academic, 2012.

King, Stephen. "Stephen King's Screen Addiction." *Entertainment Weekly*, July 24, 2009.

Kingsley, Patrick. "The Art of Slow Reading." *Guardian*, July 15, 2010.

Kirk, Andrew. *Counterculture Green: Whole Earth Catalog and American Environmentalism.* Lawrence, KS: The University Press of Kansas, 2007.

Kiron, David, Nina Kruschwitz, Holger Rubel, Martin Reeves, and Sonja-Katrin Fuisz-Kehrbac. "Sustainability's Next Frontier: Walking the Talk on Issues that Matter Most." *MIT Sloan Management Review*, December 2016.

Klein, Naomi. *This Changes Everything: Capitalism vs. the Climate.* New York: Simon and Schuster, 2014.

Konnikova, Maria. "The Multitask Masters." *New Yorker*, May 7, 2014.

Konrath, Sara, Edward H. O'Brien, and Courtney Hsing. "Changes in Dispositional Empathy in American College Students over Time: A Meta-Analysis." *Personality and Social Psychology Review* 15, no. 2 (May 2011): 180–198.

Kovach, Bill, and Tom Rosenstiel. *Warp Speed: America in the Age of Mixed Media.* New York: Century Foundation Press, 1999.

Kummer, Corby. *The Pleasures of Slow Food: Celebrating Authentic Traditions, Flavors, and Recipes.* San Francisco: Chronicle Books, 2002.

Langer, Ellen. *Mindfulness.* Cambridge, MA: Da Capo Press, 1989.

Lanier, Jaron. *You Are Not a Gadget: A Manifesto.* New York: Knopf, 2010.

Lasn, Kalle. *Culture Jam: How to Reverse America's Suicidal Consumer Binge—and Why We Must.* New York: William Morrow and Co., 1999.

Laufer, Peter. *Slow News: A Manifesto for the Critical News Consumer.* Corvallis, OR: Oregon State University Press, 2011.

Le Masurier, Megan. "Slow Journalism: An Introduction to a New Research Paradigm." *Journalism Practice* 10, no. 4 (2016): 405–413.

Le Masurier, Megan. "What is Slow Journalism?" *Journalism Practice* 9, no. 2 (2015): 138–152.

Leigh, David. "Are Reporters Doomed?" *Guardian*, Nov. 12, 2007. www.theguardian.com/media/ 2007/nov/12/mondaymediasection.pressandpublishing3.

Leonard, Annie. "The Story of Electronics: Annotated Script." *The Story of Stuff Project.* 2011. http://storyofstuff.org/wp-content/uploads/movies/scripts/SoElectronics_Annotated_ Script.pdf.

Levine, Robert, and Kathy Bartlett. "Pace of Life, Punctuality and Coronary Heart Disease in Six Countries." *Journal of Cross-Cultural Psychology* 15 (1984): 233–255.

Levine, Robert, and Ara Norenzayan. "The Pace of Life in 31 Countries." *Journal of Cross-Cultural Psychology* 30, No. 2 (1999): 178–205.

Levitin, Daniel. *The Organized Mind: Thinking Straight in the Age of Information Overload.* New York: Plume Books, 2014.

Levy, David. *Mindful Tech: How to Bring Balance to Our Digital Lives.* New Haven, CT: Yale University Press, 2016.

Lewis, Justin. *Beyond Consumer Capitalism: Media and the Limits to Imagination.* Cambridge, UK and Malden, MA: Polity, 2013.

Lief, Judy. "The Dharma of Distraction." *Shambhala Sun*, September 2014.

Loeb, Zachary. "Warding Off General Ludd: The Absurdity of the Luddite Awards." *Boundary 2*, January 7, 2015. http://www.boundary2.org/2015/01/warding-off-general-ludd-the-absurdity-of-the-luddite-awards-2.

Lopez, Antonio. *Greening Media Education: Bridging Media Literacy with Green Cultural Citizenship.* New York: Peter Lang, 2014.

Lopez, Antonio. *The Media Ecosystem.* Berkeley, CA: Revolver, 2012.

Lopez, Antonio. "Putting the Eco Back in Ecosystems." In *Media and the Ecological Crisis*, edited by Richard Maxwell, Jon Raundalen, and Nina Lager Vestberg, 152–176. New York: Routledge, 2015.

MacDonald, Scott. "Toward an Eco Cinema." *Interdisciplinary Studies in Literature and Environment* 11, no. 2 (Summer 2004): 107–132.

MacGillis, Alex. "Revenge of the Forgotten Class." ProPublica, November 10, 2016. https://www. propublica.org/article/revenge-of-the-forgotten-class.

Madrigal, Alexis. "The Machine Zone: This Is Where You Go When You Just Can't Stop Looking at Pictures on Facebook," *Atlantic*, July 21, 2013.

Mander, Jerry. *In the Absence of the Sacred: The Failure of Technology and the Survival of the Indian Nations*. San Francisco, CA: Sierra Club Books, 1991.

Mander, Jerry. "Six Grave Doubts about Computers." *Whole Earth Review* 44 (1985).

Marche, Stephen. "Is Facebook Making Us Lonely?" *Atlantic*, May 2012.

Marcus, Ruth. "After Shirley Sherrod, Time for the Slow Blogging Movement." *Post Partisan* (blog), *Washington Post*, July 23, 2010. http://voices.washingtonpost.com/postpartisan/ 2010/07/after_shirley_sherrod_time_for.html.

Mark, Gloria J., Stephen Voida, and Armand V. Cardello, "A Pace Not Dictated by Electrons: An Empirical Study of Work Without Email," *Proceedings of the SIG CHI Conference on Human Factors in Computer Systems* (2012): 555–564.

Marr, Lisa, and Paolo Davanzo. "The Sound We See: Growing a Global Slow Film Movement." *Echo Park Film Center*, 2015. http://www.echoparkfilmcenter.org/blog/sound-we-see.

Marron, Maria. "Content Creation Spans All Aspects of J-Programs." *Journalism and Mass Communication Educator* 69, no. 4 (2014): 347–348.

Maxwell, Richard, and Toby Miller. *Greening the Media*. New York: Oxford University Press, 2012.

Maxwell, Richard, and Toby Miller. "Greening the Media." *Huffington Post*, June 15, 2012. https:// www.huffingtonpost.com/richard-maxwell/greening-the-media_b_1601492.html.

Maxwell, Richard, and Toby Miller. "The Fantasies of Marshall McLuhan." *Greening the Media* (blog). *Psychology Today*, November 3, 2014. https://www.psychologytoday.com/blog/ greening-the-media/201411/the-fantasies-marshall-mcluhan.

Maxwell, Richard, Jon Raundalen, and Nina Lager Vestberg. "Media Ecology Recycled." In Maxwell, Raundalen, and Vestberg, *Media and the Ecological Crisis*, xi–xxi. New York: Routledge, 2015.

McChesney, Robert. *Digital Disconnect: How Capitalism is Turning the Internet Against Democracy*. Boston: New Press, 2013.

McChesney, Robert, and John Nichols. *People Get Ready: The Fight against a Jobless Economy and a Citizenless Democracy*. New York: Nation Books, 2016.

McChesney, Robert, and John Nichols. *The Death and Life of American Journalism: The Media Revolution That Will Begin the World Again*. New York: Nation Books, 2010.

McGregor, Lyn Christine. *Habits of the Heartland: Modern Life in Small-Town America*. Ithaca, NY: Cornell University, 2010.

McKibben, Bill. *Deep Economy: The Wealth of Communities and the Durable Future*. New York: Times Books, 2007.

McKibben, Bill. *Enough: Staying Human in an Engineered Age*. New York: Henry Holt, 2003.

McLelland, Mac. "Shelf Lives." *Mother Jones,* March/April 2012.

McLuhan, Marshall. *Understanding Media: The Extensions of Man*. New York: McGraw-Hill, 1964.

McLuhan, Marshall, and Bruce Powers. *The Global Village: Transformations in World Life and Media in the 21st Century*. New York: Oxford University Press, 1992, 97.

McSweeney's. "A Look at the San Francisco Panorama." January 2, 2010. https://www. mcsweeneys.net/articles/a-look-at-the-san-francisco-panorama.

Misra, Stalin, Lulu Chenge, Jamie Geneva, and Miao Yuan. "The iPhone Effect: The Quality of In-Person Social Interactions in the Presence of Mobile Devices," *Environment and Behavior* (2014), 124.

Moeller, Susan. "A Day Without Media." International Center for Media and the Public Agenda and the University of Maryland, 2010. https://withoutmedia.wordpress.com.

Morgans, Julian. "Your Addiction to Social Media is No Accident." *Vice*, May 19, 2017. https:// www.vice.com/en_us/article/the-secret-ways-social-media-is-built-for-addiction.

Moore, Martin. "Churnalism Exposed." *Columbia Journalism Review*, March 3, 2011.

Morozov, Evgeny. *The Net Delusion: The Dark Side of Internet Freedom*. New York: Public Affairs, 2011.

Morozov, Evgeny. "Only Disconnect: Two Cheers for Boredom." *New Yorker*, October 28, 2013.

Moser, Miriam. "Slow Media: Using Digital Media Responsibly." *AlumniPortal Deutschland Career Magazine*, August 2014. https://www.alumniportal-deutschland.org/en/jobs-careers/career-magazine/slow-media-digital-media-digital-safety-at-work.

Nail, Jim. "If It's Not 'Green,' What is 'Sustainability Communications'?" *Speaking Sustainability* (blog), Nov. 30, 2010. https://web.archive.org/web/20120227032853/http://speakingsustainability.com:80/2010/11/30/if-its-not-green-what-is-sustainability-communications/

Narratively. "About." *Narratively*, February 24, 2013. https://web.archive.org/web/20130224053212/http://narrative.ly/about.

Natural Resources Defense Council, "America's Data Centers Are Wasting Huge Amounts of Energy," Issue Brief, August 2014.

Negativland. "Shiny, Aluminum, Plastic, and Digital." *The Baffler* 8 (1996).

Neveu, Erik. "On Not Going Too Fast with Slow Journalism." *Journalism Practice* 10, no. 4 (2016): 448–460.

Nielsen, "U.S. Music Industry Year-End Review 2013." *The Nielsen Company*, January 27, 2014. http://www.nielsen.com/us/en/insights/reports/2014/u-s-music-industry-year-end-review-2013.html.

Nielsen, "2017 U.S. Music Year-End Report." *The Nielsen Company*, January 3, 2018. http://www.nielsen.com/us/en/insights/reports/2018/2017-music-us-year-end-report.html.

Nielsen, Jakob. "The End of Legacy Media." *Nielsen Norman Group*, August 23, 1998. https://www.nngroup.com/articles/the-end-of-legacy-media-newspapers-magazines-books-tv-networks.

Noble, David. *Progress without People: New Technology, Unemployment, and the Message of Resistance*. Toronto: Between the Lines, 1995.

Ofcom. "The Communications Market Report: UK." August 4, 2016. https://www.ofcom.org.uk/research-and-data/cmr/cmr16.

O'Hagan, Sean. "Analogue Artists Defying the Digital Age." *Observer*, April 23, 2011. http://www.theguardian.com/culture/2011/apr/24/mavericks-defying-digital-age.

Oliver, Laura. "Delayed Gratification: New Magazine Launches Dedicated to 'Slow Journalism.'" *Journalism.co.uk*, December 13, 2010. https://www.journalism.co.uk/news-freelance/delayed-gratification-new-magazine-launches-dedicated-to-slow-journalism-/s12/a541963.

Ophir, Eval, Clifford Nass, and Anthony D. Wagner. "Cognitive Control in Media Multitaskers." *Proceedings of the National Academy of Sciences USA* 106, no. 37 (September 15, 2009): 15583–15587.

Osnos, Evan. "On Slow Journalism." *New Yorker*, January 31, 2013.

Pachal, Pete. "Why the iPad 2 is Far More Likely to Break than the Original." *Mashable*, March 3, 2012. http://mashable.com/2012/03/13/ipad-breakage.

Pang, Alex Soojung-Kim. *The Distraction Addiction: Getting the Information You Need and the Communication You Want, without Enraging Your Family, Annoying Your Colleagues, and Destroying Your Soul*. New York: Little, Brown and Co., 2013.

Pang, Alex Soojung-Kim. *Rest: Why You Get More Done When You Work Less*. New York: Penguin, 2016.

Parkins, Wendy. "Out of Time: Fast Subjects and Slow Living." *Time and Society* 16, nos. 2 and 3 (2004): 311–332.

Parkins, Wendy, and Geoffrey Craig. *Slow Living*. Oxford and New York: Berg, 2006.

Parks, Lisa and Nicole Starosielski. *Signal Traffic: Critical Studies of Media Infrastructures*. Champaign, IL: University of Illinois Press, 2015.

Parikka, Jussi. "The Geology of Media." *Atlantic*, October 11, 2013.

Parramore, Lynn Stuart. "Six Reasons Your Apple Product Has Become Very Uncool." *AlterNet*, June 3, 2013. http://www.alternet.org/economy/apple-not-cool.

Parnham, John. *Green Media and Popular Culture: An Introduction.* London: Palgrave, 2015.

Pea, Roy, et al. "Media Use, Face-to-Face Communication, Media Multitasking, and Social Well-Being Among 8- to 12-Year-Old Girls." *Developmental Psychology* 48, no. 2 (2012): 327–336.

Perlow, Leslie. *Sleeping with Your Smartphone: How to Break the 24/7 Habit and Change the Way You Work.* Cambridge, MA: Harvard Business Review Press, 2012.

Petrini, Carlo. *Slow Food Nation: Why Our Food Should Be Good, Clean, Fair.* New York: Rizzoli, 2007.

Petrini, Carlo. *Slow Food: Collected Thoughts on Taste, Tradition, and the Honest Pleasures of Food.* White River Junction, VT: Chelsea Green, 2001.

Petrini, Carlo. "Three Ideas, One Project." *Slow* 1 (2005): 6–7.

Pfauth, Ernst-Jan. "How We Turned a World Record in Journalism Crowd-funding into an Actual Publication." *Medium*, November 27, 2013. https://medium.com/de-correspondent/how-we-turned-a-world-record-in-journalism-crowd-funding-into-an-actual-publication-2a06e298afe1.

Pickerill, Jenny. *Cyberprotest: Environmental Activism Online.* Manchester, UK: Manchester University Press, 2003.

"The Playboy Interview: Marshall McLuhan." *Playboy*, March 1969.

Poe, Edgar Allen. "A Descent into the Maelstrom." 1841.

Pollan, Michael. *The Omnivore's Dilemma: A Natural History of Four Meals.* New York: Penguin Press, 2006.

Portinari, Folco. "The Slow Food Manifesto." December 10, 1989. http://www.slowfoodusa.org/manifesto.

Postman, Neil. *Amusing Ourselves to Death: Public Discourse in the Age of Show Business.* New York: Penguin, 1985.

Postman, Neil. "The Reformed English Curriculum." In *High School 1980: The Shape of the Future in American Secondary Education*, edited by A. C. Eurich. New York: Pittman, 1970.

Postman, Neil. *Technopoly: The Surrender of Culture to Technology.* New York: Vintage, 1993.

Powers, William. *Hamlet's Blackberry: A Practical Philosophy for Building a Good Life in the Digital Age.* New York: Harper Books, 2010.

Przybyliski, Andrew, and Netta Weinstein. "Can You Connect with Me Now? How the Presence of Movie Communication Technology Influences Face-to-Face Conversation Quality." *Journal of Social and Personal Relationships* (2012): 1–10.

Pynchon, Thomas R. "Is It O.K. to Be a Luddite?" *New York Times Book Review*, October 28, 1984.

Rademaker, Claudia. *Green Media: Exploring Green Media Selection and its Impact on Communication Effectiveness.* Dusseldorf: Lambert Academic Publishing, 2013.

Rauch, Jennifer. "Activists as Interpretive Communities: Rituals of Consumption and Interaction in an Alternative Media Audience." *Media, Culture and Society* 29, no. 6 (2007): 994–1013.

Rauch, Jennifer. "Are There Still Alternatives? The Relationship between Alternative and Mainstream Media in a Converged Environment." *Sociology Compass* 10, no. 9 (2016): 756–767.

Rauch, Jennifer. "Constructive Rituals of Demediatization: Spiritual, Corporeal, and Mixed Metaphors in Popular Discourse about Unplugging." *Explorations in Media Ecology* 13, nos. 3–4 (2014): 231–246. doi: 10.1386/eme.13.3-4.231_1.

Rauch, Jennifer. "Exploring the Alternative-Mainstream Dialectic: What 'Alternative Media' Means to a Hybrid Audience." *Communication, Culture and Critique* 8, no. 1 (2015): 124–143.

Rauch, Jennifer. "Hands-on Communication: Zine Circulation Rituals and the Interactive Limitations of Web Self-Publishing." *Popular Communication* 2, no. 3 (2004): 153–169.

Rauch, Jennifer. "Is There a Slow Media Movement, or Is It Just Me?" *Slow Media* (blog), September 2009. http://slow-media.org.

Rauch, Jennifer. "Living Offline: Artifacts of Life Before the Smartphone." *Medium*, March 5, 2015. https://medium.com/@jenniferrauch.

Rauch, Jennifer. "The Origin of Slow Media: Early Diffusion of a Cultural Innovation through Press and Public Discourse." *Transformations* 20 (2011). http://www.transformationsjournal.org/wp-content/uploads/2016/12/Rauch_Trans20.pdf.

Rauch, Jennifer. "Slow Media as Alternative Media: On the Cultural Persistence of Print and Analog Forms." In *The Routledge Companion to Alternative and Community Media*, edited by Chris Atton, 571–581. Oxford and New York: Routledge, 2015.

Rauch, Jennifer. "Superiority and Susceptibility: How Activist Audiences Imagine the Influence of Mainstream News Messages on Self and Others." *Discourse and Communication* 4, no. 3 (2010): 263–277.

Rauch, Jennifer. "Three Reasons I Don't Own a Smartphone." *Huffington Post,* March 18, 2014. https://www.huffingtonpost.com/author/jennifer-rauch-.

Ray, Paul, and Sherry Ruth Anderson. *Cultural Creatives: How 50 Million People are Changing the World.* New York: Harmony Books, 2000.

Reynolds, Simon. "Back to the Future." *Salon,* May 12, 2007.

Reynolds, Simon. *Retromania: Pop Culture's Addiction to its Own Past.* New York: Farrar, Straus and Giroux, 2011.

Rheingold, Howard. *Net Smart: How to Thrive Online.* Cambridge, MA: MIT Press, 2012.

Rheingold, Howard. "Technology 101: What Do We Need to Know About The Future We're Creating?" *Howard Rheingold* (blog), May 5, 1998. http://www.rheingold.com/texts/techcrit/technophiles.html.

Ricard, Matthieu, Antoine Lutz, and Richard Davidson. "The Mind of the Meditator." *Scientific American* 311, no 5. (November 2014): 38–45.

Rifkin, Jeremy. *Time Wars: The Primary Conflict in Human History.* New York: Touchstone, 1987.

Roach, Sean. "The Constant Gardener: My Two Years Tending AOL's Hyperlocal Experiment." *Columbia Journalism Review,* March/April 2012.

Robins, Kevin and Frank Webster. *Times of the Technoculture: From the Information Society to the Virtual Life.* New York: Routledge, 1999.

Romney, Jonathan. "In Search of Lost Time." *Sight and Sound,* February 2010.

Rosa, Hartmut. *Social Acceleration: A New Theory of Modernity.* New York: Columbia University Press, 2013.

Rosenberg, Howard, and Charles S. Feldman. *No Time to Think: The Menace of Media Speed and the 24-hour News Cycle.* New York: The Continuum International Publishing Group, 2008.

Rosnick, David. "Shorter Work Hours as a Means of Slowing Climate Change," Center for Economic and Policy Research, February 2013. http://cepr.net/documents/publications/climate-change-workshare-2013-02.pdf

Rosnick, David, and Mark Weisbrot. "Are Shorter Work Hours Good for the Environment? A Comparison of U.S. and European Energy Consumption," Center for Economic and Policy Research, December 2006. http://cepr.net/documents/publications/energy_2006_12.pdf.

Rushkoff, Douglas. *Program or Be Programmed: Ten Commands for a Digital Age.* Berkeley, CA: Soft Skull Press, 2010.

Rushkoff, Douglas. "Remember the Sabbath? Douglas Rushkoff Pleads for a Respite from E-Commerce." *Guardian,* March 8, 2000.

Rushkoff, Douglas. *Throwing Rocks at the Google Bus: How Growth Became the Enemy of Prosperity.* New York: Portfolio, 2016.

Rust, Stephen, Salma Monani, and Sean Cubitt. *Ecomedia: Key Issues.* Abingdon, UK and New York: Routledge, 2015.

Rutten, Tim. "AOL? HuffPo. The Loser? Journalism." *Los Angeles Times,* February 9, 2011.

Safire, William. "The Return of the Luddites." *New York Times Magazine,* December 6, 1998.

Sale, Kirkpatrick. *Rebels against the Future: The Luddites and Their War on the Industrial Revolution: Lessons for the Computer Age.* Boston: Addison-Wesley, 1995.

Salzberg, Sharon. "The Myth of Multitasking." *Shambhala Sun,* May 2014.

Salzberg, Sharon. *Real Happiness: The Power of Meditation.* New York: Workman Publishing Group, 2010.

Sax, David. *The Revenge of Analog: Real Things and Why They Matter.* New York: Public Affairs, 2016.

Schmidt, Charles W. "E-Junk Explosion." *Environmental Health Perspectives* 110, no. 4 (April 2002): 188–194.

Schlosser, Eric. *Fast Food Nation: The Dark Side of the All-American Meal*. New York: Houghton Mifflin, 2001.

Schull, Natasha Dow. *Addiction by Design*. Princeton, NJ: Princeton University Press, 2012.

Schor, Juliet B. *The Overworked American: The Unexpected Decline of Leisure*. New York: Basic Books, 1992.

Schor, Juliet B. *True Wealth: How and Why Millions of Americans are Creating a Time-Rich, Ecologically Light, Small-Scale, High-Satisfaction Economy*. New York: Penguin, 2011.

Schulevitz, Judith. *The Sabbath World: Glimpses of a Different Order of Time*. New York: Random House, 2010.

Schumacher, E. F. *Small is Beautiful: Economics as if People Mattered*. New York: Harper Perennial, 2010.

Schwartz, Barry. *The Paradox of Choice: Why More Is Less*. New York: Harper Perennial, 2005.

Segal, David. "Apple's Retail Army: Long on Loyalty but Short on Pay." *New York Times*, June 23, 2012.

Senge, Peter. *The Necessary Revolution: How Individuals and Organizations Are Working Together to Create a Sustainable World*. New York: Crown Business, 2010.

Shah, Neil. "The Biggest Music Comeback of 2014: Vinyl Records." *Wall Street Journal*, December 11, 2014. https://www.wsj.com/articles/the-biggest-music-comeback-of-2014-vinyl-records-1418323133.

Sharma, Sarah. *In the Meantime: Temporality and Cultural Politics*. Durham, NC: Duke University Press, 2014.

Shapiro, Walter. "After Breitbart and Shirley Sherrod, We Need a Slow-News Movement." *Politics Daily*, July 27, 2010. https://web.archive.org/web/20100728230512/http://www.politicsdaily.com/2010/07/27/after-breitbart-and-shirley-sherrod-we-need-a-slow-news-movemen.

Shea, Christopher. "Slow-Media Movement." *Boston Globe*, January 25, 2010. http://archive.boston.com/bostonglobe/ideas/brainiac/2010/01/the_slow-media.html.

Shenk, David, Andrew Shapiro, and Steven Johnson. *Technorealism* (blog). 1998. http://technorealism.org.

Shteyngart, Gary. *Super Sad True Love Story*. New York: Random House, 2011.

Shi, David. *In Search of the Simple Life*. Leyton, UT: Gibbs Smith, 1986.

Siegel, Daniel. *The Mindful Brain: Reflection and Attunement in the Cultivation of Well-Being*. New York: W.W. Norton, 2009.

Siegel, Lee. *Against the Machine: Being Human in the Age of the Electronic Mob*. New York: Spiegel and Grau, 2008.

Slack, Jennifer Daryl. *Communication Technologies and Society: Conceptions of Causality and the Politics of Technological Intervention*. Norwood, NJ: Ablex Publishing, 1984.

Slack, Jennifer Daryl. "Environment/Ecology." In *New Keywords: A Revised Vocabulary of Culture and Society*, edited by Tony Bennett, Lawrence Grossberg, and Meaghan Morris, 106–108. Oxford, England: Blackwell, 2005.

Slaughter, Anne-Marie. "Why Women Still Can't Have It All." *Atlantic*, July/August 2012.

Society of Professional Journalists. "SPJ Code of Ethics." September 6, 2014.

Sorrel, Charlie. "Ten Things Missing from the iPad." *Wired*, January 28, 2010. https://www.wired.com/2010/01/ten-things-missing-from-the-ipad.

South By Southwest, "Tech Detox: Can You Survive a Day Without Technology?" 2012. http://schedule.sxsw.com/2012/events/event_IAP11664.

Speth, James Gustave. *The Bridge at the Edge of the World: Capitalism, the Environment, and Crossing from Crisis to Sustainability*. New Haven, CT: Yale University Press, 2008.

Spira, Jonathan B., and Cody Burke. "Intel's War on Information Overload: A Case Study." Basex, August 2009. http://iorgforum.org/wp-content/uploads/2011/06/IntelWarIO.BasexReport1.pdf.

Standing, Guy. *The Precariat: A Dangerous New Underclass*. London and New York: Bloomsbury Academic, 2014.

Starosielski, Nicole. *The Undersea Network: Sign, Storage, Transmission*. Durham, NC: Duke University Press, 2015.

Starosielski, Nicole, and Janet Walker. *Sustainable Media: Critical Approaches to Media and Environment*. New York: Routledge, 2016.

Stearn, Gerald, ed. *McLuhan: Hot and Cool*. New York: The Dial Press, 1967.

Stone, I. F. "Con Games," speech delivered at Sylvan Theater, Washington, DC, April 22, 1970.

Stone, Linda. "The Connected Life: From Email Apnea to Conscious Computing." *Huffington Post*. May 7, 2012. https://www.huffpost.com/entry/email-apnea-screen-apnea-_b_1476554.

Stone, Linda. "Conscious Computing." *Linda Stone* (blog), April 20, 2012. https://lindastone.net/2012/04/20/conscious-computing-36.

Stone, Linda. "Continuous Partial Attention." *Linda Stone* (blog). https://lindastone.net/2009/11/30/beyond-simple-multi-tasking-continuous-partial-attention/.

Stone, Linda. "Just Breathe: Building the Case for Email Apnea." *Huffington Post*. February 8, 2008. https://www.huffpost.com/entry/just-breathe-building-the_b_85651.

Strayer, David L. and Jason M. Watson. "Supertaskers and the Multitasking Brain." *Scientific American Mind*, March/April 2012.

Sweeney, Chris. "Is Your Phone Smart Enough Not to Poison the People Making It? This One Is." *Yes! Magazine*, October 11, 2013. http://www.yesmagazine.org/issues/the-human-cost-of-stuff/smart-phone-why-its-time-for-a-kind-phone.

Tam, Daisy. "Slow Journeys: What Does It Mean to Go Slow?" *Food, Culture and Society* 11, no. 2 (2008): 208–218.

Thompson, E. P. *The Making of the English Working Class*. New York: Vintage Books, 1963.

Thorpe, Nick. "The Love of Stuff: Why We Should Love Material Things More, Not Less." *Aeon*, March 3, 2014. https://aeon.co/essays/we-should-love-material-things-more-than-we-do-now-not-less.

Thoreau, Henry David. *Walden; or, Life in the Woods*. New York: Viking/Penguin, 1854/1983.

Tierney, John. "Jaron Lanier Is Rethinking the Open Culture of the Internet." *New York Times*, January 12, 2010.

Tomlinson, Bill. *Greening through IT: Information Technology for Environmental Sustainability*. Cambridge, MA: MIT Press, 2010.

Tomlinson, John. *The Culture of Speed: The Coming of Immediacy*. Thousand Oaks, CA: Sage Publications, 2007.

Turkle, Sherry. *Alone Together: Why We Expect More from Technology and Less from Each Other*. Cambridge, MA: Basic Books, 2011.

Umble, Diane Zimmerman. *Holding the Line: The Telephone in Old Order Mennonite and Amish Life*. Baltimore, MD: Johns Hopkins University, 1996.

Unruh, Gregory et al. "Investing For a Sustainable Future." *MIT Sloan Management Review*, May 2016.

Urls, Yalta T., et al. "Five Days at Outdoor Education Camp Without Screens Improves Preteen Skills with Nonverbal Emotional Cues." *Computers in Human Behavior* 39 (2014): 387–392.

Walker, Rob. "Replacement Therapy: Why Our Gadgets Can't Wear Out Fast Enough." *Atlantic*, September 2011.

Wang, Zheng, and John M. Tcherhov. "The 'Myth' of Media Multitasking: Reciprocal Dynamics of Media Multitasking, Personal Needs, and Gratifications." *Journal of Communication* 62 (2012): 493–513.

Waskow, Rabbi Arthur. "Can America Learn from Shabbat?" In *Take Back Your Time: Fighting Time Poverty and Overwork in America*, edited by John de Graaf, 123–132. San Francisco: Berrett-Koehler, 2003.

Wasserstrom, Jeffrey. " 'Civilization' and its Discontents: The Boxers and Luddites as Heroes and Villains." *Theory and Society* 16 (1987): 675–707.

Waters, Alice. "Fast Food Values and Slow Food Values." In *Ecological Literacy: Educating Our Children for a Sustainable World*, edited by Michael K. Stone and Zenobia Barlow, 49–55. San Francisco, SF: Sierra Club Books, 2005.

Watson, Leon. "Humans Have Attention Spans Shorter Than Goldfish, Thanks to Smartphones." *Telegraph*, May 15, 2015.

Weaver, David, and Lars Willnat. *The Global Journalist in the 21st Century.* New York: Routledge, 2012.

White, Micah. "Clicktivism is Ruining Leftist Activism." *Guardian*, August 12, 2010. https://www.theguardian.com/commentisfree/2010/aug/12/clicktivism-ruining-leftist-activism.

Williams, Ray. "Why It's so Hard to Unplug From the Digital World." *Wired for Success* (blog), *Psychology Today*, May 6, 2012. https://www.psychologytoday.com/blog/wired-success/201205/why-it-s-so-hard-unplug-the-digital-world.

Williams, Raymond. *Marxism and Literature.* New York: Oxford University Press, 1977.

Wilson, Jeff. *Mindful America: The Mutual Transformation of Buddhist Meditation and American Culture.* New York: Oxford University Press, 2014.

Winn, Marie. *The Plug-In Drug: Television, Computers, and Family Life.* New York: Penguin, 1977/2002.

Winner, Langdon. "Look Out for the Luddite Label." *MIT Technology Review*, November/December 1997.

Wolf, Maryanne. *Proust and the Squid: The Story and Science of the Reading Brain.* New York: Harper Perennial, 2008.

Wortham, Jenna. "Raised on the Web, But Liking a Little Ink." *New York Times*, October 22, 2011.

Zhang, Peter. "Deleuze's Relay and Extension of McLuhan: An Ethical Exploration." *Explorations in Media Ecology* 10, vols. 3 and 4 (2011): 207–224.

Index

Abbey, Edward, 110
Absence of the Sacred (Mander), 114
abstinence, from media. *See* unplugging
activism, 8, 67–68, 111–12. *See also* protest(s)
   on device production and disposal, 66–68
   and media use, 9, 141n8, 150n55
   in Slow movement, 18, 30, 31
   in sustainability movement, 3, 5–6
Adbusters, 118, 128, 140n32
addiction, to media or technology, 80–81, 86,
   153n12, 153n16
advertising, 45, 63, 147n57
Agger, Ben, 123
Alone Together (Turkle), 119
Alter, Adam, 80, 93, 98
alternative media, xix, 7, 8–9, 28, 62, 72
Alternative Media (Atton), 8
Amazon, 54, 66, 150n56
Amish, xx, 114, 140n22
Amusing Ourselves to Death (Postman), 59, 106. *See*
   also Postman, Neil
analog media, 23, 28, 29, 71–73. *See also*
   typewriters; vinyl records; zines
Anderson, Sherry Ruth, 5
anthropocentrism, 60
anti-globalization movement, 112
apnea, email or screen, 92
Apple, 4, 53, 68–71, 150n63
Atavist, 43
Atlantic, 43
attention, 36, 82–86, 91–95
Atton, Chris, 8
Australian Broadcasting Corp., 140n24, 143n27

Bauerlein, Mark, 106
Belt, 46
Berg, Maggie, 124
Berkey-Gerard, Mark, 38
Berry, Wendell, 107, 116
Binfield, Kevin, 102
bioregions, 107, 114

Bittman, Mark, xiv–xv
Blessed Unrest (Hawken), 6
Blumtritt, Jorg, 25. *See also* Slow Media Institute
Borsook, Paulina, 100, 117–18
Boston Consulting Group, 89, 132
Brand, Stewart, 2, 141n5, 152n88
Brûlé, Tyler, 41
Buddhism, 83–84, 97
Bush, Mirabai, 90
Butterworth, Trevor, 41–42
Buy Nothing Day, xxii, 128

Callenbach, Ernest, 114
Carey, James, 130
Carr, Nicholas, 73, 100
   on cognitive effects of media, 85, 106
   on disconnecting from media, xi, xxii, 94
churnalism, 33, 35, 145n13
citizen journalism, 48
"Click Clean" (Greenpeace), 53–54, 66, 70
climate change, 2, 39, 111, 135, 148n24
Clinton-Lewinsky scandal, 41
cloud computing, 54, 151n81
"Code of Ethics" (Society of Professional
   Journalists), 40
coloring books for adults, 97, 98, 156n88
Comcast, 62
commercialism, 25, 28–29, 45, 61, 133, 140n32
community-supported agriculture (CSA), 5–6, 9,
   15, 18, 48, 134
compact discs (CDs), 27–28, 151n83
compulsion loops, 81
computers, 3, 54, 84, 107, 109, 141n10
conscious breathing, 95
conscious computing, 92–93
consumerism, 19, 68, 74–76, 134
contemplative computing, 92, 155n71
co-production, 48, 50, 51
Cowan, Ruth Schwartz, 126
Craig, Geoffrey, 13, 17, 23, 32
Cubitt, Sean, 56

cultural creatives, 5, 62, 135–36, 141n15
culture jamming, 128
Culture of Speed (Tomlinson), 30
Cyberprotest (Pickerill), 9

data centers, 54–55, 66, 148n9
David, Sabria, 25. *See also* Slow Media Institute
Davidson, Richard, 85
Davis, John, 71
De Correspondent, 34, 46
De Michiel, Helen, 18
dead media, 56, 73
default mode, 82, 85, 87, 95
Delayed Gratification, 33–34, 35, 40, 43, 49
detox, digital or tech. *See* unplugging
Dewey, John, 59
diet, information or media. *See* unplugging
Digital Detox Week, xxii
digital devices, 69, 72–73, 74, 80–81, 83, 144n47.
    See also addiction; product design: for
    engagement
  environmental consequences of, xxii, 54–56,
    57–58, 65–66, 67
  human consequences of, 64, 65–66, 68, 70, 71
  for mindfulness, 92–93, 97
digital maximalists, 128
disconnection, digital. *See* unplugging
distraction, 79–83, 86, 92, 94–96
Distraction Addiction (Pang), 92
Doctorow, Cory, 60
dopamine, 85, 86
Driftless Centre for Slow Media, 134
Dumbest Generation (Bauerlein), 106

Earth Day, 1, 58, 62, 111, 148n25
ecocentrism, 60
eco-cinema, 19, 143n18
Ecodefense (Foreman), 110
eco-gastronomy, 16
ecological ethics, 60–61
ecological time, 6
Ecology of Commerce (Hawken), 6
ecomedia studies, 56, 74
ecosabotage, 110
ecosystem, 3, 60
Ecotopia (Callenbach), 114
education, 125, 128, 132
  Green Media approaches to, 63–65, 76
  mindful approaches to, 90–91, 158n8, 159n27
  Slow approaches to, xxi, 22, 51, 130,
    140n24, 144n62
  about sustainability, 14, 16, 76
Edwards, Andres, 1, 5
efficient time, 6
Eggers, Dave, 41
electronic waste (e-waste), 64, 65–66, 74, 150n60
  growing volume of, 3, 55, 74
  options for reducing, 56, 66, 67, 132–33

e-mindfulness, 91
empathy, 12, 80, 90, 94, 125
employment. *See* labor practices
environmentalism, 8, 111
epicurianism, 22
e-waste. *See* electronic waste
executive function, 85–86

Facebook, xii, 22, 53, 66, 140n18, 153n10
Fairphone, 67, 70, 150n59
fair trade, 49
fake news, 36, 42, 133
fast food, 15–16, 36
fasting, from media. *See* unplugging
Fast Food Nation (Schlosser), 15
flow (state of mind), 153n16
Food, Inc., 15, 16
Food Rules (Pollan), 16
Foreman, Dave, 110
Forgotten Works Warehouse, 134
Four Arguments for the Elimination of Television,
    (Mander), 106, 107
Foxconn, 69–71, 151n66–67. *See also* Apple
Franklin, Benjamin, xvi, 26, 130–31
free time (leisure time), xii, 51–52, 129
Freeman, John, xxiii, 21–22

Gabrys, Jennifer, 57
Gallagher, Winifred, 82
Genuine Progress Indicator (GPI), 75–76
Gess, Harold, 39
Gladwell, Malcolm, xiii–xiv, 121, 141n8
Glendinning, Chellis, 105, 111
globalization, 17, 69, 111–12, 142n9
"Good, Clean, Fair" (slogan), 16, 38–40
GoodElectronics Network, 68
Google, 53, 66, 90, 98, 131
green advertising, 61, 63
green communication, 7
green/sustainable consumption, 68, 75–76
green consumerism, 74–74, 125
green cultural citizenship, 76–77, 125
Green IT movement, 1, 3, 57–58, 67. *See also*
    product design
green marketing, 61–62, 63
Green Media, 56, 58, 63–65, 74, 76
Greenberg, Susan, 37, 42–43
Greening the Media (Maxwell and Miller), 58, 64
Greening Media Education (Lopez), 60, 64
Greenpeace, 53–55, 66, 67, 70, 150n55
greenwashing, 49, 60, 61, 64, 75, 149n25
growth, vs. "degrowth," 75–76
Guide to Greener Electronics (Greenpeace), 67, 70

Hamlet's Blackberry (Powers), xv, 128
Harris, Tristan, 80–81, 93
Harper's, 42
Hawken, Paul, 6

hedonic treadmill, xvi. *See also* pleasure
Herships, Sally, xiii, 21
Honoré, Carl, 13–14, 124
Horstra, Rob, 34–35
Huffington, Arianna, 44, 45, 47, 92
Huffington Post (HuffPost), xiv, 44, 146n47
human agency, 14, 27, 73, 108, 133
    and false choices, 120–21, 123, 130
    and freedom of choice, 120, 158n8
    individual vs. collective aspects of, 81, 120,
        124–25, 131–32
    amid proliferation of choices, 47, 51, 128
    in Slow media use, 25, 30–32, 48–49, 50

industrialization, 125–26
    criticism of, 14, 17, 107, 109
    environmental effects of, 16, 58, 61
    influence on food systems of, 16–17, 30, 39
    of journalism/news, 36, 44
    vs. pre-industrial society, 107, 111, 114, 157n27
    protests against, 102–4
    social effects of, 114, 129
In Praise of Slowness (Honoré), 13, 44, 124
Information Technology and Innovation
    Foundation (ITIF), 113, 117–18
Intel, 88
International Campaign for Responsible
    Technology (ICRT), 67–68
International Forum on Globalization (IFG),
    112, 119
Irresistible (Alter), 80, 98

James, William, 82–83
Johnson, Joel, 71
Johnson, Steve, 117
Jones, Nick, 21
Jot Down, 34, 46, 50
journalism. *See also* journalists; Slow Journalism
    business practices in, 145n16, 146n47, 147n57
    corporate-commercial structure of, 45, 51, 133
    criticism of speed in, 33, 35–36, 41
    ethics of, 39–40, 133
    long-form narrative in, 34, 35, 37, 42, 147n57
    proposed subsidies for, 133
    transparency in, 49
    working conditions in, 43, 44–45, 50, 51
journalists. *See also* journalism; Slow Journalism
    attitudes toward Slowness of, 34, 36,
        47, 143n27
    overwork and stress among, 44
    vs. PR professionals, 145n13, 146n52
    undercompensation of, 43, 44–45
Journatic, 36, 50, 145n18
Joy, Bill, 100, 156n2

Kabat-Zinn, Jon, 83, 85, 153n19, 159n28
Kaczynski, Ted, 109–10, 157n33
Kakutani, Michiko, 28

Katz, Jon, 107
Kelly, Kevin, 108, 109, 110, 152n88
Kelly, Maura, xxiii, 22
King, Jr., Martin Luther, 75
King, Stephen, xiii–xiv
Klein, Naomi, 132, 134, 135, 149n25
Koehler, Benedikt, 25. *See also* Slow Media
    Institute
Kovach, Bill, 35–36
Kummer, Corby, 30

labor issues, 102, 104, 133, 146n47, 147n53,
    156n3. *See also* journalists: under-
    compensation of; overwork
    domestic labor, 125–26, 157n27, 158n6
    forced labor/slavery, 71, 151n74
    working hours, 31, 125, 127, 157n27, 158n9
    workplace health and safety, 67–68, 69–70
Langer, Ellen, 87–88
Lanier, Jaron, xxiii, 119, 121
Lasn, Kalle, 128
Law of Progressive Simplification, 108
Leigh, David, 43
leisure time. *See* free time
Le Masurier, Megan, 37, 48, 50, 51
Leonard, Annie, 65–66
Levy, David, 79, 90–91, 93, 94, 158n8
Lew, Jack, 131
Lewis, Justin, 51–52
Lian Jian, 70. *See also* Apple
Long Play, 34
Lopez, Antonio, 60, 63, 64, 76
Ludd, Ned, 101
Luddism, 99–100, 102–4, 107, 112, 113, 114–15
Luddite Awards, 113
Luddites (historical), 11, 99, 100–104, 156n5. *See
    also* Luddism; Neo-Luddism
    achievements of, 104
    destructive/violent actions of, 102, 103–4
    and environmentalism, 111
    and protest strategy, 102, 104
    official responses to, 102, 104
    socio-political context of, 103, 111

MacDonald, Scott, 19
machine zone (state of mind), 81, 153n16
Maher, Bill, 68–69
Mander, Jerry, 106, 107, 112, 114
manifesto(s), xxiii, 120
    Neo-Luddite, 105, 106
    Sabbath, xxiii
    Slow Books, xxiii
    Slow Communication, xxiii
    Slow Food, 17
    Slow Media, xxiii, 24
    Slow News, 47
Marcus, Ruth, 47–48
Marketplace, xiii, xviii

Maxwell, Richard, 58, 60, 61, 64, 67, 118,
    148n25, 149n44
McChesney, Robert, 28–29, 44, 51, 133, 135
McDonald's, 14–15. *See also* fast food
McGregor, Lyn, 134
McKibben, Bill, xx, 75, 107, 109, 112,
    140n22, 156n2
McLuhan, Marshall, xii, 2, 58–59, 96, 106, 129n49
McNews, 36
McSweeney's, 41
media archaeology, 56
media ecology, 56, 59–61
Media Ecology Association, 59
media ecosystem, 55, 60–61
Media Ecosystem (Lopez), 60
media environment, 59–60
meditation, 83, 85, 86, 91, 96, 97–98
Miedema, John, 22
Miller, Toby, 58, 60, 64, 67, 148n25, 149n44
Mindful America (Wilson), 96
mindful emailing, 90
mindful media, 93, 94, 95–97
Mindful Nation (Ryan), 132
mindfulness, 83, 92–93, 97, 132
Mindful Tech (Levy), 91, 158n8
    in corporate culture, 97–98
    scientific evidence of benefits, 84–85, 87–88
    as Slow principle, 81, 93–94
    in spiritual traditions, 81, 83, 154n27
Mission and State, 46
mobile phones. See *digital devices*
monkey mind, 79, 82
Monkeywrench Gang (Abbey), 110
Monocle, 41
monotasking, 24, 86, 95
More Work for Mother (Cowan), 126
Morozov, Evgeny, 141n8, 155n71
multitasking, 21, 84, 86–87, 93, 95, 152n5
My Dinner With André, xi, xviii, 139n17

Narratively, 34, 42, 43, 45
Nathaniel, Naka, 34–35, 37
National Day of Unplugging, xiv–xv, 44, 129
National Public Radio, xiii, 21, 47, 143n27
nature, 23, 56, 60, 154n45
Neo-Luddism, 99, 105, 107, 114, 115
    attitudes towards television, 105–7
    criticism of, 107–8, 114–15
    and environmentalism, 107, 110–11, 114
    and globalization, 111–12
    misperceptions of, 108, 111
    and violence, 102, 103, 109–110
Netflix, 53–54, 66
neuroplasticity, 85
Neveu, Erik, 38
new media materialism, 56
news. See journalism; journalists
New Yorker, 34–35, 42

New York Times, xiv, 27, 34
Nichols, John, 44, 133, 135
Nietzsche, 22
Noble, David, 107, 112
nonmaterialism, 75–76, 108
No Music Day, 20, 143n21
nostalgia, xxi, 25, 28, 144n40
"Notes toward a Neo-Luddite Manifesto"
    (Glendinning), 105, 106
No Time to Think (Kovach and Rosenstiel), 35

Occupy Wall Street, 112
Orchard, Rob, 33. See also *Delayed Gratification*
Out of Eden Walk, 34–35
overload, information and email, xxiii, 79–80,
    88–89, 106, 130
overwork, 32, 125–26, 127, 129, 158n10. *See also*
    labor issues; time scarcity

pace of life, 31–32
Pang, Alex Soojung-Kim, 92, 93, 156n84
Paradox of Choice (Schwartz), 128
parasympathetic nervous system (PNS), 84–85
Parikka, Jussi, 56
Parkins, Wendy, 13, 17, 23, 32
Patch, 44
payphones, xvii
People Get Ready (McChesney and
    Nichols), 133
Perlow, Leslie, 89
Peters, Dorian, 100
Petrini, Carlo, 14–15, 16, 30, 144n56
    critique of global capitalism, 9, 16–17, 24, 142n7
    on motto "Good, Clean, Fair," 38–39
    on product labeling, 39, 51
Pickerill, Jenny, 9
Plain, 108
pleasure, xvi, 22, 75–76, 97, 130–31,
    139n14, 150n59
    as Slow Food value, 16, 17, 30, 38
    in Slow Media use, 26, 28, 41, 72
Plug-in Drug (Winn), 105–6
politics of time, xvi, 12, 31–32, 125. *See also*
    overwork; time scarcity
Pollan, Michael, 16, 22
positive computing, 93, 155n73
Post-Luddism, 11–12, 101, 115, 118, 120
    exemplars of, 118–20, 121
    principles of, 116–17
Postman, Neil, 56, 59, 99, 106, 107, 116
Powers, William, xv, 128, 130
Predictable Time Off (PTO), 89
producer responsibility, 66, 68, 74
product design, 65–66, 69
    for engagement, 80–81, 153n16
    ethical and green approaches to, 57, 66,
        67–68, 93, 98
    for print magazines, 40–41

product labeling, 48–49, 51
product longevity, 25, 29, 36, 72–73
product obsolescence, 25, 28–29, 36, 68–69, 71–73
product takeback. *See* producer responsibility
Program or Be Programmed (Rushkoff), 118
progress, 75–76, 104, 108, 113, 120
  relationship to speed, 21
  skepticism toward, 9, 61, 73, 116, 119
Progress without People (Noble), 112
protest(s), 3, 5, 101–2, 104, 112
Proust and the Squid (Wolf), 94, 130
provenance of media products, 37, 39, 43, 48–49, 51
public relations (PR), 35, 145n13, 146n52
puppy mind, 82, 96

quality of life, 3, 7, 39, 75
Quiet Time (experiment), 88

Rapt (Gallagher), 82
Raundalen, Jon, 61
Ray, Paul H., 5, 141n15
realtechnik, 119
Rebels against the Future (Winner), 107–8
Reboot, xiv, 129
records. *See* vinyl records
Record Store Day, 73. *See also* vinyl records
recycling, 56, 66, 70, 72, 74, 111
renewable energy, 53–54, 66
reporting. *See* journalism; journalists
residual media, 73
rest, xiv, xv, xx, 84, 95–96, 156n84
Retromania (Reynolds), 20
Revenge of Analog (Sax), 28
Reynolds, Simon, 20
Rheingold, Howard, 117, 119, 121
Rifkin, Jeremy, 6, 112
rituals, xiv, xx–xxi, 104, 128–29, 130, 131
Rosa, Hartmut, 31
Rosenstein, Justin, 81
Rosenstiel, Tom, 35–36
Rushkoff, Douglas, 117, 118–19, 121, 159n33
Ryan, Tim, 132

Sabbath, religious, xx, 129, 131, 140n20
sabbath, secular, digital, Internet, or
    technological. *See* unplugging
Sabbath Manifesto, xiv, xxiii, 129
Sale, Kirkpatrick, 107–8, 109, 110, 111
Salopek, Paul, 34–35, 37
Salzberg, Sharon, 83–84
San Francisco Panorama, 41
satisficing, digital, 128. *See also* pleasure
Sax, David, 28–29, 118
Schlosser, Eric, 15, 16
Schumacher, E.F., 105
Schwartz, Barry, 128, 139n14
Screen Free Week, 128
Search Inside Yourself, 90, 98

Second Luddite Congress, 109, 110
Seeber, Barbara, 124
self-denial, philosophical, xvi, 130, 139n14
Senge, Peter, 58
server farms. *See* data centers
Shabbat, xx. *See also* Sabbath, religious
Shallows (Carr), 85, 106
Shapiro, Andrew, 117
Shapiro, David, 26
Shapiro, Walter, 47
Sharma, Sarah, 29, 30, 31, 32
Shenk, David, 117
Sherrod, Shirley, 47–48
Shteyngart, Gary, xii
Simpsons, 106–7
Slake, 46
Slaughter, Anne-Marie, 131
Slow Blogging, 47–48. *See also* Slow Journalism
Slow Books, xxiii, 22
Slow Cinema, 18–19
Slow Communication, xxiii, 21–22
Slow Film, 19
Slow Food, 14–17, 30, 38–39, 48, 124
Slow Food Nation (Petrini), 16, 38
Slow Journalism, 10, 30–31, 33–38. *See also*
    journalism
  alternative business models for, 45–46
  audience support for, 45–48, 50
  and collective action, 48, 52, 133–34
  emergence of, 37
  examples of, 31
  and fair-trade movement, 49–50
  good, clean, and fair aspects of, 39–40
  key characteristics of, 37–38
  marketing of, 41–42, 51
  obstacles to, 50, 51
  similarities to traditional journalism, 35, 38
  voluntary product labeling in, 48–49, 51
Slow Journalism Company, 30. See also *Delayed*
    Gratification
Slow Listening, 20, 95
Slow living. *See* Slow movement
Slow Media, xxi, 25, 29, 123
  and alternative media, 8–9, 28
  and collective actions, 32, 124–25, 132–33
  connections to Slow Food, xxi, 14, 17, 134
  critique of corporate-commercial media, 28, 45
  and human agency, 32, 49, 72
  origins and growth of, xii, 20–21, 134
  practices and strategies of, 23, 124–25
  values and principles of, 17, 23
Slow Media (blog), xi, 120
Slow Media Institute, 25–26
Slow Media Manifesto, xiii, xxiii, 24–25
Slowmodernity, 123
Slow movement, 14, 23, 25, 93, 140n24
  critical responses to, 29, 30, 32
  growth of, 13, 16, 50, 124

Slow News, 44, 47. *See also* Slow Journalism
Slow Reading, 22, 93–94, 95
Slow Reading (Miedema), 22
Slow-washing, 49
"Small is Beautiful" (slogan), 105
smartphones. *See* digital devices
Smith, Ted, 67–68
snail (Slow Food logo), 15, 30, 42
Sochi Project, 34–35
Society of Professional Journalists, 40
South by Southwest, xv
Starosielski, Nicole, 7, 56
Stone, Linda, 92–93
Story of Electronics, 65–66
Story of Stuff, 65
streaming video, 53–54
stress, 44–45, 80, 92–93, 95, 97–98, 152n6
sustainability, 3, 68, 75–76
    and alternative media, 8–9
    in media and device industries, 57, 61–62,
        67, 68, 71
    origin and growth of, 1–4
    principles of, 5–6
    in Slow movements, 14, 16, 18, 19, 25,
        38–40, 43, 49
    sustainability communication, 62, 63
    sustainability movement, 75, 114
sustainable communication, 7
sustainable media, 7–8, 25, 132
Sustainable Media (Starosielski and
    Walker) 7, 56
sympathetic nervous system (SNS), 84–85

Take Back Your Time, 129
Technopoly (Postman), 59, 99, 107, 116. *See also*
    Postman, Neil
Technorealism, 117–18, 119
techno-utopianism, 2, 28, 73, 117
television, xx, 59, 105–7, 128, 141n8, 150n55
Thoreau, Henry David, 1, 22, 75
time politics. *See* politics of time
time scarcity, xvi, 31, 51, 125, 128. *See also*
    overwork; politics of time
time spent with media, xiii, 79–80, 133
Tomlinson, Bill, 1, 3, 57. *See also* Green IT
    movement
Tomlinson, John, 30
Toynbee, Alfred, 108
transmission (mode of communication), xx

Turkle, Sherry, 95, 98, 119, 121
Turn Here Sweet Corn (De Michiel), 18
TV Turnoff Week, xxii, 128
typewriters, xxii, 23, 29–30, 72, 73
Tyranny of Email (Freeman), xxiii, 22

Unabomber, 109–10
unitasking. *See* monotasking
unplugging, 4, 20, 84, 89–90, 96, 129,
        140n29, 144n62
    abstinence, from media, xxi, xxii, 81
    detox, digital or tech, xiv–xv, xx–xxii, 7,
        24, 140n29
    diet, information or media, xiv, xx–xxii, 8
    disconnection, digital, xiv, xvi, 47, 90,
        119, 128
    fasting, from media, xx, 4, 20, 24
    sabbath, secular, digital, Internet, or
        technological, xv, xx, 7–8, 24, 118–19,
        129, 131

Van Bruggen, Arnold, 34–35
Vestberg, Nina Lager, 61
vinyl records, xxi, 27–28, 72, 73

Walker, Janet, 7, 56
Waskow, Rabbi Arthur, 129
Waters, Alice, 16
Webb, Marcus, 40. See also *Delayed Gratification*
well-washing, 97
White, Micah, 118, 141n8
Whole Earth Catalog, 2
Wilson, Jeff, 96, 97
Winfrey, Oprah, xiv
Winn, Marie, 105–6
Winner, Langdon, 107, 112
Wired, 2, 100, 107–8, 109, 110
Wolf, Maryanne, 94, 130
"World Unplugged," 89–90
Writings of the Luddites (Binfield), 102
Wortham, Jenna, 26–27

XXI (Vingt-et-Un/Twenty-One), 34

You Are Not a Gadget (Lanier), xxiii, 119

Zerzan, John, 110
zines, xxii, 26–27, 72
zombie media, 73